Slashing!

Slashing!

Hockey's Most Knowledgeable Critic
Tells What Should Be Done
to Save the Game

Stan Fischler

Thomas Y. Crowell Company
New York   Established 1834

The publisher wishes to thank the following for permission to use photographs from their files (Photo section follows page 128.):

Dan Baliotti: page 6 (top right, middle right and left, bottom left), 8 (top), 11 (top right), 12 (top); Terry Foley: 5 (bottom); Melchior Di Giacomo: 2 (bottom), 3, 7 (bottom); Wide World Photos: 1 (top and bottom), 2 (top), 4 (top and bottom), 5 (top), 6 (top left and bottom right), 7 (top), 8 (bottom), 9 (top and bottom), 10 (top and bottom), 11 (all except top right), 12 (bottom).

Manufactured in the United States of America

ISBN 0-690-00674-8

Library of Congress Cataloging in Publication Data

Fischler, Stan.
    Slashing!

    1. Hockey. I. Title.
GV847.F464   796.9'62   74-12481
ISBN 0-690-00674-8

To Frank Boucher, who, more than anyone,
knew how hockey should be played, and
played and taught the game that way

The author wishes to thank Richard Friedman, Howard Hyman, Reyn Davis, Melinda Muniz, Nancy Demmon, Mike Rubin, Bob Verdi, Tom Henshaw, Anita Latner, Robert Stampleman, Helene Elliot, Jay Acton, and the many others who helped so much in the preparation of this book. And a special thanks to the inspirational crew, Shirley and Benjamin.

Introduction

DURING THE 1973–74 SEASON a minor yet significant event took place in my life. After following hockey for more than thirty-five years I walked out of a major-league game before it was over. It was the first time I had ever committed such hockey heresy.

It happened in Madison Square Garden. The Rangers were playing the St. Louis Blues, and the match was so dreadful in every conceivable way that I told my wife Shirley, "You won't believe this, but I can't stand this hockey game."

She didn't believe it because I have long considered myself an absolute and irrevocable hockey fanatic. I have driven through blizzards to watch Montreal play Detroit at the Forum. And I have sped through the night to see minor-league games in Baltimore and Hershey on Friday and Saturday nights and then ridden a milk train home to catch the Sunday evening Rangers match in New York.

But that was long ago. Long ago, that is, if you consider 1966 yesteryear. I, for one, do, because hockey was a different game then—a much better game, with higher-quality players and better people.

Then along came expansion, and the game went to hell. Not that expansion in and of itself is bad. Big-league hockey in its purest form is a wonderful sport, and I love it. But I hate uncontrolled expansion, and I loathe the stupid management and the nearsightedness of hockey players who have stripped the game of its inherent glamour.

I love hockey as much as I revere a work by Rembrandt. I would be terribly depressed if some graffitti artist defaced that Rembrandt. Nowadays I have the feeling that my game of hockey has been defaced by the cretins who are running and playing the sport.

I passionately hope that hockey, as I and many others once loved it, can be salvaged before it's too late. This book is dedicated to that goal.

New York, May, 1974

Contents

Part One

How Violence
Is Killing Hockey

1

The Roots of Hockey Violence

IT WAS A TYPICAL NIGHT in Boston Garden, a funereal arena known to visiting National Hockey League players as the "Zoo." They call it that because over the years the home team—the Bruins—have taken a bloodthirsty delight in being known as the "Animals." On this evening they were intent on devouring the Toronto Maple Leafs while more than fifteen thousand customers played Romans at Caesar's Circus. It is the thing to do at Boston Garden as it is in Philadelphia's Spectrum, the Forum in Los Angeles, and most hockey arenas up, down, and across North America.

"C'mon, Bobby," a rinkside fan snapped at local folk hero Bobby Orr. "Lessee some blood!"

Before Orr could oblige, Brian Conacher, a tall, husky Toronto forward, found himself on a collision course with Orr. Reacting with the natural self-preservation reflex, Conacher brought his pound-and-a-half white ash stick up to face level. Orr's head lurched back like a man who had just taken a bullet in the stomach. He fell to the ice as blood spurted from his just-broken nose.

Before Conacher could conduct an orderly retreat he was surrounded by the Animals, who mauled him long enough for Orr to clamber to his feet, jump Conacher, and punch the fallen Leaf so brutishly and ruthlessly that even the partisan *Boston Globe* printed an open letter the following day condemning the brutality.

Orr promptly copped the traditional hockey player's plea—he who sees blood on himself must extract blood from the attacker. "Conacher got me in the nose, and I was bleeding like a stuck pig," Orr explained. "I didn't want to fight, but if they see you backing up in this league, it's no good."

By contrast, Conacher found the bloodletting too nauseating for his constitution and quit big-league hockey in the prime of his career. In a parting warning, Conacher predicted that such violence for "bloodthirsty American fans" might ultimately destroy hockey.

That was like saying gasoline might ultimately destroy automobiles, or blood might cause arteries to wither. Conacher was unrealistic. Violence has been part of the woof and warp of hockey since the first game was played in Montreal on March 3, 1875.

As early as 1907 hockey was alternately being denounced and hailed— depending on your metabolism—as the bloodiest of modern games. In a contest that season between Ottawa and Montreal there was so much blood spilled on the ice the *Montreal Star* headlined it as "an exhibition of butchery."

The official NHL history described the quasi-massacre this way:

> Baldy Spittal [of Ottawa] was said to have deliberately tried to split Cecil Blachford's skull by bringing down his hockey stick upon it with all his force using both hands. Blachford was carried off with his blood pouring on the ice. Alf Smith was said to have skated across and hit Rod Stuart across the temple with his stick, laying him out like a corpse. Harry Smith was credited with cracking Ernie Johnson across the face with his stick, breaking Johnson's nose.

Judging by that heartwarming atmosphere, it hardly was surprising that later in the same season a player died as a result of a clubbing he absorbed in a hockey game. The victim was Owen McCourt, leading scorer on the Cornwall, Ontario, team. His crime was getting in the path of a stick wielded by an opponent named Charles Masson.

McCourt was carried from the ice bleeding from a cut on his head. He died in the hospital the following morning. As a result of a coroner's inquest it was determined that McCourt "came to his death by a blow from a hockey stick."

As for Masson, the report added: "Although there was no evidence of ill-feeling previous to the assault, there was no justification or personal provocation for the blow at the hands of the said Masson.

"After hearing the evidence, your jury further recommends that legislation be enacted whereby players or spectators encouraging or engaging in rough or foul play may be severely punished."

But alas, history has demonstrated that such pious suggestions to humanize hockey have melted like the ice in spring. In 1968 Bill Masterton of the Minnesota North Stars cracked his head on the hard, rutted ice and died the next day in the hospital. In 1973 Greg Neeld, a gifted Junior A player, took a stick in his right eye and eventually had to have the eye removed. His father correctly assailed hockey "butchery"; several wails were heard from do-gooders and politicians. And less than three months later another teenage boy was beaten up by a rival hockey player and was pronounced dead on arrival at the hospital near Toronto.

Why does a game that combines ballet and bloodshed always seem to accent the crimson? Why have fans literally crashed down doors to see the "Big, Bad Bruins" and the "Ferocious Flyers," while treating the more pacific but more artistic Montreal Canadiens with virtual disdain?

For starters, hockey was invented by Canadians, developed by Canadians, and until recently has been virtually monopolized by Canadians. Despite rumors to the contrary, Canadians have been a hell-for-leather people whose passion for raucousness and the grape was a legend of two world wars.

"Much of the appeal of hockey," wrote Canadian author Scott Young, "is the combination of blood, sweat and beauty. Perhaps these qualities in juxtaposition have an extra meaning for a nation that still is engaged in pushing back its fierce and beautiful frontiers."

Exposure to bloodshed and death are part of hockey's *machismo*, which is somehow related to the Canadian psyche. "Hockey reflects us," said the late Lloyd Percival, Canada's physical-fitness expert. "In a game like hockey you have to have the emotional ability to keep going despite the knocks, without overreacting to the dangers."

The roots run deep; from the bitterly frigid outdoor rinks of Canada's prairie provinces to the comfortable innards of a new, brilliantly lit arena in Toronto. Education of a hockey player begins as early as age three. "Don't fight," a mother tells her pre-school son on an outdoor municipal rink in Elmira, Ontario. The boy has discarded stick and mittens to wrestle a friend to the ice. "Don't fight!" she pleads again.

For a split-second the lad looks up only long enough to shout: *"BUT HOCKEY PLAYERS FIGHT."*

They fight because savagery is sanctioned by the NHL and WHA. The crash of body against body is legal in many cases and even illegal acts are frequently overlooked by the referees. That, of course, is when the real trouble starts.

Many fans experience a bestial satisfaction—bordering on the sadistic—in totalling the stitches and broken bones of their sworn enemies. Few players have all of their own teeth and those who do are often regarded as softies.

Gordie Howe, who played twenty-six years for the Detroit Red Wings and more recently for the Houston Aeros, would judge a season by goals, assists, and stitches. "I had fifty stitches in my head one year," said Howe. "That was a bad year. I only got ten stitches the following season. *That* was a good year."

The *machismo* integrated into the Canadian psyche causes hockey players virtually to dismiss serious injuries. Denis Potvin, the young defenseman of the New York Islanders, played nearly two months of the 1973–74 season despite a broken leg. Gilles Marotte of the New York Rangers once suffered a broken jaw and leg as well as a nasty thigh cut that took weeks to heal, but when asked if he had ever been hurt badly, he shook his head. "No," he said, "I guess I just been lucky."

They are toughened up at an early age. Derek Sanderson's father used to collect his son's hockey stitches in a glass jar. "When I reached a hundred," said Derek, "he threw the bottle away and figured I was tough enough for organized hockey."

The result is adult intensity and stoicism at precocious ages. A Junior C player in Elmira, Ontario, rated highly as an NHL prospect, broke two of his ribs. He went home, spat blood, and waited four days to see a doctor. "If you keep running to the doctor with something minor," he explained, "they don't look at you after that."

Among the young man's souvenirs is a broken nose, never set by a doctor. Urged to wear a protective mask, the player rebelled with this rationale: "You wear a nose mask, and it sets you up as a target. They come after you with high sticks."

Canadians accept the stitches and breaks and scars as matter-of-factly as snow in winter. "What's so dangerous?" said a Kitchener mother with two sons in organized hockey. "Accidents can happen anywhere."

No athlete underreacts like a hockey player. During a Stanley Cup final, defenseman Bob Baun of Toronto suffered a broken leg. He calmly requested a shot of painkiller from the doctor, returned to the ice, and scored the winning goal in sudden-death overtime. Or take the case of Elmer Lach, former star center of the Montreal Canadiens. Knocked out during a game at Olympia Stadium in Detroit, Lach was carried to the rubbing table in the arena hospital. His face was pale and drawn, and his light, spiky hair was matted wetly across his forehead. A trickle of blood ran out of the side of his mouth and down his chin to the white sheet that covered the table, and there it formed a spreading red blot. There was a pervasive fear among the Canadiens that Lach would never lace on skates again.

When the doctor looked down at the victim Lach winked back. "I can't breathe when I skate because of the blood, is all that's the matter," said the Montreal forward. "I was thinking, maybe if I plugged my mouth with cotton. . . ."

Lach's teammate Maurice "Rocket" Richard once was bludgeoned to the ice by Leo Labine of the Boston Bruins during a Stanley Cup series. Lying unconscious in a pool of blood, Richard appeared to be dead. He finally was helped from the ice and revived in the dressing room. Late in the game he quietly returned to the bench and eventually skated through the Boston defense to score the winning goal. After the game Richard revealed he could not recall a single move he had made from the time Labine had hit him to the dressing-room interview.

What obviously makes hockey bloodier than other major sports is the fact that for sixty minutes of playing time each of the twelve players carries a large weapon in his hand—a stick that measures five feet in length and has a pointed tip, the better with which to jab your opponent in the gut.

Some of hockey's more adept "infighters" claim that the stick is too obvious a weapon to use on a foe, that the referee can easily see it from thirty feet away. They claim that it's more practical to use one's skates to separate an enemy from his head along the boards. The razor-sharp skate blades have a machetelike effect. It also has been discovered that a swift jab of the skates against an opponent's boot will knock an opponent right off his feet. Hence the expression "kicking skates."

According to insiders one of the best skate-kickers was George "Red" Sullivan, a peppery center who played for the Boston Bruins and New York Rangers and is now Washington's chief scout. One evening, it is said, Sullivan made the mistake of kicking the skates of All-Star defenseman Doug Harvey of the Montreal Canadiens. As expected, Harvey landed on his derriere, but carefully made a mental note of the injustice. Several games later he encountered Sullivan along their common alleyway on the ice. Harvey's stick dented Sullivan's jersey and plunged deeply into the Ranger's skin. An hour later Sullivan was in St. Clare's hospital as a priest prepared to administer to him the last rites of the Catholic Church.

Fortunately Sullivan recovered and played again. As for Harvey, his explanation was accepted by all who've played big-league hockey: "He kicked skates!" And that's not nice.

Curiously enough, large amounts of blood usually are not spilled as a result of the ubiquitous fistfights that occur in hockey games. A noteworthy exception was a collision in 1951 between "Wild" Bill Ezinicki of the Boston Bruins and Ted Lindsay of the Detroit Red Wings. When it was over, Ezinicki required nineteen stitches in his head while Lindsay accepted one. Years later, in a calmer moment, Lindsay offered an interesting insight into why his and other hockey fights start:

"Ezinicki always liked to give you a last shove. When he jostled me, I gave it back to him. Then he cut me with his stick, and I cut him. We went at it with our fists, and I was lucky enough to land the best punch I ever threw in hockey. It was a right, and it landed on the button. After that, Ezzie kept comin' at me without protectin' himself. . . . All that began with a couple of shoves."

The thing to remember is that shoves are legitimate in hockey; it says so in the rule books except that they are called body checks. Blood starts gushing when the shove is delivered with unusual indiscretion. Ed Van Impe, defenseman of the Philadelphia Flyers, once received such a shove from Claude Laforge in Pittsburgh. Van Impe was catapulted headfirst into the hard boards and awoke dazed but not foggy enough to forget who had done him in.

He remembered Laforge's number and later in the season intercepted the French-Canadian with such impiety that Laforge suffered a broken jaw and spit out nine teeth in the process. When poor Claude woke up in the recovery room he vowed to get Van Impe "if it's the last thing I do in hockey."

But hockey players are funny people when it comes to bad blood, and a few years later both Laforge and Van Impe became teammates on the Flyers. Captain Ed suddenly regarded little Claude as if he were his long-lost cousin from Brittany.

In more pious moments owners of NHL teams have been known to condemn the bloodletting, but few observers take them seriously—any more than one believes a pitchman at a carnival.

Hockey's violence was accepted and encouraged by the owners a long time ago, and nothing since Conn Smythe was boss of the Toronto Maple Leafs has changed the prevailing philosophy. Smythe's theme became a coaching credo: "If you can't beat 'em in an alley, you can't beat 'em on the ice." Smythe realized, as many other hockey promoters have since, that the prospect of bloodletting lures fans to a rink like hyenas to a carcass. But every so often, the damage inflicted is so awesome that even the most savage rooters are stunned to the core. Just such an episode occurred on December 12, 1933, when Eddie Shore of Boston charged Toronto's Ace Bailey from behind with so vicious a blow Bailey spent two weeks on the critical list and never played hockey again.

Equally frightening was a one-way decapitation contest conducted by Bernard "Boom Boom" Geoffrion of the Montreal Canadiens against Ron Murphy of the Rangers at Madison Square Garden in the early fifties. Murphy made the mistake of massaging Geoffrion's face with the side of his stick while they battled along the sideboards. Geoffrion was offended principally because *he* did not have a stick at the time. Not content with three massages of Geoffrion, Murphy tried for six. Exasperated, Geoffrion finally broke free and found a stick of his own. By this time Murphy had retreated to center ice where he suddenly appeared mummified by the oncoming Montrealer. Geoffrion wound up and swung like Hank Aaron going for the grand slam, but he missed Murphy's head by a fraction of an inch. Strike one!

Since Murphy remained firmly—and rather unintelligently—implanted in the same spot, Geoffrion wound up a second time. This time the full cut of his stick blade cut a wide swath of air and struck Murphy in the jaw, breaking it into many pieces. The Ranger eventually was carted away and years later discussed the phenomenon of hockey stick-swinging. "After the first swing," said Murphy, "you go crazy. All you can think about is trying to protect yourself, and the only way to do it is to get the other guy. When you start swinging, there's no place to run."

Another reason for the frequency of hockey bloodshed is that players expect it and accept it as part of their working day. One night superstar Frank Mahovlich was being mended after colliding with an enemy defenseman's stick. Mahovlich had one red welt about six inches long and the width of a hockey stick across the lower part of his neck, just above the collarbone, and his left shoulder was bleeding in two places from abrasions. Yet he discussed the injuries like a man describing an episode on his front lawn.

"I was getting ready to take a pass when somebody high-sticked me," said Mahovlich. "I saw the stick coming and pulled my head back so it got me lower." And that was that.

Being sensitive souls, hockey players will sometimes take arms at the mere drop of a verb. A classic example of that occurred in the early forties when Jimmy Orlando, a veteran Detroit Red Wings defenseman, took exception to rookie Gaye Stewart of the Toronto Maple Leafs.

"You're pretty fresh for a rookie," snarled Orlando, renowned for his perennial five-o'clock shadow.

"Why don't you get yourself a shave?" cracked Stewart.

Outraged by the rookie's impudence, Orlando delivered a left uppercut from the knees that knocked Stewart unconscious. In time the Leafs forward was revived and returned to the game.

Stewart seemed to have forgotten the humiliation and led several Toronto attacks into Red Wing zone. On one such assault, he personally carried the puck along the left side of the rink when he noticed Orlando moving over to stop him. Stewart promptly discarded the puck, raised his stick like an ax, and cracked Orlando across the head.

"The only time I ever saw more blood," said Canadian author Jim Coleman, "was the day I was taken on a tour of the cattle-killing floor of an abattoir."

Such displays of woodchopping inevitably inspire cries of barbarism in the Canadian Parliament and from ladies' sewing groups. When that happens, the league front office replies with promises of a crackdown. Of course nobody connected with hockey really believes it. Every new season brings promises of elimination of bloodshed, and every new season brings new instances of near-manslaughter.

In August 1974 the National Hockey League was singled out as "the strongest influence contributing to increased violence in amateur hockey in Ontario." The league, with its emphasis on winning and the use of violence as a tactical instrument to achieve that goal, was cited in the report of a provincial government inquiry into the sport conducted by Toronto lawyer William McMurtry.

Not long ago a Quebec judge observed that while homicide was not permitted to go unpunished on the streets of Montreal, everything seemed to be allowed in a hockey rink. "One gets the impression," the judge explained, "that hockey players believe that there will be no police intervention and no criminal charges regardless of what they do on the ice."

To a large extent the judge is right. Ever since Owen McCourt was killed on a hockey rink in 1907, judges have been issuing warnings and hockey players have gotten away with murder—or close to it. Neither judges, nor owners, nor the players themselves really want to legislate against mayhem on skates.

"It's part of the game," said Lorne Henning of the New York Islanders. "Eliminate it, and people just wouldn't pay to see a hockey game."

Perhaps he's right. Violence has been part and parcel of the Canadian and American way of living since the arrival of Columbus. Perhaps hockey's appeal as sanctioned savagery can be understood in terms of a report by the National Commission on the Causes and Prevention of Violence. It helps explain why Americans, in particular, have become more and more infatuated with hockey's bloodshed.

"Our nation was conceived and born in violence," said the Report. "In the violence of the sons of liberty and the patriots of the American port cities of the 1760s and 1770s.

"The patriot, the humanitarian, the nationalist, the pioneer, the landholder, the farmer and the laborer (and the capitalist) have used violence as a means to a higher end. For all our rhetoric, we have never been a very law-abiding nation, and illegal violence has sometimes been abundantly rewarded."

Nowhere is it so abundantly rewarded as it is in the NHL, where the 1974 world champion Philadelphia Flyers have turned butchery into a money-making art form. "One night," said former California Seals coach Fred Glover, "the Flyers just chopped us up. I had a guy slashed so bad his wrist was almost broken."

And the fans love it. Within a year after the Flyers turned killers they became the biggest drawing card in pro hockey. Perhaps that is not necessarily a bad thing. Perhaps the hockey arena has become a legitimate outlet for our stopped-up aggressions.

It is suggested that technology has robbed man of what Austrian anthropologist Konrad Lorenz calls "the legitimate outlets" for the aggressive drives bred into him over thousands of years.

Sigmund Freud said that "the tendency to aggression is an innate, independent, instinctual disposition in man." Lorenz contends that prehistoric man developed his aggressive tendencies purely as a matter of survival—to kill for his food and defend himself.

"We began, after all, as a people who killed red men and enslaved black men," said Arthur Schlesinger, Jr., the Pulitzer prize–winning historian. "No nation, however righteous its professions, could act as we did in Vietnam without burying deep in itself—in its customs, its institutions and its psyche—a propensity toward violence."

Perhaps that is what veteran hockey promoter Conn Smythe had in mind when a bunch of "nervous Nellies" urged him to curb the amount of blood being spilled by his Toronto Maple Leafs on the ice.

"Yes," snapped Smythe, "we've got to stamp out this sort of thing or people are going to keep on buying tickets!"

2

The Hockey Cop: Epitome of the Violent Player

IN THE VIOLENT WORLD of professional hockey there are hard checkers, deft bodyblockers, and assorted players who, from time to time, display their belligerence. These skaters are to be differentiated from the hockey cop, a player who is acknowledged by his teammates to be a very special breed of hard guy.

The hockey cop didn't get that way overnight—nor in one season or even two. It takes years and years to build a reputation and sustain it against challengers, both in the major and minor leagues. It takes seasons of battles and hundreds of stitches, dozens of broken bones, and the firm knowledge implanted in the opposition that the hockey cop, despite all his wounds, will come back for more.

Almost without exception the hockey cops are, as George Frazier IV once put it, a "strange species of marvelously durable brutes, men who are uniquely and superhumanly (or perhaps *sub*humanly) insensitive to physical pain." Perhaps surprisingly, they are also remarkably mild-mannered human beings *off* the ice.

Nobody more epitomized the hockey cop than Larry Zeidel, who skated for the Philadelphia Flyers from 1967 through 1969 as well as a Stanley Cup–winning Detroit Red Wings club and a cellar-dwelling Chicago Black Hawks team. Zeidel, now a respected Philadelphia stockbroker and commissioner of a local high-school hockey league, was involved in one of the bitterest and bloodiest ice battles the game has known. Zeidel and

Boston Bruin Eddie Shack raked each other murderously during a game in 1968, swinging sticks like machetes. When the battle was over they looked as though they had been in a terrible traffic accident as blood coursed down their dazed faces. According to Zeidel the stitches he accumulated from that encounter lifted his embroidery total over the seven-hundred mark encompassing twenty years as a professional "hit" man of the rinks.

To understand what motivated Zeidel one must flash back to his childhood.

For Zeidel it all began on the streets of Montreal where he was born on June 1, 1928. The son of immigrant Jews, Zeidel quickly learned the meaning of anti-Semitism on the streets of the tough Park Extension neighborhood of Montreal. The Zeidels were the only Jewish family in the community, a fact literally punched home to him at the age of five.

"I got my first taste of anti-Semitism when I started school," said Zeidel. "The kids knew I was a Jew. They'd gang up on me. First it was one gang, then another."

His mother wanted him to go to college and be a doctor; a nice Jewish boy should get into a profession. Larry obliged with first-rate grades in school. He was clearly Phi Beta Kappa material except that he was already carrying a chip on his shoulder and actually enjoyed the raw spirit of his community. The jungle law of Park Extension was not much different from the jungle law of professional hockey. In that blue-collar, working-class community, the toughest kids survived, and Zeidel was one of the toughest on the street or in the neighborhood rink. When he walked out of the house he consciously—and sometimes unconsciously—told the world this was one Jew-boy who wouldn't take any crap. If anyone disagreed he only had to take a shot at that chip.

"There was only one thing to do," Larry recalled, "and that was fight. So I fought. I didn't have that much time to think, I had to survive. My scheme was to go after the ringleaders, the bullies. I figured that if I could take them, I could take anybody and I'd get the respect I needed. I did that and I won the fights and I got a reputation that I was a guy to be left alone—or else!"

A psychological root had been planted and soon took firm control of Zeidel's personality. He remained a discreet youngster at home and in the classroom where survival was a simple matter, but when he skated onto the hockey rink where his WASP enemies were carrying long, sharp sticks, the chip on his shoulder appeared and the nice Jewish boy from Park Extension became as murderous as the neighborhood laws would permit.

"I needed every bit of toughness at my command," Zeidel remembered. "Toughness with the fist and toughness with the stick because my opponents were ruthless. They'd put the stick right through me if they were given a chance, so I had to be sure and hit first. I went after the bullies, and I discovered that I was doing all right and that I'd last for a long time."

In those pre-1967 days the mother NHL consisted of only six teams. There was no draft system, and the "have" teams—Toronto, Detroit, and Montreal—stockpiled their minor-league clubs with talent that could have been playing elsewhere in the National League. "You were a body," said Zeidel, "virtually a slave. Like slaves, you had a basic impulse—self-preservation."

A player was totally at the mercy of the club that owned him. There were no unions, no player agents; only an employers' market. Larry Zeidel's only friend was Larry Zeidel. His mentor was Hap Emms, a hard-nosed, junior hockey manager.

"Every second word out of Emm's mouth was *guts*," Zeidel pointed out. "I remember one Emms' pep talk. I was on his junior team in Barrie, but Hap was also scouting for the pro team in Buffalo and had just returned from a trip.

"We were all standing around the dressing room when Hap came in. He just stood there in the center of the room and looked around at all of us. Then, in a very low voice, he began to speak. 'You know I was on a scouting trip. Well, while I was at a game I saw a player who could skate faster than the late and great Howie Morenz, the fastest of them all. Not only that, but this guy could shoot better than Morenz. In fact he could do almost *everything* better than the great Howie Morenz.'

"Then, Emms paused. 'There was only one thing wrong,' he went on, still in a very low tone. All of a sudden Hap went out of his mind, 'ONLY HE DIDN'T HAVE ANY GUTS!' And he was just spitting the words out, like it was something dirty to say, just ranting and raving about this guy who didn't have any guts."

Zeidel eventually graduated to the Detroit Red Wings and stickhandled and bludgeoned his way to the Stanley Cup victory party in April, 1952. The Red Wings, led by Ted ("I hate *everyone* on the opposition") Lindsay and the tough Gordie Howe, completed Larry's education.

"Detroit had its eye on a kid named Bob Solinger who had been burning up the American League," said Zeidel. "But before they'd sign him they put him through the guts wringer during an exhibition game."

Larry watched in awe as Solinger took the ice for the Cleveland Barons and the Red Wings cast a bloodthirsty eye on their prey.

"It was like we were executing a mission at the front lines," Zeidel recalled. "Everyone on the Detroit bench was saying, 'All right, they've got this guy Solinger who's supposed to be so good. Well, we'll have to put him through the wringer and test him.' Believe me, they did. They nicked him in the face with their sticks and cut him wide open. Like good burglars, they escaped without penalties."

Solinger escaped with his life but never made it with the Red Wings. "Howe and Lindsay walked into the dressing room when the game was over, shook their heads, lowered their eyes, and whispered, 'No guts. The guy hasn't got it!' "

Even if your teammates believe that you've "got it," you have to keep it. At any time in a player's career he can be so traumatized by an injury or a fight that he suddenly finds himself run out of the league. For Zeidel the end almost came in May, 1953, when he stopped a shot with his temple.

"The last thing I remember was going down to the ice feeling a heavy *clop* when the puck hit me and then hearing a buzzing in my head exactly like a telephone busy signal."

When Larry awakened he was being carried off the ice to the trainer's room. Red Wings coach Jimmy Skinner and trainer Carl Mattson were waiting for him. He was frightened.

"I figured I had had it as a hockey player," Zeidel said. "If my reflexes were any good I would have ducked in time. I knew that the shot could have killed me. Then I tried to touch the hairs on my chest but I couldn't feel anything. My fingertips felt like lightning bolts."

Skinner slowly walked to the table and leaned over Zeidel. "How do you feel, Rock?" he asked quietly.

Zeidel shook his head. "I can't figure it out, coach. I can't feel the hairs on my chest. It's like electricity when I touch them."

The coach leaned forward and smiled. Slapping Zeidel on the shoulder, he scoffed, "Aw, they don't call you 'Rock,' for nothing, do they?"

Larry got the message. His guts were on the line. "There I am, lying on my back with a busy signal still going off in my head. I'd been hit in the temple by a shot, and he's standing there feeding me this stuff—'They don't call you "Rock" for nothing.' "

At that precise moment Zeidel noticed the trainers carrying in another injured teammate. He had two welts on his head like golf balls. Zeidel looked at Skinner, turned to his injured colleague, and leaped off the table like a jack-in-the-box, shouting, "Goddamn right they don't call me the 'Rock' for nothing!"

He didn't know it at the time but that telephone sound in his head was a signal that he had a fractured skull.

"It took me ten days in the hospital before I even regained my appetite. But hurt as I was, I really bought all that 'They-don't-call-you-"Rock"-for-nothing' stuff. As soon as I could eat again, I grabbed my clothes and sneaked out. I wanted to play again, but the doctor caught me and said I might die if anything happened on the ice. Skinner didn't bug me, so I guess I proved I had guts. By this time it was clear to me that guts was the name of the game."

Zeidel covered most of the hockey map during his career. By the time he was thirty he had engaged in three of the most chilling bouts in hockey history, and each for a different reason. In his classic stick-swinging encounter with Jack Evans, Larry was the cop protecting his smaller teammates. The Zeidel–Bill Shvetz bloodbath was purely a case of personal retribution; Shvetz, a Cleveland defenseman, had sliced open Zeidel's face with the point of his stick. "I spent two days just looking at that thing in the mirror," Zeidel recalled, "and all I could see was Shvetz's face."

Envy was the motivation in the Eddie Shack–Zeidel encounter. The two had had a fistfight during an exhibition game between Shack's Rangers and Zeidel's club, the Hershey Bears. Superficially, at least, it appeared that Shack was the winner.

"I was bleeding," Larry explained, "and Shack didn't have a scratch on him. I was madder than hell. Besides, I had built up a reputation by this time."

In the vendettas with Evans and Shvetz, Zeidel nearly killed both his enemies. "I put my sharpened stick into Shvetz," he said, "and just then the shaft broke. In retrospect it was a good thing because that stick was like a bayonet. If it hadn't broken I would have killed him."

He nailed Shack after the two had been evicted from their game and were in civvies watching the game from the grandstands. Larry approached Shack from the side, tapped him on the shoulder, and administered a blazing right cross. Minutes later, Zeidel and Shack were arrested. Larry didn't mind all that much. "I had settled the score," he said.

At least for a decade. He had survived by using the uppercut, the sucker punch, the spear, and whatever weapon would ensure a weekly paycheck. "I did anything to survive," he said. "After a while, I had the other guys thinking I was some kind of a nut. Mostly it was like those days in Park Extension. I couldn't let *anybody* think he could take liberties with me. A guy named Phil Maloney once tried it, putting his stick between my legs and lifting up on me. I got him later—punched him in the eye. I think his eye is still a little off center because of my punch. But he deserved it after what he had done to me."

When you're a cop like Zeidel, you know that many—like Maloney—don't come back to trouble you or haunt you. But Shack did. It took him a decade to catch up with Zeidel, but when he did, he extracted his pound of flesh.

Larry had turned thirty-nine and was making an NHL comeback with the Philadelphia Flyers. He tried to go straight. It was like Capone going soft. Word got around.

"The only reason I changed my style," Larry explained, "was that my manager [Bud Poile] and coach [Keith Allen] both had me in my wild days in the minors. They knew the Flyers were a weaker team, so they begged me not to go crazy and get a lot of penalties. So, I stayed calm."

But too many among the foe remembered Zeidel as Attila the Hun, not Howdy Doody.

It took nearly a season before Zeidel was cut down. Shack and Shack's team, the Boston Bruins, were big and bad, and their ringleader, "Terrible" Ted Green, was feared like the wrath of God throughout the NHL. "Teddy could shake us up just by staring," said his teammate Derek Sanderson. "His eyes made me quiver. One look from Greenie was worth a thousand-word tongue-lashing."

Huskier than their opponents and infinitely more aggressive, the Bruins used intimidation as a basic form of strategy. Gang-fighting was their specialty. If one Boston player was involved in a bout, chances were that another would grab the enemy from behind, and even a third might become involved if necessary. "We practiced violence," said Sanderson, "because we knew it won hockey games. The other teams were afraid of us. Which meant we had the puck most of the time."

In addition to their sticks and fists the Bruins used their tongues to advantage, slicing up their enemies with invective and threats. Because he was the only Jew in the NHL, Zeidel was an ideal target.

To throw Zeidel off stride, the Bruins barbed him with stinging epithets: "We'll see you in a gas chamber, Jew-boy!" Zeidel counted to ten and minded his business. He remembered the warnings from Poile and Allen. There was a play-off berth to attain, and getting penalties was not going to do him or the Flyers any good.

"Jew-boy . . ." The zingers continued on that February night in 1968. "I took a lot of dirt in that game," said Zeidel. "We were down 2–0 when Green came down the ice on a rush, one-on-one against me. In a matter of seconds he practically put his stick down my throat and ran me into the net."

The "new" Zeidel turned the other cheek. The sidewalk battles of Park Extension were erased from his mind. He knew that he had made a critical strategic mistake. "You can't be intimidated in this game," he said, "and I was, in this case."

For a month Larry tortured himself over the episode with Green: "I knew I couldn't be Mr. Nice Guy anymore. *I had to get even.*"

March 7, 1968, was his day of retribution: "I was psyched high. I knew there would be blood. I figured the one I came into contact with first would be the one to get it. But the Bruins were working on me, too. They were telling me to watch out, that they were out to get me."

Eddie Shack, whom Zeidel had sucker-punched way back when, ran at Larry just as he released a shot on goal. Zeidel took a crunching elbow in the jaw. "That," said Zeidel, "was my cue. The next time Shack came along I gave him the stick, up high. He came back at me, madder than hell, and gave me a shot with his stick."

Joe DiMaggio, Willie Mays, and Stan Musial never swung harder than the two players doing their macabre dance around the rink. Soon, blood burst forth from their respective faces. They looked like a pair of gored bulls. "I remember thinking," said Zeidel, "while all this was happening that 'this is crazy,' but we kept swinging at each other."

Eventually officials intervened before both players killed each other. They were taken to the infirmary for repairs. Zeidel needed six stitches, Shack three. The Flyers tried to make a case of the Bruins' anti-Semitic needling but only succeeded in getting a lot of headlines. Boston's strategy of intimidation had worked.

Both Shack and Zeidel were brought on the carpet by NHL president Clarence Campbell. After a relatively mild wrist-slapping both were able to resume playing.

Except the Flyers' front office believed that Zeidel had had it. They did not want the "old" troublemaking Larry the Rock, and they realized that a Zeidel who turned the other cheek was as good as no Zeidel at all.

Before the next season was a month old, Zeidel was dropped by the Flyers.

Ironically, Zeidel's exit coincided with the ascendancy of Ted Green as the number-one cop in professional hockey—a role that almost cost him his life.

Like Zeidel, Green was the offspring of Canadian parents who were less than wealthy. Unlike Zeidel, Green had an older brother, Tony, against whom he played hockey. Tony Green was an easygoing kid, Teddy was the opposite.

"I was tough and hard-nosed," said Green, "always in fights on the ice, always bashing the nearest someone with something—stick, elbows, or bare hands. I wasn't mad at anybody. As a defenseman I had a job to do, and that was my way of doing it."

Green made it to the NHL because of his aggressiveness more than his ability. The Bruins were a weak team and needed all the color they could get in order to fill Boston Garden. "I played a hard game," Green explained, "because management expected it of me at the time. It was the only way I was going to stay in the league. If I didn't knock people down, which is what the fans expected me to do, I wasn't going to keep my job."

It was a question of economics, of survival.

Yet if you took Teddy Green away from the rink, he could pass for Casper Milquetoast. "I was sort of shocked to learn he was supposed to be the tough guy of the NHL," said his wife, Pat Green. "At first I couldn't understand it. He may have been a terror on the ice, but he was a lamb off it—a sweet, considerate guy who acted as if he wouldn't swat a fly."

In time the Bruins acquired so many bashers Green found that he had less and less protecting to do. He began accenting his offensive skills, his stickhandling, playmaking, and shooting, while deemphasizing his brawling. But like Zeidel he couldn't shake the "Terrible" mantle. "Once you acquire a reputation," he lamented, "you seldom lose it. Sure I kept getting into fights, but I didn't look for them."

On the night of September 21, 1969, Teddy Green was to face his most violent moment as a hockey player. In his autobiography *High Stick*, Green detailed his account of the tragedy. It is the most simple yet precise anatomy of a hockey fight ever written; each player was right, and yet each was wrong. What Wayne Maki of the St. Louis Blues did to Green, Green had attempted to do to other opponents earlier in his career. The young gunslinger went after the old-timer, and it was high noon on the ice.

"As I trapped the puck behind the net," wrote Green, "the kid hit me from behind, and I got a little ticked off, as I always do when that happens. But my first obligation was to clear the puck. I kicked it with my skate up to my stick, and shot it around the boards to our right wing. Then I turned to take care of the guy who hit me (Maki). By that time we'd both moved in front and a little to the left of our net. I reached out with my gloved hand and shoved Maki in the face. He went down by the side of the net. Figuring that was the end of that, I turned away, but then Maki speared me in the abdomen.

"Now I was sore as hell, and I hit Maki with my stick just below the shoulder at the bicep, knocking him off balance and, I think, down on one knee. I say 'I think' because I'm not really sure, and I wouldn't know what happened next except from pictures and from what I was told. Seeing Maki on the ice is the last clear memory I have. My last thought was, *Well, I guess that'll straighten him out*, and, again, I turned to skate away.

"The next thing I knew, I was lying on my stomach with my head turning violently. I remember trying to stop it from moving, but I couldn't because I had no control over it. It was whipping back and forth."

Green was rushed to a hospital where he teetered on the brink of death. He had suffered severe brain damage. At first it was believed that he would never regain the normal use of his legs, arms, and mouth. Certainly nobody ever expected Ted Green to play hockey again.

He sat out the 1969–70 season but slowly and painfully worked his way back into shape. "While recovering," said Green, "I could skate, handle a stick, and carry a puck before I could write my name."

Green persisted in his exercises and eventually recovered to the point where he was able to return to the Bruins lineup for the 1970–71 season. Soon he was confronted by Maki, the man who had nearly killed him a year earlier.

"I just don't want to have anything to do with him," said Green. "Maybe he felt the same way. The few times we were on the ice together we hardly went near each other. Frankly, if I saw him coming at me, I'd go the other way. Maybe I was afraid of myself, of what I might do to the guy. All I know is the less I saw of him the better."

Those who remembered the "old" Ted Green and the one who emerged from the hospital to skate again in the NHL and later the WHA, were dumbstruck by the change in his decorum. The erstwhile "Terrible Teddy" learned from his misfortune.

"I'm not trying to sound religious or anything," said Green, "but I did a lot of praying in the hospital, and I lived. I realized afterwards how delicate life is, how short it is, too. Before the first game we played against Wayne Maki, after he got back from his suspension, I wrote a letter to my team telling the guys not to go after Wayne.

"The guys had told me how they were going to get Maki for me. So I wrote the letter. Eddie Johnston, who was our goaltender and player rep at the time, got up in the dressing room and read it out to the guys. A lot of them couldn't understand my thinking. Couldn't see it at all. But I understood, and that's all that mattered."

Green saw little enough of Maki and played two full seasons with the Bruins before switching to the New England Whalers of the World Hockey Association. His play was competent but consciously more temperate than in his NHL days.

"That bad-guy stuff," said Green, "was built all out of proportion. It was kept alive by the papers. I've never been quite as terrible as they made me out to be."

Maki emerged as the tragic figure in the dispute. He was dealt to the Vancouver Canucks and in December, 1972, underwent a four-hour emergency operation for removal of a brain tumor. He died of the tumor in May, 1974.

Why did a seemingly innocent clash develop into so awesome an incident? "It started," said Green, "when he speared me with his stick and I retaliated with mine. Except I don't think I'll ever do so again. I realize now more than anyone what can happen."

Why did it happen? Larry Zeidel said the reaction was rooted in the hockey cop's psyche. It was a conditioned reflex. "We were brought up like Pavlov's dog," said Zeidel. "We were trained by coaches and managers to shove our sticks down the enemy's throat. Fortunately for me I didn't end up with a plate in my head like Teddy Green. When all is said and done," Zeidel concluded, "the excessive bloodletting occurred—and still occurs—because we were taught that it's a badge of honor to go onto the rink and kill!"

3

The Role of the Fan in Hockey Violence

ON THE NIGHT OF JANUARY 7, 1972, the St. Louis Blues and the Philadelphia Flyers were playing at the Spectrum in Philadelphia. The Blues were coming off a 9–1 defeat by the New York Rangers and a severe tongue-lashing by their coach, Al Arbour. Worse, they were in fifth place, faced with the possibility of missing the play-offs for the first time since their entry into the NHL in 1967.

So they were on edge, more so since they trailed the fourth-place Flyers 2–0 after two periods. The Blues also felt that Philadelphia's second goal, near the end of the second period, should have been disallowed. The Blues claimed that the score had come about because referee John Ashley dropped the puck on a face-off before St. Louis center Garry Unger was ready.

At the end of the period Arbour walked onto the ice to continue his protest. Ashley responded by calling a two-minute bench penalty against the Blues, and then he started walking to the officials' dressing room.

Arbour followed. Then, as the St. Louis coach moved along a walkway leading to the area beneath the stands, a fan poured beer on his head. That ignited one of the worst donnybrooks in the history of the NHL and emphasized how frequently fans become caught up in the whirlpool of hockey violence.

Fourteen St. Louis players charged across the ice and surged onto the walkway. The fans threw cups and debris at the players. Some of the Blues retaliated by swinging their sticks at fans. Punches were exchanged. Police reinforcements were called—150 cops in all responded—and soon they and some of the Blues were brawling.

"When I saw the Blues start coming I ran over to the rail," fourteen-year-old Anthony Bordini said later. "When I tried to get back to my seat, the crowd pressed me and I couldn't get free. Then the Blues started climbing the fence and swinging their sticks. I got hit on top of the head. One of my buddies got hit, too."

Mrs. Betty Kania, who was at the game with her daughter and son-in-law, said she became hysterical. "Garry Unger was swinging like I don't know what," she recalled. "Barclay Plager was trying to tell me to get down low, so I wouldn't get hit."

The fight lasted thirty minutes. Coach Arbour needed ten stitches to close a head wound, and defenseman John Arbour took forty stitches, also for a head wound. Four fans were injured, and several policemen suffered an assortment of cuts and bruises. The two Arbours, plus St. Louis wingers Phil Roberto and Floyd Thomson, were arrested. (Charges against them were dismissed a few months later.)

For the most part, the Philadelphia press blamed the riot on Arbour and the Blues. Certainly they had to bear a good part of the blame. And there is no excuse for the players who swung their hockey sticks at some of the fans. But the spark was supplied by the fan who poured beer on Arbour's head. And there isn't any excuse for that, either. Which prompts the question: What's wrong with hockey fans?

The fact is that there is an increasing number of hockey fans who believe, apparently, that buying a ticket gives them the right to shout obscenities, to threaten, and to hurl objects at hockey players. True, this type of fan is in the minority. But he is becoming increasingly dangerous—so dangerous, in fact, that some hockey officials are now looking for ways to neutralize him.

"Hockey players don't have much protection on the bench from fans who want to throw things at them," says Bill McCreary, a former NHL player. "I would hate to see it come to putting a cover over the bench to protect the players. That would take away a lot of the appeal from the normal, well-behaved fans who like the closeness they have to the players on the bench."

As McCreary said, closeness is part of hockey's appeal. But it's also part of its problem. Everything is magnified, and since hockey is by its very nature a violent sport, the speed, contact, and on-the-ice fisticuffs generate spectator emotions unlike those associated with any other professional sport. And often it takes just a small incident to push those emotions out of control. That's when hockey fans go crazy.

Sometimes the actions of an individual player can trigger violent reaction. Case in point: Derek Sanderson.

A few years back, again at the Spectrum, Sanderson was serving a minor penalty when he took exception to some of the remarks being directed at him by two Philadelphia fans. Suddenly, he went after them, trying to scale the glass wall that separates the penalty box from the stands. The fans grabbed Sanderson and began pulling him over. At that point, half of the Bruins jumped in. That started a fair-sized brawl involving the Bruins, the fans, the police.

No one was badly hurt. But Sanderson, playing the incident for all it was worth, skated around on the ice after peace was restored while the irate Philadelphia fans booed their lungs out. Sanderson responded by thrusting both arms up in defiance and jabbing his stick in the air. That only goaded the "hate-Sanderson" crowd to a greater frenzy.

"One of those guys in back spit on me," Derek said. "I stood up on the bench, and he hit me. I decked him, and a couple of others moved in.

"I knocked that one down and took on the others," he continued. "It might have been very tough, but pretty soon Swoop [Carleton] and Ace [Bailey] were in there with me, too, so we had things kind of isolated. Shocker [Danny Schock] was there, too, and some of the other guys."

Nobody in the Spectrum management appeared greatly disturbed by the brawl.

You wouldn't think so, anyway, in view of the message that was flashed on the illuminated screen of the scoreboard:

THE FANS INVOLVED IN THE FIGHT ARE ALIVE AND WELL . . . 18 BRUINS COULDN'T HURT THEM.

But just as often incidents occur without apparent reason. During a regular-season game at Madison Square Garden, a fan jumped Minnesota goalie Cesare Maniago as he and his teammates were on their way to the dressing room after a 5–0 win over the Rangers. About ten other North Stars came to Maniago's rescue and gave the fan a good going-over.

"You don't know if he's got a gun or a knife," Dennis Hextall remarked after the incident. "All you know is that one of your teammates is down there."

Usually, of course, fan-player fights involve home crowds and visiting teams. But there are times when the reverse is true.

Back in 1965, for example, at the old Madison Square Garden, the Rangers and Detroit Red Wings were locked in a tight game when, following a pileup outside the New York net, the red light went on signifying a Detroit goal. Emile Francis, then the general manager but not the coach, jumped from his seat as soon as the red light went on and rushed to the goal judge's area. "I was watching that play clearly," Francis shouted, "and that puck never crossed the red line."

Suddenly, a burly spectator sitting near the goal judge got into the act. "Get lost, Francis," he yelled, "that puck was in!" Then, before Francis really knew what was happening, that fan and two others jumped him. One tore the coat off Francis' back, and a second crawled on top of Francis and started pelting him with lefts and rights.

Fortunately for Francis, left wing Vic Hadfield saw what was happening and led a dozen of his teammates over the glass barrier to Francis' rescue. They grabbed two of the three fans who had punched the general manager and turned them over to police. Francis, meanwhile, needed stitches to close cuts on his left cheekbone and over his left eye.

The spectators who attacked Francis were not necessarily Detroit fans. Some hockey buffs get just as much of a charge out of riding the home team as they do riding the opposition. This is especially true of fans who have rooted for a team that has suffered defeat after defeat and disappointment on top of disappointment. The Rangers and their fans are good examples of that. They used to expect the worst, and usually they got it. And as a result, though the Blueshirts are on top, the relationship between the Rangers and their fans is something of a love-hate match.

So it was not surprising that during the 1972 Stanley Cup play-offs some balcony fans at Madison Square Garden shouted obscenities at some of the New York players, and this while the Rangers were in the process of sweeping the Chicago Black Hawks.

A few weeks later, however, some of these same Madison Square Garden fans put on a disgraceful exhibition before and after the third game of the Stanley Cup final between the Rangers and the Bruins. Only this time the Bruins were the target.

During the pregame warm-ups, hundreds of spectators swarmed to rinkside and shouted obscenities and made vulgar gestures at the Bruins. (One wonders how this affected the women and children within earshot. One wonders how soon they'll go back to a hockey game.)

Then, after the game, the Bruins were forced to skate off the ice with gloved hands protecting their heads from a barrage of missiles that included lighters, keys, transistor batteries, oranges, and apple cores.

"It made me sick," former Boston goalie Gerry Cheevers said later. "I was scared. Don't those people know it's wrong? Don't they know they can hurt somebody? They've got to be nuts. Imagine what happens if one of those batteries hits you? Sure, they're throwing at us, but they could hit a Ranger or a fan near the ice. The crowd here is the worst in hockey. You should hear the filthy stuff they call us."

Ranger defenseman Brad Park agreed. "It's got to be stopped," he said. "It's not good for hockey, for us, or for New York City. We've got a lot of fans, and they can help put a stop to the throwing of things by pointing out the idiots who do it."

The fourth game was also at Madison Square Garden. After the general outcry in the press about the incidents in the third game, the fans behaved themselves. But the players did not. There were a half dozen fights and over a hundred minutes in penalties. Which moved *New York Post* sports columnist Larry Merchant to observe: "Such disorderly conduct [by the players] might incite the fans to do all those disorderly things the Rangers and Bruins didn't want them to do."

The fans' role in contributing to the violence varies. Sometimes the spectators are goaded into their animalistic behavior, and other times they themselves inspire the players to shed blood and more blood.

In Philadelphia, for example, the Flyers have undergone a systematic image transformation from what has been described as "Pattison Avenue Patsies" to "Broad Street Bullies." "Come," beckons a Flyers promotional brochure, "and see the Mean Machine!"

Before a year had elapsed, the sight of the Philadelphia Mean Machine skating in an enemy rink was like waving a red flag in front of seventeen thousand bulls. "As soon as I saw the Flyers coming out on the ice with those evil-looking orange sweaters and broken beaks," said a Montreal hockey fan, "and skating around with their asses away up in the air, I said to myself, 'My God, this is an old-time Gashouse Gang. That Bob Kelly and Dave Schultz. They look like reincarnations of Dracula."

The fans in Montreal fling remarks like *"Tueur"* ("killer, butcher") and *"Salaud"* ("dirty player") at the Flyers.

On St. Patrick's night, 1955, a Montreal mob rioted in protest against NHL president Clarence Campbell's suspension of Maurice Richard for the season, for slashing an opponent and slugging a linesman. Moved to a fury pitch by Campbell's decision, the Forum audience cuffed, pelted, and very nearly killed Campbell before he was barely whisked to safety by police. Someone threw a gas bomb. The Montreal fire department cleared the Forum. Montreal forfeited the game to Detroit, and in the ensuing hours a crazed mob smashed windows, looted, and overturned vehicles for nearly a mile along Montreal's main drag, Ste. Catherine Street.

That represented the extreme example of a fan uprising, but they have continued in more limited forms. During the 1973–74 season Bruins defenseman Bobby Orr incited a near riot at Boston Garden after disputing a referee's decision. Orr smashed his stick on the sideboards in a temper tantrum, and soon the spectators began filling the air with beer cans and bottles.

Maintenance men were so fearful of the audience they refused at first even to attempt to clear the ice. "Someday," warned a Garden cop, "some of those nuts on the Bruins are going to start a riot, and there's no way we can stop them."

Many responsible observers believe that controlled violence in the arena has a positive cathartic effect on spectators as if a sore had been lanced and the poison drained off.

"After their display of hostility," wrote G. E. Mortimore of the Forum crowd, "you might expect them to be scowling as they make their way down to the snowy street. In fact, many of them are laughing. They look thoroughly happy."

It is this blood lust that more and more appears to dominate the spectators' interest, and where it will stop nobody knows.

During April, 1974, Fred Shero, the Philadelphia Flyers coach, was mugged by Atlanta fans *after* a game in the Omni. So violent was the attack that Shero was compelled to return to Philadelphia for treatment while an aide coached his team a night later.

At the rate fans are intervening, it appears that only a juicy case of manslaughter will appease their thirst for gore. Or will it?

4

The Modern Marauders:
Individual Killers

PRECISELY WHAT ARE THE INGREDIENTS that motivate a hockey player to commit violent acts in a game that is so thoroughly beautiful?

It is a sport so artistic in its concept that an organizer of the Canadian National Ballet never missed a Toronto game for years because, she said, the game has a quality of beauty and discipline of the body that, as a dancer, she understands.

And yet it is a game mottled with roughnecks who often prefer to drink an opponent's blood rather than score a goal. It is a sport in which one Hall of Famer, Edouard "Newsy" Lalonde, boasted that in his career, "I was involved in fifty stretcher-case fights."

Lalonde was not the exception, he was the rule. Another Hall of Famer, Dick Irvin, once had his front teeth crosschecked into his tongue by an opponent named Cully Wilson. Wilson's five-minute penalty was considered miles too mild for Irvin, who took the law into his own hands and clubbed Wilson over the head so hard that even the hard-bitten Newsy Lalonde was horrified.

"I've never seen more damage done by one man to another in my life," said Lalonde. "After they revived him Wilson needed enough stitches in him to weave an Indian blanket."

Such acts of violence are often taken for granted on the ice. Lalonde's skull was nearly detached from his torso one night by a chap named

Sprague Cleghorn, who once disabled three players in one night. Cleghorn was arrested for nearly killing Lalonde, but Newsy hardly was vindictive about the accident. The next day Lalonde pleaded before the judge on Cleghorn's behalf and was so successful that Cleghorn escaped with a $200 fine.

Cleghorn apparently wasn't moved to pacifism. Shortly thereafter he stickwhipped huge Lionel Hitchman so viciously that Cleghorn's own manager, Leo Dandurand, fined him $200.

One reason why violence is so rampant is that hockey players very early in their careers are conditioned to be indifferent to pain. "It's a basic part of the game," said NHL veteran Glen Sather, who majored in child psychology. "Our ability to withstand pain while we're playing stems from the time we were youngsters. We'd watch the other kids with facial lacerations continuing to play although blood was streaming out of a cut. At that level there was no one stitching wounds.

"You just kept on playing, accepting the injury as a minor affliction. It was an attitude we picked up from our coaches. A player gets to realize that violence on ice is spontaneous, something a hockey player learns to forget."

Hall of Famer Tom Johnson was one who learned to forget. Johnson's career was abruptly ended by a kick in the calf from an opponent's razor-sharp skate. It slashed his muscles and nerves so badly Boston Bruins trainer John Forristall described it as "the worst thing I ever saw." But Johnson was casual about it and dismissed his enemy as some type of assailant.

"He might have meant to kick me, sure," said Johnson, "but I don't think he meant to hurt me *badly*."

Like Sather, Johnson is a native of Western Canada where the "tough life" tends to inure youngsters to brutality on ice. "When I was a child," said Sather, "I saw cattle slaughtered. I remember helping dehorn cattle when I was twelve—seeing blood shoot all over the place. But there were men there with us, and we wanted to be men just like them."

So, resistance to pain enables most hockey players to tolerate the violence around them. That, plus the innate speed of the game, which solidifies this condition. "The brain," said Dr. John Bonica, head of the Pain Clinic at the University of Washington at Seattle, "is unable to handle more than a few things at one time. Concentrating intensely, the hockey player is able to ignore pain because the brain is unable to perceive the problem. Only so many impulses can flow along the spinal cord to the brain, and pain is low down on the scale of perceivable impulses."

What about the personalities of players who perpetuate violence? Are they using violence to conceal a basic dearth of talent? Are they naturally aggressive? Sadomasochistic? Insecure? Do some feel a need for punishment?

The answers are almost as numerous as the more than five hundred players in hockey's major leagues. There are, however, some basic generalizations that can be made. To wit:

Small Players

Skaters in this group overcompensate for their lack of size as a means of self-defense. Hall of Famer Ted Lindsay is the classic example of a little man who became an NHL terror.

"I've been slashed, speared, elbowed, butt-ended, and boardchecked as much as anybody who ever played the game of hockey," said Lindsay. "I had a broken shoulder, a broken instep, a broken hand, and a couple of hundred stitches in my face. *I just wanted to keep the ledger balanced.*"

Henri Richard, captain of the Montreal Canadiens, is smaller than Lindsay. Apart from his size, Richard was burdened with the Richard name. His brother, Maurice the "Rocket," was the most exciting scorer in hockey history and one of the most prolific. Young Henri thus became a natural target for NHL bullies and was compelled to establish himself with—and against—the hit men. His singular triumph on New Year's Day, 1958, is regarded by veteran linesman Matt Pavelich as the most memorable fight he's seen.

Pavelich, who has been breaking up NHL fights for nearly two decades, had total recall of the episode:

"Henri hadn't been in the league very long at the time, and the fans and players used to get on him, saying he was only there because of his brother, the Rocket, who was still playing.

"Henri was going along the boards, and big Fern Flaman of Boston, one of the toughest players in history, was rubbing him. Then Leo Labine, another hard-nosed Bruin, leaped off the bench and took a swing at Henri. The players had been giving him a rough time all night.

"Well, Henri hauled off and hit Labine and split his eyebrow for eight stitches. That put Labine out. Then, Jack Bionda, another big, tough defenseman who was also a great lacrosse player, came into it. Jack was about two hundred ten pounds and six-one. A real rough, tough customer.

"Richard hit him and split his nose—twisted it across his face. That put him out. Flaman came after Henri next. Flaman didn't lose too many, but he didn't beat Henri. It was a saw-off. To tell the truth, I wouldn't have believed it if I hadn't seen it with my own eyes. The linesmen still talk about that one."

The little men, therefore, go out of their way to prove their masculinity in what many observers consider the most masculine of the popular spectator sports. "Hockey players are born into a tradition," said Dr. Allan Levy, team physician for the New York Islanders. "It's a *machismo* tradition.

"I remember one night little Bobby Lalonde of Vancouver was hit so hard in the shoulder that his glove flew thirty feet in the air. When he was helped up I told him to go immediately to the hospital for X rays. He told me he'd only go after the game. He played the whole third period on innate aggressiveness."

Bryan Watson is another smallish player who, according to Sather, is "the toughest guy I know." Watson's size and limited talents militate against him; therefore he must compensate, and he does so physically.

"In the corners," said Watson, "I have to use all my resources. Maybe I'll be dirty. But I have to get the job done. My best trick is tripping people and getting away with it. There's a way to get a guy to fall on his face without getting called for a penalty. Disguise it, hide it, but get him down. I'll hit a guy when he's looking the other way. I'll give him some crap if I can get away with it."

Away from the rink Watson is calm, courteous, intelligent, and surprisingly, somewhat squeamish. "Off the ice," said Sather, "let a doctor stick Bryan with a needle, and he passes out."

What, then, would enable a Watson to maraud the enemy yet blanch before a doctor?

"The player's motivation," explained Dr. Bonica, "is a strong factor. There are suggestions to him from several sources in the rink—the coach, the fact that he's a member of the group, the screaming and cheering of the crowd—that are key factors."

New York Islander Garry Howatt's motivation was two-fold. Like Richard and Lindsay he's small by hockey standards. And he is an epileptic. Ever since promotion to the NHL in 1973, Howatt has taken a special delight in battling with the biggest and toughest of the foe.

Once, during the 1973–74 season, Howatt (5 feet, 9 inches; 170 pounds) challenged Pat Quinn (6 feet, 3 inches; 215 pounds) of Atlanta. "He surprised me," said Quinn. "I didn't know the little guy was ready to fight, and before I could get my gloves off he landed a couple of good ones."

Howatt was asked why he didn't pick on somebody his own size. He grinned: "There isn't anybody on the ice my size."

Perhaps it is not all that surprising that little men like Howatt react so violently. One night in March, 1974, Howatt, who has the instincts and reflexes of a terrier, captured the imagination of fans in Maple Leaf Gardens when he outpointed the bigger Darryl Sittler of Toronto.

"I'm not surprised at the small guy being a good fighter," said Martin O'Malley of the *Toronto Globe and Mail.* "In my neighborhood, and I suspect in many other neighborhoods, the one to fear always, always, was the small, chippy boy with the choirboy face and large capacity for anger. Always, always, he was so incredibly quick and tenacious. Even if a bigger boy won, he didn't win. And if he lost—God, the humiliation!" Which brings us to . . .

Big Players

Skaters in this category are looked upon, by the very nature of their physique, to protect the smaller members of the tribe. Some of the big ice cops develop a concern for the smaller, defenseless skaters early in their careers. John Ferguson, one of the toughest big men the game has known, was one of them. He was a thirteen-year-old stickboy for the Vancouver Canucks when an incident on the ice left an indelible impression on Ferguson's psyche. The culprit, incidentally, was Larry Zeidel, then playing for Edmonton.

Zeidel was big, Phil Maloney small, a high-scorer and a pacifist. As Ferguson remembered it, Zeidel and Maloney clashed within arm's length of the Canucks' bench.

"Zeidel," said Ferguson, "sneaked up from behind. He just killed Maloney and nearly cost Phil the sight of an eye. I stood there and looked at the other players on that Vancouver team. Not one guy went to help. I hated the whole team and made up my mind that if I ever become a hockey player, I'd never stand by and watch something like that happen to one of my teammates."

Referee Art Skov has said that Ferguson epitomizes the player who used violence to conceal a lack of talent. "Ferguson," said Skov, "was a good boxer and brawler, anything you wanted him to be. He played tough hockey because he had to. He wasn't a very good skater and he played rough to compensate for his lack of ability as a player."

By contrast, Gordie Howe has been called by many respected critics the best and dirtiest player of all time. The charge has also been leveled by several players who should know, such as Derek Sanderson and Carl Brewer, both less than pantywaists.

"Howe," said Sanderson, "is the dirtiest, filthiest ever."

"Howe," said Brewer, "is a great player, but the dirtiest who ever lived."

"Hockey," replied Howe, "is a man's game."

Why was Howe violence-prone? Many of those who have known the superstar well believe that it was a function of his childhood. Gordie was an intelligent youngster who suffered a very limited schooling before leaving his native Saskatoon, Saskatchewan, to become a professional hockey player. In his early years with Detroit in the NHL, he remained an introverted youngster off the ice who seemed to release his social frustrations and aggressions against the enemy.

"He got into so many fights," said his manager Jack Adams, "that I told him he was wasting a great talent. I begged him to concentrate on scoring and stop fighting."

By April, 1950, Howe had become the best all-round player in the NHL. It was then that he suffered a serious injury that completely altered his psychology on aggression. Ted Kennedy, captain of the Toronto Maple Leafs, collided with Howe, sending the Red Wing plummeting headfirst into the sideboards.

For several days Howe teetered on the brink of death, having suffered a fractured skull. He eventually recovered and returned to the ice wars determined never to let his bumper down—in fact to get the first blow in if necessary to protect himself. One by one, the enemy fell before Gordie's quick stick.

"Howe," said former Rangers manager Muzz Patrick, "became the meanest and toughest in the NHL. Once I saw Howe nearly take the ear off my defenseman, Lou Fontinato. Gordie didn't think twice about it. His stick flashed up, and Fontinato almost lost an ear. It took twelve stitches to sew it back on."

Fontinato remembered the words of All-Star defenseman Doug Harvey: "Either you give it right back or the next thing you know, everybody and his brother will be trying you on for size."

In what many observers believe to be one of the most vicious one-on-one bouts on ice, Fontinato ran at Howe during a Rangers/Red Wings game at Madison Square Garden. Referee Art Skov was a linesman at the time and officiated that day.

"At that time," said Skov, "Fontinato was reputed to be the toughest man in the league. He'd fought and beaten everybody."

The bout erupted when Howe and Eddie Shack of the Rangers fenced with their sticks behind the net. Fontinato, who was at the blue line, skated to the fray, moved in on Howe, and began raining blows at him with no appreciable effect.

"Then," said Skov, "Howe began smashing him with lefts and rights and then fired an uppercut that smashed Lou's nose. I just stood back and said, 'No way, I'm not going in to break up this one.' Big George Hayes was the other linesman in the game, and he told me to stay out of it.

"It was a vicious thing, but Howe cleaned Fontinato like you've never seen. Louie was never feared much in the league after that."

In fact the demise of Fontinato was followed closely by the demise of the Rangers. The onetime cop was finally traded to Montreal where his career ended. He was smashed into the boards by the Rangers' new young cop, Vic Hadfield, and suffered a broken neck.

Each season from the moment hockey went big time, coaches, managers, and even referees have drummed the survival theme into the players' psyches. When Howie Morenz, one of the greatest players ever, was in his teens, a friendly referee, Lou Marsh, once told him, "Listen, kid, don't let anyone out there make a fool of you. Show 'em you can take it, and they'll leave you alone."

Wayne Cashman of the Bruins, one of the biggest players in the NHL, quickly adopted the hit-first philosophy and challenged Orland Kurtenbach, one of the league's best fighters, early in his career, whipped Kurtenbach, and has remained at the top of the hit parade.

To the amusement of many, Cashman has frequently played down his aggressiveness. "I pay no attention to the people who call me dirty," said Cashman. "I'm rough and I like body contact."

With Dennis Hextall, son of a former truculent major leaguer, Bryan Hextall, the feeling is mutual. One afternoon Cashman and Hextall collided. The result was a test-tube example of a battle of the big guys.

The turbulence was caused by the opening of a wound. Cashman slashed Hextall. Hextall cracked Cashman across the throat with *his* stick.

Cashman's version: "Hextall gave me a two-hander across the back of the legs. I chased him and slashed him in the ankles. Then he speared me in the throat, cutting off my wind."

Hextall's version: "Cashman hit me three times across the ankles, and I tried to jam my stick right down his throat. The guy used his stick on me like an ax."

Such behavior is expected of Hextall and Cashman; or at least when they swing sticks it hardly is surprising. But every so often a pair of exceptionally mild-mannered types engage in vicious bloodletting. Which brings us to . . .

The Boy Scout Battlers

Even nonviolent skaters become ensnared in hockey's bloody whirlpool. Hall of Famer Doug Harvey always preferred defending and scoring to fighting, but one night he nearly killed Red Sullivan by bayoneting him with his stick blade because, as Harvey put it, Sullivan had been trying to kick his skates out from under him.

"Maybe it was unintentional," said Harvey, "maybe not. How am I to know? All right, it could be an accident, so I give the guy the benefit of the doubt that time. If it happens again, then I've got to take a stand.

"Hockey is our bread and butter. You're going to think twice before you let another fellow take it away from you."

Which is precisely what Ab DeMarco, Jr., was thinking one evening while lying in a St. Louis hospital bed in November, 1972. DeMarco is regarded as one of the cleanest, easiest-going defensemen in the majors—the type who is a perennial candidate for the Lady Byng (good-conduct) Trophy. Yet that night DeMarco had murder on his mind.

Earlier in the day DeMarco was skating for the Rangers against the Blues on St. Louis ice. At one point DeMarco took the puck away from Garry Unger, an equally nonbelligerent type, and skated to the St. Louis blue line.

Unger pursued DeMarco up the ice, "hacking at his back with his stick," as the *New York Post* described it. Suddenly, DeMarco jammed his skates at right angles, crunching to a halt so that he could make a pass play. "As Ab applied his brakes," the *Post* noted, "Unger speared [bayoneted] him from behind, knocking him to his knees with a cross check to the lower back."

"It was a cheap shot," said DeMarco, who had a reputation for never delivering cheap shots, "and I can't figure out why he did it. Unger doesn't have the reputation for being a dirty hockey player."

DeMarco was hospitalized with a bruised kidney. A day after the episode DeMarco was still woozy from a heavy dose of pills when, to his utter amazement, Unger walked into the hospital room.

"When I saw him [Unger] I thought I was dreaming," DeMarco recalled. "Then, I realized that he actually had the nerve to come and visit me after what he had done."

A cutting pain in the back reminded DeMarco of Unger's vicious lance the night before. He winced as he lurched forward in an attempt to obtain revenge.

"They had me strapped down," said DeMarco, "and a good thing, too.

I'd have liked to have gotten up out of that bed and popped him and knocked his block off.

"If what he'd done had been an accident, I could see how he'd want to come to see me in the hospital to see how I was doing. But what he pulled was no accident."

Unger was accompanied by teammate Floyd Thomson. He handed DeMarco a few books and said, "I hope it's not too serious."

DeMarco was unimpressed. "Boy," he snapped, "have you got some nerve to come here after what you pulled!"

Unger said, "Sorry," turned, and walked out of the room. Why had he injured DeMarco in the first place? Unger was never regarded as being among the league's hatchet men but rather as an exceptionally gifted young scorer.

"The incident," explained one hockey writer who witnessed the clash, "stemmed from frustration—Unger's frustration for having lost the puck. And also because his club had been playing poorly."

Hockey's jungle law called for DeMarco to get *his* pound of flesh from Unger when next they met. "I told Ab," said his manager Emile Francis, "that maybe someday when Unger came to New York he [DeMarco] could visit *him* in a hospital."

DeMarco got the message. Soon after he returned to action the Rangers and Blues played again. With fifty-two seconds remaining in the second period, Unger struck DeMarco with a thudding—but clean—body check.

When he recovered from the blow, DeMarco shouted, "You've got a helluva nerve!" Instinctively, both players dropped their gloves. Unger missed three right-handed punches to the head and landed one. DeMarco had one hit and two misses, but his head felt better.

"I feel I settled the score enough to satisfy myself," said DeMarco. "I think I showed him two can play the game, but I didn't hurt him like he hurt me. At least now he knows that I didn't forget about what he pulled before."

Unger was less eloquent but no less explicit. "There's no feud," he said, "between Ab and me." Curiously, DeMarco soon was traded to St. Louis and became close friends with, of all people, Unger.

Neither Unger nor DeMarco had to compensate for any lack of ability by resorting to violence. Both are gifted players who, in any given season, could achieve All-Star status. But there are others—the authentic hatchet men—who survive because of brutality alone. They are the spear-carriers for teams that practice intimidation as a *modus operandi,* or conversely, are hired to prevent *their* clubs from suffering intimidation. They are . . .

The Woodchoppers

Violence clearly covers their lack of skills. Sometimes it's subtle, but usually not. "My surefire method of enraging the other guy," said Glen Sather, "is to put my big leather glove in a superstar's face before twenty thousand people. I'll mush the glove in his face for a few seconds, and he'll be real embarrassed." The trick is to goad the superstar into retaliating and hope that he gets a penalty.

Bob "Hound Dog" Kelly of the Philadelphia Flyers typifies the woodchopper who understands his role as a violent player and makes absolutely no bones about it. "I know," said Kelly, "that I'm supposed to be dirty but I don't have to admit it. Really, I know they pay me to hit. Actually, I think it's a reflex action with me. I feel it in me to hit someone, so something clicks inside my head and I grab the guy and get my knee way up high into him. And if a guy has the guts to try and maim me, I'll try to maim him back."

Frequently Kelly will not wait for someone to maim him first. During a game against Pittsburgh early in the 1973–74 season Kelly single-handedly inspired the Pittsburgh management to alter its roster after he had intimidated the Penguins club.

"We were down 1–0," explained Pittsburgh manager Jack Button, "and it was a helluva game. All of a sudden Kelly sweeps through our goal crease and gives our goalie an elbow smash, knocking him dizzy. None of our guys even let on that they noticed, and none of them did anything about it. As a result, we got whipped, 7–0."

Button promptly went into the player market and made some deals. He was looking for woodchoppers and soon obtained J. Bob Kelly (no relation to Hound Dog) and Steve Durbano, two of the best sluggers in the big leagues.

"Now," said Button, "if anybody wanted to start trouble, they'd have to contend with those big guys."

Both J. Bob Kelly and Durbano had established reputations for themselves in the minors. J. Bob was known as the smiling killer. "He always seems to laugh after a fight," said a team spokesman. "Of course he always seems to win." Before J. Bob's rookie season was a week old he had beaten up such notorious badmen as Dave Schultz (twice) and Pat Quinn.

The son of a Canadian hockey impresario, Durbano marauded through the Ontario Hockey Association's Junior A division before terrorizing the NHL. "There's no getting around it," said Durbano, "I'm dirty. I admit it. I have to be. I'm trying to make a name for myself. Any name. I'll do some mucky things."

One of the muckier things occurred in March, 1973, when during a game against Philadelphia Durbano clouted Flyers assistant trainer Jim McKenzie with his stick. Why would a regular player attack the enemy's defenseless trainer?

"I had been near the Philadelphia bench," Durbano explained, "and happened to hear some guys yelling at me, so I take my stick and swing it in the area, and it just happened to hit the trainer in the face. Frankly, I was sorry it hit him. It should have hit every one of the Flyers."

Durbano was promptly pummeled by the Flyers' Bob Kelly. "Hound Dog followed with so many blows," wrote Jack Chevalier in the *Philadelphia Bulletin*, "that Durbano covered up and refused to punch back."

Was Durbano penitent? Did the pasting he received teach him to change his ways? Hardly.

"I'm doing my job," Durbano explained. "It's what I get paid for. I'm a ruffian. I'm tough. I like it."

Durbano lost the bout, but every hatchet man loses a fight once in a while. *That* is not the point. What matters in the hockey jungle is the thirst for combat—an iceman's credo.

"It's not who wins the fights that's important," said Barclay Plager, one of the most notorious of the NHL bad men, "it's being *willing* to fight. If you get challenged and renege, everyone will take a shot at you."

In almost every hockey game someone is being challenged, and someone always accepts the challenge. Perhaps that, more than anything, is what inspires the endless violence and the emergence of the individual killers of the sport.

"The bottom line," said Larry Zeidel, "is survival!"

5

The Modern Marauders: Total Team Violence— The Philadelphia Flyers

OF ALL THE TEAMS ever to skate in major-league hockey, none ever executed so complete a physiological, psychological, and artistic a metamorphosis as the Philadelphia Flyers, 1974 world champions.

From the very first game played by the Flyers in 1967 through the spring of 1972, Philadelphia's NHL representative was generally likened to the ninety-five-pound weakling who always is the unfortunate recipient of sand kicked in his face by the beach bully.

Eventually, the ninety-five-pound weakling went to Charles Atlas, grew muscles, and emerged a latter-day Popeye, belting the bully while pretty ladies cheered. Likewise, the Flyers found happiness—if not serenity—in big muscles and the bloodletting that goes with them.

During their nonbelligerent days the Philadelphia sextet was dotted with peace-loving lightweights such as Andre Lacroix, Jimmy Johnson, and Garry Peters. They put the accent on finesse, with a conspicuous aversion to ferocity. Time after time they got the crap beaten out of them by behemoths, especially those wearing St. Louis Blues uniforms.

The Blues discovered they could defeat the Flyers as early as the 1968 Stanley Cup play-offs, when huge St. Louis defenseman Noel Picard—a former barroom bouncer—beat up on the smaller Philadelphia players. "The Flyers," said one observer of the series, "were the better club, but Picard and some of the other monsters frightened all the little Philadelphia guys. Once they were frightened, they didn't want any part of the puck, and it belonged to the Blues."

One of the more intimidating Blues was Bob Plager, a product of a lusty northern Ontario town called Kapuskasing, where brawling had been a way of life. "I fought in bars when I was sixteen," said Plager, "on the street when I was seventeen, and on the ice everywhere, from that point on."

The humiliation of the Flyers by the Blues continued through the 1968–69 season, reaching its embarrassing nadir on April 6, 1969, Philadelphia's day of infamy on ice. On that afternoon the Blues completed a four-game sweep of the Flyers on Spectrum ice, using the hammer-and-tongs blueprint that had worked so well a year earlier. The Blues chased them, and the Flyers ran scared. "The Flyers knew it," wrote Chuck Newman of the *Philadelphia Inquirer*, "and so did the Blues."

More important, so did Ed Snider, the dapper, graying president of the Flyers. Immediately after the series he called a meeting of his high command.

"I wasn't angry," said Snider. "I observed what went on during the series. It was quite simple—we were intimidated. I said to myself that it would not happen to a team of mine again."

Snider's lieutenants, manager Bud Poile and his assistant Keith Allen, agreed. The Flyers would fight fire with fire. If the Blues had big brawlers, the Flyers would go out and find a stable of fighters of their own.

"We put an emphasis on size," said Snider. "At the same time we did not want to deemphasize talent. We wanted a blend, but we knew we needed some horses. If we came across two players of equal ability, we decided to go for the bigger guy."

The transformation from a collection of Dr. Jekylls to Mr. Hydes required adroit selection. In one draft the Flyers obtained Bobby Clarke—eventually to become the NHL's most valuable player and one of its most violent checkers—as well as Dave Schultz, who ultimately set a league record for penalty minutes. They were abetted by Don Saleski, a 6-foot, 2-inch, 200-pounder, and Bob "Hound Dog" Kelly, who beat up one of his own teammates, defenseman Joe Watson, in one of his first scrimmages.

The Flyers soon added a coach, Fred Shero, who once had been a professional boxer. Shero understood the decisiveness that intimidation could have in a hockey game, and when the 1972–73 season began, he instructed Schultz not to let opponents take liberties with any Flyers.

Results were obvious from the opening game—against St. Louis. "From the outset," said the *Philadelphia Inquirer*'s Chuck Newman, "it was evident that things had changed. Bob Plager made an early run at a Flyer but intimidated no one. Shero put Schultz into the game and everything got quiet." In one fell swoop, the Blues had been neutralized.

Schultz was abetted by a few other toughies, including newly acquired left wing Ross Lonsberry, but mostly it was Schultz who carried the Flyers' banner.

"Dave gave us courage on the road," Shero explained. "The big guys don't intimidate us anymore because they know Schultz will be after them. You can't measure the value of a man like that. Schultz's roughness has created a vacuum around him."

Some victims have measured Schultz. Montreal defenseman John Van Boxmeer had a go with the Flyers' cop and was dropped for the count after one punch was thrown.

"I wasn't knocked out cold by Schultz," said Van Boxmeer, "but I was damn near."

The significance of Schultz's one-punch decision did not elude former hatchet man Ted Lindsay, who was handling the "color" commentary for the National Broadcasting Company's "Game of the Week" telecast that afternoon.

While teammates were helping Van Boxmeer off the ice, Lindsay told the viewers that now they would see how much of a man Van Boxmeer was, because when he came back to the ice the name of the game would have to be "Get Schultz." He was insinuating that if Van Boxmeer didn't come back and hit Schultz, other players around the league would think he was a coward and run him out out of the rink. Von Boxmeer never did retaliate.

Schultz, however, did find a Montreal battler in Pierre Bouchard, son of the former NHL heavyweight Butch Bouchard. In a vicious bout that took place in March, 1973, Schultz pummeled Bouchard, and Montreal writers conceded that the Flyer had earned the decision. Bouchard won the second bout between the pair, one in which the two sluggers were so impressive that Montreal boxing promoter Regis Levesque invited them to come into his Forum boxing ring. "I'll guarantee them twenty-five thousand dollars each and a percentage of the gate," said Levesque. "It has to be a natural because it will draw boxing fans and hockey fans."

Bouchard refused the offer, although Schultz accepted, but the Flyers continued their rampage through the NHL.

By March, 1973, many of the Flyers' victims had already complained officially and unofficially about the Flyers' fanaticism. Following a game against the Red Wings in Detroit, the then Red Wings coach, Johnny Wilson, beefed bitterly about the Flyers' Pier 6 style.

"Something should be done about this," said Wilson. "They're letting brutality get into the game. They [the Flyers] have lawsuits pending against them all over the league. No team will back down, man-to-man, but all that holding, hooking, and spearing doesn't make sense. You don't win hockey games playing like animals."

Wilson's point was clear, but his facts were wrong. The Flyers did have a lawsuit against them, but only one. Several teams have backed down from the club coached by Shero. And yes, the Flyers have been winning hockey games by using the old Conn Smythe philosophy. "Fighting," says Shero, who played NHL hockey for the Rangers, who dubbed him "Ferocious Freddie," "is part of the game."

What has disturbed several coaches and managers is the obvious delight the Flyers take in bashing heads, bodies, and anything else. Montreal coach Scotty Bowman accused the Flyers of intentionally injuring his defenseman Guy Lapointe, who was hit in the eye by the stick of the Flyers' Bill Barber in a game at the Forum. That episode followed two major brawl-games in Vancouver, where the Flyers battled the Canucks and their fans.

The first major upheaval took place on December 29, 1972, at the Pacific Coliseum in Vancouver. As a result of the brawl seven Philadelphia skaters—Barry Ashbee, Bob Taylor, Joe Watson, Ed Van Impe, Saleski, Lonsberry, and Bill Flett—were charged with creating a disturbance "by using obscene language and by fighting with spectators with fists and by wielding hockey sticks against and in close proximity to spectators in the general seating area for spectators."

In addition, Taylor, a goalie, was charged with assaulting police corporal Don Brown, Flett with common assault on spectator Joe Cavallo, Van Impe with assault on spectator Harry Woolley, Lonsberry with common assault on spectator Bruce McColl, and Lonsberry and Saleski with common assault on spectator Jack Lederman.

Taylor was later sentenced to thirty days in jail for his part in the brawl.

Vancouver fans and writers have accused the Flyers of inciting the spectators to violent behavior with *their* violent behavior. This, naturally, has happened elsewhere. In Detroit's Olympia Stadium on the night of February 28, 1973, the audience was stimulated by four intense fights and 134 record-breaking minutes in penalties.

In one encounter, Bobby Clarke, the lone Flyers' superstar, grappled with Detroit defenseman Thommie Bergman. In a trice, Barber and Flett of the Flyers intervened on their teammate's behalf. "That's the difference between the teams," said Clarke, "two guys helped me, and nobody helped Bergman."

Some members of the Flyers' family did lose in that one. Mrs. Ed Snider, wife of the Flyers' president, was pelted by peanuts, popcorn, and assorted other debris hurled at her husband's team. "They gave me some men's cologne for being on TV between periods," said Mrs. Snider, "and I felt like shoving it down the throat of the guy behind me."

One of the interesting aspects of the Flyers is that they rarely miss fulfillment of their notices. When Shero's Mean Machine returned to Vancouver for a rematch on February 9, 1973, a few naive observers believed that this time the Flyers would maintain decorum. They were, of course, wrong. Some seventy-one penalty minutes were called, including three game misconducts. The fight-filled first period took sixty minutes to complete, and once again the Flyers zeroed in on the enemy's top-scorer, Bobby Schmautz.

Schmautz fought with Schultz and Dupont of the Flyers and was thrown out of the game. John Wright of the Canucks was thrown out of the game for pulling Schultz off Schmautz. Then Schultz beat up Dale Tallon of Vancouver, and the fights continued.

Occasionally the Flyers have grown penitent. "We're going to have to cut down on these penalties," said a Philadelphia forward, "because we're going to get crucified by the teams that can work the power play."

Yet other Flyers believe the league will have to adjust to their Mean Machine. "The referees are going to have to change," said Barber. "They can't make us change our style.

"We've got a lot of tough guys like Schultz, Kelly, and Dupont, but we're not doing anything differently than the other teams. I'm beginning to think we're being blackballed."

Added defenseman Van Impe: "The referees are watching us closer because we're the most penalized team. Things other teams get away with, we get caught at."

"The Flyers," said Montreal ace Yvan Cournoyer, "will never win the Stanley Cup playing that way, because by the time they get to the second round of the play-offs they're all knocked out from fighting and have nothing left for scoring."

That's what happened in the 1973 Canadiens–Flyers series. But a year later, the Flyers did win the Stanley Cup.

"Sure we'll hit," warned coach Shero. "I think we should all be grateful there are still a few players around willing to hit!"

Despite the warnings from NHL president Clarence Campbell and the pessimistic predictions from experts such as Cournoyer, Philadelphia's Mean Machine was tougher, more arrogant, and infinitely superior in its second season of marauding, 1973–74.

In the Flyers' first meeting with the Toronto Maple Leafs, then Philadelphia forward Bill Flett challenged rookie Inge Hammarstrom, an import from Sweden. After hearing what Flett had to say, Hammarstrom realized that everything he had heard about the brutal Flyers was true.

"I told him," Flett later admitted, "that the first time he touched the puck I'd break his arm! After that the Swede was two steps behind me the rest of the night." To Philadelphians the end justified the means—total team violence helped win the championship. Toronto signed Flett a year later.

Flett's message was reinforced by teammate Ed Van Impe, a defense-man whose quick, rapierlike thrusts of his stick blade have earned him notoriety as one of the NHL's most ruthless spear-carriers. A typical Van Impe maneuver was executed against Borje Salming of the Maple Leafs. In a split second, Salming fell to the ice, clutching his stomach in pain.

"It was," said veteran hockey reporter Red Burnett of the *Toronto Star*, "a vicious thrust of the stick to the stomach. It was the second time Van Impe had speared Salming."

After the game, reporters asked Van Impe about the episode. They suggested Salming could have been badly hurt by such a deliberate attempt to injure. Van Impe, who frequently has the innocent look of a choirboy, replied that the newsmen took an unfortunate view of his behavior.

"I was only falling backwards," Van Impe explained in a desperate attempt to maintain a straight face, "and my stick accidentally came up and caught him in the stomach." Then, after a pause: "He couldn't have been hurt too bad, could he? I noticed he came back and finished the game."

If Van Impe looks like a choirboy, teammate Bobby Clarke suggests a Boy Scout with his winsome, gap-toothed grin. A diabetic, Clarke evolved as the Flyers' titular leader, their most dependable scorer, most tenacious checker, and in the minds of many opponents, dirtiest player.

Dirty play, of course, is in the mind of the beholder. Ted Lindsay has gone to great lengths defending Clarke as a persistent forechecker with an unquenchable passion for winning.

"It's not dirty hockey," Lindsay said of Clarke's style. "It's competitive. That's his job. It's not a kid's game. If you haven't got the guts, leave it."

Opponents such as Murray Wilson of the Canadiens are less charitable. During a game in February, 1974, Wilson scored a goal against the Flyers. "After I put the puck in the net," said Wilson, "Clarke whacked me a good two-hander in the left arm."

The two-hander was obviously part of Clarke's offensive repertoire. During the Team Canada–Russia series in September, 1972, Clarke gave the NHL skaters a distinct edge when he personally—and violently—dis-patched Soviet star Valery Kharlamov, Russia's ace forward, from the series.

"Clarke cracked Kharlamov's ankle," said Canadiens coach Scotty Bowman, "and put him out of the series."

Since Clarke was a Canadian and Bowman a Canadian, that bit of brutality was perfectly all right with Bowman. But God forbid Clarke should do the same to one of Bowman's Montreal skaters!

Clarke has been doing the same, give or take a fracture, to many opponents. He does so with the endorsement of coach Shero. "Bobby," said Shero, "is the ultimate as a competitor. Anybody who expects to be great has to be mean. I mean truly great like Gordie Howe, Rocket Richard, Milt Schmidt. They were mean. They took care of the opposition.

"That's Clarke's game, too. He wants to be hacking and hitting and all of that. He seems to be initiating everything. He knows he's got to get the best of the other guy immediately—with his body, with his stick, with whatever it is."

Whatever the Flyers' strategy, *it* has worked. No longer ninety-five-pound weaklings, they finished on top of the West Division in 1974, and during the regular schedule proved capable of whipping and intimidating every team in the NHL—occasionally even Boston's big, bad Bruins.

The Flyers were aware that the Bruins, led by superstar Bobby Orr, had repeatedly beaten them over the past three years. They also had been working on blueprints to overcome the dilemma. Typically, coach Shero had the answer.

"To beat Boston, you do the same thing to Orr that Clarke did to Kharlamov. Break his ankle!"

The Flyers didn't break Orr's ankle in the 1974 Stanley Cup finals, but they broke the Bruins' spirit with their hard-nosed play and scored one of the NHL's biggest upsets when they defeated Boston to become the first expansion team to win the Cup.

6

A Psychoanalyst Looks at Hockey Gore

THERE HAVE BEEN NUMEROUS clean-playing craftsmen in the National Hockey League—skaters who would rather switch than fight, who believe that a deft feint or a spurt around the defense is more valuable to their team and more appreciated by the fans than a jab in the mouth or a spear in the groin.

None, however, epitomized the clean, spectacular skater more than Bobby Hull, the "Golden Jet" of the Chicago Black Hawks, and more recently, the Winnipeg Jets. Hull, who would never start a fight unless suitably provoked, was Mr. Clean of the NHL. He didn't have to play dirty, because he was the fastest skater, the hardest shooter, and curiously, the strongest player in the game.

His antithesis was John Bowie Ferguson, a ham-fisted forward on the Montreal Canadiens who interpreted his role rather simply: "Fighting? I couldn't say it was my job, but I *felt* it was." One evening Ferguson proved his point by breaking Hull's jaw. A few weeks later, Hull returned to combat wearing a massive guard around his wound. Before the night was up, Ferguson had engaged Hull once more in a fight, displaying no compunctions, no concern about his foe's injury.

Was Ferguson some kind of psychopath? Was his behavior antisocial? Should he have been barred from the sport?

Not according to the neo-jungle rules of hockey. "When I became coach of the Bruins," said Harry Sinden, "I would have taken Ferguson over anybody in the league. *Anybody!* His aggressiveness could lift an entire team and keep it hitting and fighting long after it had passed the point of exhaustion."

How would a Ferguson, or the brawling Philadelphia Flyers, or the fight-happy Islander, Garry Howatt, be judged by a social scientist? Does the violence of a hockey rink beget more violence in the outside world?

Some critics believe it does, and they insist that hockey leaders should be condemned for, at the very least, condoning the bloodletting that regularly takes place on ice. When the National Broadcasting Company signed former brawler Ted Lindsay to handle commentary on its "Game of the Week" telecasts, the "eye-for-an-eye" philosophy was transmitted to millions of fans, including a huge percentage of youngsters.

When a defenseman whacked his stick across an opposing player's back, Lindsay frothed with admiration. "That's layin' the ol' lumber on 'im. Gotta keep that area clear." It was clear to those who didn't already know him that Lindsay's devotion to violence, brutality, and mayhem on ice was being drummed into American living rooms with all the subtlety of a sledgehammer.

"The hockey stick," Lindsay bubbled, "is the great equalizer."

Was Lindsay being antisocial? Was he ill-equipped to comment on a magnificent game, or was he making a realistic comment on a pastime that really is just a violent parody of sport? Some observers rejected Lindsay's attitude.

"Hockey," said columnist Gary Deeb of the *Chicago Tribune*, "is a sport of poetic beauty, charm, and not just a little adventure. Somebody had better get that message to Lindsay whose hockey mentality seems locked in a 1950s time capsule. As it now stands he is neither ethically nor emotionally equipped to broadcast big-league sports over a major network. Championship wrestling is more in his ballpark."

A reporter from *The New York Times* was even more critical of Lindsay's accent on guts and more guts. "Presumably," said the man from the *Times*, "some children without guts now will give up the game on Lindsay's advice. Presumably, those who remain in kids' leagues across North America will be those with guts."

However, some viewers of the social scene have taken a more relaxed view of hockey's brawling and its brawlers. Ted Saretsky, a group therapist and associate professor of clinical psychology at Adelphi University's Psychotherapy Institute, believes some positive factors emerge from the brouhahas on ice.

"Fights," said Saretsky, "allow the audience to act out their fantasies, which is one reason why fans encourage the fighters. Many of these fans have little control over their lives. They live in an age of bureaucracy and they don't often get to see the little man smash the big man. This is what it's all about—the good guys versus the bad guys. Watching players fight or smash each other into the boards is a process of letting the animal out. In addition, the speed builds a rising excitement in the spectators; it brings a potential danger right up to the fans' eyes. It's the horror that makes hockey attractive."

That helps explain why John Ferguson, despite the fact that he destroyed such nice people as Bobby Hull, was one of the most popular skaters in the NHL. "The fans loved me," said Ferguson. "When I first retired I received thousands of letters from fans in every town in the league, all asking me to come back."

Why would a fan who on the one hand would shout, "Fergie, I hope you break your neck," turn around and write a passionate letter, urging his sworn foe to keep playing hockey?

"I was the villain who made the game interesting," said Ferguson. "Without me, they'd have nobody to hate."

Ferguson grew up in a lower-class neighborhood in Vancouver, British Columbia. According to Dr. Saretsky, such an environment contributed to Ferguson's violence. "In a low-class society," said Dr. Saretsky, "violence is part of the everyday life. It's not just capricious. In the Canadian family there's great respect for the father, self-restraint, self-discipline, and hardiness. Quitters are weak."

Ferguson, obviously, was not weak nor was he ever a quitter. But did he carry his brutality too far? In a game against the New York Rangers he once flattened Ken Schinkel with a massive body check that dispatched Schinkel to the hospital with a broken collarbone.

When the Rangers' trainer, Frank Paice, asked Ferguson how hard he had hit Schinkel, Ferguson shook his head, sucked in his cheeks, and formed a perfect O with his lips.

"A kiss," said Ferguson, "I gave him just a kiss."

Ferguson's reaction enraged his opponents. Many called him an animal, a brute with no redeeming qualities. "There's a thin line," says Saretsky, "between being aggressive, intimidating, fearless, and someone who's a vicious, murderous person.

"If a person is only relying on punishment—if he wouldn't maim only because he's afraid of being caught—he's a dangerous person in hockey or in life and should be banned from hockey."

What, then, can be done about such potential threats? Dr. Saretsky believes there are a few rudimentary curbs available. "If a player showed dangerous tendencies early in his career he should be called out to discuss his problems. Some things are truly dangerous such as stick-swinging, kicking skates, two players jumping on one. However, I don't believe it's possible to weed out the real troublemakers with a diagnostic test. If you gave me twenty players for three hours each I could tell you which are the most dangerous but I couldn't tell which one would break another's head."

The therapist believes that some sort of psychological evaluation should be done on players in the minor leagues before they reach the big-league level. "That," said Dr. Saretsky, "would be for prevention; not cure. To do an effective job I would have to live with a team and relate to it as a family, to see how the family climate affects performance; and observe the daily social interactions.

"It's impossible to separate out inferiority, aggression, and other traits unless you look at a single individual and look often. It's an interactional thing—and it would have to relate to the players' prehockey career attitude to certain experiences, to aggression and the like. The problem is you can't tell by behavior what a person's motives are. What if you saw him leaning against a subway pillar in an apparent stupor? He could just be contemplating; he could be a drunk or he could be suicidal."

Dr. Saretsky believes that in certain cases a therapist could be helpful. The New York Rangers' Derek Sanderson, for example: "Sanderson's behavior over the years suggests to me something very destructive. Some people have said that Sanderson just didn't care about hockey anymore because of all the money he's made, but I disagree. I think he's doing destructive things to himself because he's acting out depression."

Dr. Saretsky visited the Nassau Coliseum in Uniondale, New York, one night in March, 1974, when the New York Islanders played the fearsome Philadelphia Flyers. He sensed a very special aura about the crowd the moment he took his seat.

"There was a different kind of noise level," he recalled. "Like the Christians being fed to the lions. I sensed a state of anticipation while listening to the people. The crowd wanted the bad team—the Flyers—to be so bad that the good team—the Islanders—would be justified in striking back."

The therapist, however, did not condemn the reaction because "while on the surface our society doesn't condone violence, there is very often a murderous instinct underneath that's trying to come out and looking for justification to come out."

Less than ten minutes after the game began, Philadelphia bully Dave Schultz engaged in his first battle, and spectators throughout the building jumped to their feet to watch the fighting. Dr. Saretsky noticed that a man lifted his nine-year-old boy into the air for a better view of the brawl. Was that reprehensible? Not in the doctor's view. "It could be," Dr. Saretsky explained, "that in the father's value system it's all right to show aggression in the name of self-defense. That's consistent with American values."

He went on: "There are certain things—real things—that I would try to screen from my child. But not this; this isn't real. I would try to balance the scene by pointing out that these men are doing it for a living, that they wouldn't fight in real life.

"For professional people there are few outlets where we can expose the baser side of ourselves. A game like hockey is one of the few areas for the ventilation of primitive feelings. This deals with what one psychologist, Hartmann, called regression in the service of the ego. Every adult, no matter how mature or responsible, needs an opportunity to regress, to be something other than this mature, responsible adult, and that's what hockey does for some people."

Players like Schultz and Ferguson, who once said he "made sure I was the meanest bastard who ever went in the corners for the puck," and other hockey cops transport the fans into fanatical states of hate. Saretsky refuses to get disturbed about it.

"Basically," he concluded, "it's healthy, because it provides a controlled laboratory setting that gives an outlet and ventilation for aggression that is not a carry-over into real life.

"I think the kind of violence a little kid may see in family situations in quiet ways is more significant and damaging, and the kind of thing I cringe at more than this hockey violence.

"I see things in family life that are more cruel. The kind of thing where a father takes a kid's dog back to a dog pound because the dog has been messing up the house, and then the father laughs at the kid when the boy is upset. Real things between people in which they don't consider each other's feelings bother me more than anything I see out on the ice during a tough hockey game."

When it comes to feelings, few professional hockey players have been able to detail precisely what goes through their minds before, during, and after a battle on the ice, except for the typically trite "he-hit-me-first, then-I-hit-him-back" retorts dispensed to newsmen most nights.

There are exceptions, to be sure—players with rare insights into the cruel world of sticks, skates, and fists around them. One such skater is defenseman Jim Dorey, who entered the NHL in 1968 with such bellicosity he set penalty records in his first game as a Toronto Maple Leaf.

On October 16, 1968, Dorey received four minor penalties, two major penalties, two ten-minute misconduct penalties, and one game-misconduct penalty, which meant that he was ejected from the contest for naughty behavior.

A husky, handsome man, Dorey has since "reformed" and enjoys reflecting on his testy past and the motives behind his early truculence.

"I'm an emotional guy," said Dorey, "and hockey gives me a release for my emotions. If I get stalled in an elevator or a traffic jam, it builds up until I want to hit someone. But that's not acceptable in today's society. So I wait until I get on the ice. Then when I hit a guy, I feel good. I know he wasn't the cause of my aggression, but still it feels good. That's what I've wanted to do all day. Hockey gives a guy a chance to be himself.

"If you work in an office, you never tell people personal things that will let them know you. We all want to, but we're afraid someone might laugh or walk away. So we keep it inside. But once you get on the ice, things happen so fast you can't keep anything inside. It's impossible not to be yourself.

"You don't have time to present a facade as you would at the office. Whether that's good or bad, I don't know. Hockey brings out your deepest subconscious attitudes that would never come out otherwise. A man can find out what he's got inside him, whether he's a bad guy, a coward, a good guy, whatever. You'll see it mirrored in the faces of the other players. The problem comes up when they see just what they are and don't like it very much."

Dorey's on-ice personality changed as he grew older. In 1972 he jumped from the established NHL to the New England Whalers of the WHA. He fought occasionally but didn't go out of his way to pick a fight.

"When I fight," he said, "it's a spontaneous reaction. I'm a spontaneous guy. My reactions are honest, emotional outbursts; they're not pre-arranged. I don't go after guys. But because hockey is so fast, you have to discipline yourself beforehand to react the right way. I don't want a reputation as a fighter. I want to be a complete hockey player. I'm trying to control myself, trying not to fight as much.

"But it's hard. That's not the way I am. I'm forcing myself to react against my nature. But if I want to be a good player I have to do it."

Some players have successfully turned their hockey personalities around. For years Stan Mikita of the Chicago Black Hawks was notorious for his destructive stick and his petulance with opponents and referees alike. But after several seasons as a troublemaker, Mikita went straight and won the Lady Byng Trophy for good conduct and superior ability two years running.

"People say that Mikita stopped being mean as he got older because he wanted to protect his career," said Dorey. "I don't buy that. I think Stan saw something in himself he didn't like. It scared him, so he changed for the better. But not all guys react like that. Some guys when they see they're a bastard, get meaner. They want to hurt somebody because they've shown themselves up for what they are."

Dorey makes a very fine distinction between "mean" and "tough." He put it this way: "A tough guy will slam you into the boards every time he can, and if he fights, it's just a natural reaction from the heat of the game. But a mean player, he'll try to hurt you. He'll use his stick. He'll plot to get you when nobody's looking.

"If a guy reacts like a bastard on the ice, he knows that in life he's probably a bastard. He's revealed himself, both to the people watching and himself. Maybe he was trying to hide it from himself. But now that it's in the open, it makes him bitter, and so he takes it out on anyone he can. He becomes even meaner."

Dorey's insights are a refreshing change from much of the tough dialogue one hears in hockey. Quite often the pent-up *macho* instincts of what one author described as "the generally gray and docile Canadian psyche" seem to overwhelm the game. Some believe intimidation *is* the name of the sport.

"Every game," said Dorey, "is a test of your courage. You question yourself. Did I let up that game? Did I act like a man? Did I back off. Those questions are always there. If you doubt your courage for a minute, you have to eat it until the next game. Then you go out and hit the first guy you see."

And thousands cheer. Some critics deplore the blood, others defend it, but few will argue that the violence can be eradicated from the milky-white ice. Nearly everyone agrees that hockey would not be hockey without the brawling; even a social scientist like Dr. Saretsky.

"I had one pervasive feeling as the clock ticked off the last minute of the Flyers–Islanders game," Dr. Saretsky concluded, "and that was, *I'd like to see one more fight before the game is over!*"

7

Hockey Violence:
What Can Be Done?

What I've learned is that whatever you do in hockey, you should cheat at it. Everyone cheats in hockey. It's unbelievable how much you can get away with—if you do it when no one is looking, of course.

—TOM LYSIAK, ATLANTA FLAMES, quoted in
Sports Illustrated, April, 1974

A friend of mine was a superjock at Yale, but in his senior year he quit the varsity ice-hockey team. He organized a hockey team where you had to have a beard to play. He challenged Rhode Island School of Design to a game, and the two teams skated to the middle of the hockey rink carrying their jerseys. They made a big pile of them, then chose up sides. That was beautiful. These were friendly, cheerful people and they were doing amusing things. Their goal was to delight themselves, not to defeat each other.

—KURT VONNEGUT, JR.

Tom Lysiak is not a cynical old hockey player who has clubbed his way through the ice jungle for twenty years. His postgraduate baby face lacks the gnarled complexion of veterans like Henri Richard, whose heavily stitched head suggests a route map of American railways.

Tom Lysiak basically is a kid—a good kid who also happens to be an enormously gifted hockey player. And yet at age twenty-one, before he had completed one full season in the NHL, he had clearly doped out major-league hockey's violent world of elastic morals: "Whatever you do in hockey, you should cheat at it."

Unlike Kurt Vonnegut, Jr.'s hockey people, the characters in Tom Lysiak's ice world are neither friendly nor cheerful. They play in a team sport that uniquely accepts fighting as an asset. "In the context of baseball or football," observed author Brock Yates, "a blatant fighter would be denounced as a threat to the good order of the game. The hockey establishment's public refutation of fighting, coupled with its private acceptance, produced a schizophrenia about 'sportsmanship' that doesn't exist in other games."

To acknowledge there is sportsmanship in hockey is to insist that, at heart, Adolf Hitler was a nice guy. There has been evidence of sportsmanship in the game over the past eighty-five years, but it is extremely hard to find. What's more, the spirit of depravity is growing, particularly among the youth of North America.

They watch Philadelphia's Broad Street Bullies, alias the Flyers, on television and quickly realize that brawling produces rich rewards. If dirty play has assets, the kids include it as part of their repertoire, and head-hunting becomes as vital to them as stickhandling and shooting. They realize that by the 1974–75 season every NHL team was on the lookout for *fisthandlers* rather than stickhandlers.

I recall seeing a game between twelve-year-olds during the spring of 1974 in Winnipeg. Apart from the basic skills, which were evident, the one aspect of the match that carved a niche in my mind was the utter viciousness of many of the players. Blindsiding, high-sticking, and cross-checking were taken for granted. It was downright scary. More significant, that kind of behavior has even frightened such gnarled customers as Teddy Green.

"I go to see my sons play at the mite level," said Green, "and hell, the high-sticking, slashing, and elbowing is disgusting. Even at that level. Why? They see it in the NHL or WHA all the time.

"They think high-sticking and slashing is a part of hockey, that it draws the fans and adds color. Well, it adds color, all right—the color of blood running."

The way Green sees it, the NHL rules are egregiously too lenient about high-sticking and slashing; also too flexible and vague. "For high-sticking and slashing," said Green, "and I don't care if you hit a guy or not, you should be tossed out of the game and fined, say, a thousand dollars.

"If you come back and do it again, you should be tossed out for the *season*. That'll reduce high-sticking and slashing. I know some people say that these things are part of the game and can't be controlled. That's nonsense. I speak from experience. There were many times in the past where, if there had been the kind of penalties I'm talking about, I would have thought twice before striking."

Green speaks from the heart and the head. The rule book must be strengthened and enforced. It is an absurd rule book, because a player can rupture an opponent's spleen or emasculate him with a butt end or crosscheck and not suffer a fine, and only a measly $50 fine is imposed if an opponent is injured about the head.

Over the years there have been rumbles of discontent against the high priests of hockey about excessive bloodshed on the peewee level as well as the big-league plateau. Always, it seems, the critics are dismissed as assorted cashews infringing upon a religion so deeply rooted in people's lives that any attack on it is condemned as blasphemy. Except that the attacks are mounting both in North America and in Europe, where hockey has grown to major-league status. The disgraceful exhibition of poor sportsmanship displayed by Team Canada and its leader, Alan Eagleson, during the series in September, 1972, with the Russian National Team congealed world opinion against the NHL brand of violence.

The Russians, Swedes, Czechs, and Finns have come to hate and deride North American professionals. Curiously, it is not simply because Team Canada played a rougher brand of hockey—the Russians can bodycheck with the best of them—but rather because Team Canada expressed an alien attitude to life. This was best—or worst, depending upon your point of view—symbolized by the NHL players' attempts to decapitate, or at the very least, beat up Referee Joseph Kompalla during the tournament.

"In Europe," wrote G. E. Mortimore, "the hockey referee is almost a policeman trying to enforce a fixed set of rules. He is the agent of settled law. In the NHL he is more like a strong, respected frontier sheriff, keeping order by arresting a few men here and there as examples, while knowing that hot-tempered gunmen will shoot it out when his back is turned; sometimes in front of him."

Plenty can be done about curbing—if not eliminating—hockey violence, but first a drastic change in the philosophy of club owners must be wrought. The barons of hockey must be convinced that the game would still be salable if rules were enforced and referees respected. Unfortunately, many respected critics doubt that this worthy goal can be achieved.

> Wild hockey in Canada prospered [said Mortimore] for the same reasons that Westerns and crime movies prospered—because it harmonized with the desires, the morals, of a large number of people. The builders of hockey have created an artificial world of conflict, designed to thrill spectators.

Players are encouraged, sometimes subtly, sometimes overtly, to bash heads. When the Boston Bruins obtained Bobby Schmautz from the

Vancouver Canucks in February, 1974, Schmautz made his debut at Boston Garden as though he were middleweight champion of the world.

It seemed that Schmautz's prime motivation was to show the audience of fifteen thousand that he could behead a couple of opponents and thereby qualify as a legitimate Bruin. "If Schmautz carried his stick any higher," wrote Columnist Mike Barnicle in the *Boston Globe*, "someone in the third deck could have reached out and stolen it. Maybe a better example would be to ask Schmautz to lower his stick and concentrate on playing hockey. After a few goals, the fans might even begin to appreciate him just as much as if he had put some opposing player in the hospital."

Obviously, the Boston management, not to mention the Flyers' front office and the owners of just about every professional hockey club, sanction this brutality. In some leagues the intensity of the bloodletting is so severe that even normally fearless players such as Jim Dorey become concerned. One such organization is the North American League, formerly the Eastern Hockey League, a Class A organization with a long history of bloodshed.

"Those guys," said Dorey, "are crazy. If I ever got sent down there I think I'd quit."

Bob Giovati, a former Eastern League referee, once told me that he refereed a series involving the Syracuse club in which owners not only condoned bludgeoning, they encouraged it.

"Some of the bosses took an ad in a Syracuse paper in which they offered bonuses to their players who hurt guys on the opposition," said Giovati. "That was enough to persuade me to get out of hockey officiating."

Such barbarism isn't limited to the minors. Attorney William Jennings, president of the New York Rangers and former chairman of the NHL Board of Governors, once put a "bounty" on Ted Green's head—any Ranger who "got" Green would get a bonus. Yet Jennings frequently would scream bloody murder if one of his Rangers was victimized by a Boston hit man.

The NHL, thus, is a world of elastic morals in which the so-called good guys are allowed to hit the bad guys in the mouth and it is quite all right for the crowd to cheer such conduct. "It's a world," said Mortimore, "in which the good guys (the home team) may break the letter of the law, provided they don't get caught."

More than anyone, the referee is the fall guy. He is abused by players, coaches, managers, and frequently his own supervisors. Almost from the very start, league presidents have failed to fully support their referees, thereby lending encouragement to those who abuse them.

On a 1938 evening in Boston, defenseman Dit Clapper of the Bruins punched a referee, giving him a black eye, and was fined only $100. The referee was Clarence Campbell, who later became NHL president. At that, the fine was levied by then NHL president Frank Calder only after Campbell interceded and urged that a fine be imposed.

Campbell, however, has been more of a jellyfish official than Calder ever was. In the spring of 1960 Campbell was NHL boss when Montreal Canadiens coach Toe Blake walked eighty-five feet across the Chicago Stadium ice, following the Hawks' winning overtime goal in a play-off game, and fetched referee Dalton MacArthur a clout in the eye.

Even the most lenient of Campbell's critics assumed that he would suspend Blake for at least one year. The assumptions were wrong. Blake was fined only $2,000—traditionally the fines are paid by the club, not the offender—and Blake joked afterward: "Well, there goes my new car until next year!"

Referees who have had the misfortune of working in the NHL usually display misgivings about the whole structure and philosophy of club owners toward violence' and the enforcement of rules. One such official was Jack Mehlenbacher, who, during his five years as a big-league referee, was the best the NHL had to offer.

"The big wheels of the NHL," said Mehlenbacher, "figure they have to have blood to fill the arenas. During my years in the league that was all they were interested in."

Club owners make a basic mistake. They believe that hockey's artistic elements—the skating, passing, stickhandling, and goaltending—are insufficient to sell the game on a profitable level. They fail to realize that the institutionalized violence that now dominates pro hockey is an affront to all but the most bestial spectators.

"The fans," said John MacFarlane, coauthor of *The Death of Hockey,* "are being used. Sure, some of them enjoy the violence, but that does not mean they would not prefer displays of the athletic skill for which it is so cynically substituted. What the owners are saying is: 'It doesn't matter whether we give the suckers a good hockey game as long as we give them a fight.' "

Assuming club owners can be convinced that institutionalized violence is unnecessary and improper, hockey can be purged of its poisonous blood perversion. I submit the following ideas for improving the game:

1. Suspensions should replace fines in every area of punishment for unnecessary violence.

2. Any player who deliberately injures another with his stick should be suspended for a year.

3. A lifetime suspension should be imposed on anyone who touches an official in anger.

4. Sterner and more certain punishment should be decreed—five-minute major penalties might be adequate—for such offenses as tripping and hooking or any other tactics that mediocre players use to stop accomplished performers.

5. Younger players—peewees, mites, etc.—should be given a different kind of enforcement, allowing less violence. Eliminate professional domination of kids' hockey.

6. Reduce the referee's area of discretion, cut down opinion calls. Hall of Famer Maurice "Rocket" Richard wrote: "A player should be penalized if he lifts his stick in the air, for nothing or for anything. This would be the best way to cure certain players of using their sticks as swords."

7. Complete autonomy for levying suspensions should be removed from league presidents and given to the referees-in-chief.

NHL president Clarence Campbell has long insisted that fines are a sufficient deterrent to violence. His position, at best, is fatuous; at worst, it is cynical.

"Campbell and the governors of the NHL," said John MacFarlane, "know that fines will not eliminate fights. And that is precisely why they impose them. It permits them to *seem* to be doing something to 'stamp out this kind of stuff' while in fact doing nothing at all."

The NHL propaganda ministry has long argued that fighting is as much a part of hockey as the ice. But non-NHL experts devastate that argument. "Hockey no more leads to fighting," said Tom Watt, coach of the University of Toronto hockey team, "than playing cards leads to gambling. There's opportunity for fighting in hockey, that's all."

Watt's argument is reinforced by the mores of sports such as soccer, where fighting is practically nonexistent thanks to the automatic-suspension rule.

It is rather grimly ironic that some of the most telling cures for the sickness of hockey violence can be found in the NHL rule book, which says the following about high-sticking and slashing.

High Sticks—Section 6, Rule 58:

(a) The carrying of sticks above the normal height of the shoulder is prohibited, and a minor penalty may be imposed on any player violating this rule, at the discretion of the Referee.

(c) When a player carries or holds any part of his stick above the height of his shoulder so that injury to the face or head of an opposing player results, the Referee shall have no alternative but to impose a major penalty on the offending player. When a major penalty is imposed under this rule for a foul resulting in injury to the face or head of an opponent, an automatic fine of fifty dollars ($50) shall be imposed.

Slashing—Section 6, Rule 77:

(a) A minor or major penalty, at the discretion of the Referee, shall be imposed on any player who impedes or seeks to impede the progress of an opponent by "slashing" with his stick.

(b) A major penalty shall be imposed on any player who injures an opponent by slashing. When a major penalty is imposed under this rule for a foul resulting in injury to the face or head of an opponent, an automatic fine of fifty dollars ($50) shall also be imposed.

Referees should penalize as "slashing" any player who swings his stick at any opposing player (whether in or out of range) without actually striking him or where a player on the pretext of playing the puck makes a wild swing at the puck with the object of intimidating an opponent.

(c) Any player who swings his stick at another player in the course of any altercation shall be subject to a fine of not less than two hundred dollars ($200), with or without suspension, to be imposed by the President.

The Referee shall impose the normal appropriate penalty provided in the other sections of this rule and shall in addition report promptly to the President all infractions under this section.

Unfortunately, these rules are honored more in the breach than the observance. Worse still, rampant expansion has encouraged the breach because only by employing such illegal tactics can the inept players remain in the majors.

Campbell, the NHL's man with the power to enforce the rules, has instead chosen to fudge on hockey's laws. "I acknowledge," said Campbell, "it would be possible to set a tougher standard of rules enforcement, but I don't feel the number of injuries we have requires it.

"It would be absurd to expel a man from a game for slashing or high-sticking. The fans would laugh you out of the rink and so would the players. High-sticking has relatively few injuries—that's the best proof of all that penalties are effective.

"Hockey is not like most other team sports, say, football, where it's stop and start and the players have a chance to cool down. Much of the retaliation in hockey is instinctive because of the pace. You have to expect these things to happen. Many of the fouls are accidental."

Perhaps it would be more realistic to determine what can be done about hockey violence from a onetime hit man, a reformed hockey cop—Ted Green. Not surprisingly, Green, who nearly lost his life in a stick-swinging episode, has his own formula for reforming the bloody game. In a few words—get the sticks down!

"There's no place in hockey for high-sticking and slashing," said Green. "None at all."

What infuriates Green is the major leagues' failure to enforce the rules that prohibit these infractions. "The big shots in the NHL and WHA haven't got the guts to do what should be done," said Green.

Similarly ridiculous is NHL Rule 60, which deals with hooking and imposes a fine only if there is injury to the head or face. "A player could be caught skating to the bench with an opponent's kidneys hanging from his stick," said Lyman MacInnis, a Toronto hockey critic and chartered accountant, "but the fine would be imposed only if he removed them through the guy's mouth, thereby, presumably, injuring the other's face."

MacInnis, like Green, MacFarlane, and other NHL critics, argues that the league could easily eliminate dirty play *if it really wanted to.*

"It could impose maximum penalties anytime an injury occurs because of a foul," said MacInnis, "and would follow up with suspensions and heavy fines in particularly violent incidents. . . . Get rid of the player whose only attributes are size, strength, and a complete void where his conscience should be."

Those of us who have been privy to NHL thinking for more than two decades agree that it is virtually hopeless to expect any change in the league's attitude toward gore. "The league," MacInnis concluded, "seems to have opted for a tragic solution: Turn the game into a bloodbath; people will always line up to see that."

Perhaps he's right. Perhaps it is futile even to suggest that *anything* can be done about hockey violence. Shortly after MacInnis delivered his remarks a women's team from Cornell University played a women's team from Brown University.

When the game ended, the Cornell ladies accused the Brown ladies of unsportspersonlike play. To which Mary Leslie Ullman of Brown replied: "Hockey is hitting people. What's all the fuss about?"

Part Two

Other Things Hurting Hockey

8

The NHL Establishment:
The Preexpansionists

THREE VICES—stupidity, cupidity, and duplicity—have permeated—and contaminated—the woof and warp of the NHL Establishment ever since the league was organized on November 26, 1917, at the Windsor Hotel in downtown Montreal.

Ironically, the NHL's curious blend of knavery grew as the league expanded into the roaring twenties and once moved the *New York Daily Mirror's* muckraking columnist Dan Parker to comment, "Hockey is surviving not because of but in spite of its owners. Only the innate greatness of the game has allowed it to overcome the overwhelming burden of its leadership."

Almost from Day One, the NHL's bosses have managed to execute one damn fool mistake or another that would seem to condemn the league to mediocrity if not oblivion. Nor did any Age of Reason or Enlightenment occur fifty-six years later. In 1973, the year the NHL was bitterly challenging the upstart World Hockey Association for prestige and honor, two NHL leaders faced grave criminal charges, and both of them actually spent time in jail.

In October, 1972, Toronto Maple Leafs president Harold Ballard received a three-year sentence for theft and fraud involving $205,000 from Maple Leaf Gardens. Ballard was released on parole from Millhaven, Ontario, minimum-security prison in October, 1973, after serving one year of his sentence.

The second of the one-two punch to the NHL's solar plexus was delivered in April, 1973, when Vancouver Canucks president Thomas Scallen was sentenced to four years in prison after being told he had violated the trust placed in him by the people of British Columbia. The rap against Scallen was that he switched $3 million from one company to another to prevent his Medicor firm from sinking. After an appeal, Scallen was jailed on June 3, 1974, surrendering to the Royal Canadian Mounted Police detachment in Vancouver.

In fairness to Ballard and Scallen, it must be pointed out that they were carrying on in the grand tradition set by earlier members of the NHL Establishment. In fact NHL hockey was introduced to New York City by William "Big Bill" Dwyer, one of the biggest bootleggers in the East.

Despite his wealth and ebullience, Dwyer never became the power he might have been in NHL smoke-filled rooms, partly because he was victimized by the duplicity of his Madison Square Garden colleagues, especially George Lewis "Tex" Rickard, entrepreneur of the new Gotham sports palace.

Dwyer's problem was that his bootlegging business was booming and his hockey team played second fiddle to his distilleries. Immersed in his fortune, Dwyer discovered too late that he was being duped by Rickard and the Garden crowd.

Rickard's pals were so impressed with the drawing potential of Dwyer's New York Americans that the Garden decided to ice an NHL team of its own, which would directly compete with the Americans. There was only one thing wrong with such a move—it was directly contrary to a promise Rickard's people had made to Dwyer.

"Bringing in a new team," said respected *New York Sun* columnist Frank Graham, Sr., "was in violation of a promise to Dwyer that the Garden would not bring in a second hockey team. But Bill's protest was in vain, since he had nothing in writing to prove it."

In time, Dwyer's failure to "get it in writing" was to become the key to the Americans' downfall. The Rangers, owned and operated by the Garden, were welcomed into the NHL a year later and proceeded slowly but surely to drive the Americans out of business, a feat that was finally accomplished, thanks to agonizingly rising rental fees, by 1942.

Neither Rickard nor his accomplices achieved any position of real power in the early NHL Establishment. That dubious honor fell to Conn Smythe of Toronto, Leo Dandurand of Montreal, and Charles Adams of Boston, with New York's Lester Patrick (Rickard's deputy) pulling up the rear.

Dandurand had been a partner in a Cleveland, Ohio, racetrack in October, 1921, when the Montreal Canadiens were put on the auction block. Since Dandurand was unable to be in Montreal at the time of the sale, he phoned a friend, Cecil Hart, in Montreal and asked if he would stand in for Dandurand and bid as high as possible for the Canadiens.

Hart agreed and went to the auction where he found himself in competition with Tom Duggan, who was representing both himself and the Mount Royal Arena Company. Duggan opened with a bid of $8,000, and Hart countered with $8,500. The auction was abruptly halted when NHL president Frank Calder revealed that he was representing an Ottawa group intent on purchasing Les Canadiens. Calder said he wanted to contact his party for further instructions. At that point, the bidding was temporarily postponed for a week.

When the second auction opened, Duggan startled the audience by placing ten $1,000 bills on the table. Calder said he would top that. Now it was Hart's turn, and he was confused about his strategy on behalf of Dandurand. He asked for a time-out and dashed into the next room where he phoned Leo in Cleveland. There was no time to lose because obviously this was going to be the final auction. Dandurand decided to gamble, instructing Hart to go the limit.

The emissary returned to the room and raised the bid to $11,000, catching both Duggan and Calder unawares. The two adversaries looked at each other and conceded the decision to Hart, who, in turn, ran out and phoned Dandurand with the news. Leo didn't know whether to be jubilant or crestfallen, but he had no choice. Nevertheless, the investment paid off immediately because Les Canadiens collected a $20,000 profit in the first year after Dandurand made the deal.

Dandurand's position of eminence in the NHL Establishment rested on his seniority. His power soon would be challenged by Charles F. Adams, a New England grocery magnate, who brought NHL hockey to Boston in 1924.

Adams had become enamored of hockey after watching amateur games around the Boston area. He sponsored a team but soon became disenchanted upon discovering that some of his rivals were spreading rather large gratuities among the players, even going so far as to lure several lads down from Canada. This breach of the good-fellowship code didn't wear well with Adams, and he turned to the NHL. Only later was he to discover that the machinations of the pros were infinitely more complex than those of the amateurs in Boston.

Compared to some of his cronies in the Establishment, Adams was the very soul of honesty and had a sense of humor to boot. When he was asked about his team's sorry effort in the 1924–25 campaign, Adams smiled. "We had three teams that year—one coming, one going, and one playing!"

While Adams' team was playing, the Rangers were being organized, and once again the ugly head of duplicity was reared and another head was unfairly chopped. This one belonged to Conn Smythe, a grand character who soon was to get his revenge.

A much-decorated veteran of World War I, Conn Smythe gained acclaim in college hockey circles for his superb stewardship of the University of Toronto hockey clubs. Each year Smythe would shepherd his varsity sextet to Boston, where the Toronto skaters wowed Beantown fans on the ice while young Smythe impressed newspaper editors with his flamboyant prose and knack for headline-grabbing, a trait he refined with age. Charles F. Adams, owner of the Bruins, was fascinated by Smythe's deportment and remembered him when Colonel John Hammond, president of the Rangers, asked for a recommendation for a man to organize a group of players to be Hammond's NHL entry. "Conn Smythe is your man," said Adams. "You won't find any better."

With customary vigor Smythe spent the summer of 1926 signing players for the rookie Rangers franchise. His selections were impeccably sharp, and before the season had begun, Smythe had signed such stickhandlers as Frank Boucher, Bill and Bun Cook, Ching Johnson, Murray Murdoch, and Bill Boyd.

When the players gathered at a Toronto hotel for preseason training, Smythe felt content. His team, he believed with good reason, would be indomitable. One night after convening at the training hotel, Smythe chose to take the night off to go to a movie with his wife. It was a reasonable plan, so Smythe was flabbergasted when Colonel Hammond accosted him in the lobby upon his return.

"Where have you been?" Colonel Hammond demanded.

When Smythe revealed that he and his wife had enjoyed a leisurely dinner and a good movie, Colonel Hammond bristled with anger: "Well, that night out has just cost us one of the greatest players in the game. St. Pats just sold Babe Dye to Chicago. We could have had him for fourteen thousand dollars!"

Smythe was unimpressed, and he told Colonel Hammond so. "I wouldn't want Babe Dye on my team, no matter what the price," snapped Smythe with the brand of finality that either convinces an employer or causes a man to lose his job. "He's not the type of player we need."

Smythe was not about to be fired on the spot; the Colonel wanted more evidence, and for a one-dollar phone call he got it. Hammond phoned Barney Stanley, coach of the Black Hawks, and pointedly mentioned young Smythe's opinion of Dye. Stanley's guffaws could be heard across the continent. When he stopped laughing, the Black Hawks coach sputtered: "Smythe wouldn't want Dye on his team? Why, that man must be crazy. It only proves how little he knows about hockey players. I can't understand, Colonel, why you keep a man like that when there's an outstanding hockey man like Lester Patrick loose and ready to be signed."

The Colonel couldn't understand it either. Smythe was promptly summoned to the Colonel's office and given his discharge papers before the season even began.

"Unwittingly," wrote former Toronto hockey publicist Ed Fitkin, "Babe Dye was mainly responsible for the formation of the Toronto Maple Leafs, because Smythe, angered by the Rangers' rebuff, decided he'd get into pro hockey or bust. Within a year he was back in the NHL, this time to stay. He took over the Toronto Maple Leafs."

Although Smythe was less esteemed than Patrick as a player and an organizer, Patrick's power ebbed in the thirties while Smythe's continued to grow. The problem for Patrick was simply that his employer, Madison Square Garden, regarded hockey as something less than the number-one attraction at the New York arena, while hockey was king at Smythe's Maple Leaf Gardens.

The crowning humiliation for Patrick came every spring when the Garden would boot its own team, the Rangers, out of their home rink to make way for Ringling Brothers and Barnum and Bailey Circus. Occasionally the Rangers would be compelled to play some of their "home" games at Smythe's Maple Leaf Gardens!

Neither Dandurand nor Adams remained dynamic powers in the Establishment for very long, but the vacuum was eventually and rather forcefully filled in 1935 when a Canadian wheat baron named James D. Norris, Sr., bought the Detroit Falcons, changed the team's name to Red Wings, and completely altered the power politics of the NHL for decades to come.

With the vitriolic Jack Adams as his lieutenant, Norris built the Red Wings into an NHL power. Bald, with heavy black eyebrows and a round face, Norris emerged as a threat to Smythe on the basis of his vast wealth and his absolutely ardent love of hockey.

Norris didn't believe in contracts. His word was enough, and as a result Adams never signed a contract as long as Norris, Sr., was around. "His word was his bond," said Munson Campbell, an NHL executive who went to school with James Norris' son Bruce. "He was brought up in the grain business where every bit of activity on the Board of Trade is word-of-mouth. When you go on the Board of Trade, you raise a finger or you say 'an eight,' and you own a carload of wheat. There's no written record of it—it's all verbal." And when old Jim Norris raised a finger in the NHL executive chambers, the other members of the Establishment stopped and listened.

They kept listening to the Norris family, for soon old Jim's sons, James, Jr., and Bruce—and for a time his daughter Marguerite—moved onto the

NHL scene so forcefully that, according to New York columnist Dan Parker, "NHL meant Norris House League."

Of all the Norrises, James D., Jr., caused the most joy—as well as some grief—for the NHL. By 1942 he had become vice-president of the Red Wings, and eventually he was president of the Chicago Black Hawks as well as a stockholder in other NHL arenas.

Jim, Jr.'s,—and the NHL's—problem was that he became a patriarch of boxing in the fifties and soon became associated with the underworld. "Getting into boxing," said Norris, "was the worst thing that ever happened to me." He admitted before a United States Senate subcommittee that he associated with Frankie Carbo, a fight owner of less than unimpeachable credentials.

Jim, Jr., eventually disassociated himself from the fight mob and concentrated on running his Black Hawks while brother Bruce handled the Red Wings. By the early sixties the Norris family and the Smythe family ruled the NHL because by now Conn Smythe's son Stafford had moved into the Maple Leafs organization.

Between the Smythes and the Norrises, all attempts at expanding the NHL from six teams to eight, ten, or twelve were soundly repulsed. While baseball, basketball, and football continued to expand, hockey retained a "cottage-industry flavor," as one critic put it.

The parochial attitudes of Norris and Smythe did more to curb big-league hockey's growth than anything. When pleas were made to bring the NHL to the West Coast they were beaten down by one of the two bosses.

"I find it very difficult to sell myself the idea to get even two new teams in the NHL," said Jim Norris, Jr., in 1965. "That would mean we'd lose four games with the Canadiens and four with the Maple Leafs, and I find it difficult to believe that I'm going to substitute eight games with Los Angeles or San Francisco for eight games with the Canadiens or the Maple Leafs."

Smythe's theory was that the NHL was successful because it *was* small. "New York and Boston keep drawing because there are only six teams in the league," said Smythe. "So you've always got an attraction coming in. But if you had two more teams that couldn't win games it would be different. If you had four rotten teams in the league, you'd have a hell of a time getting people in the rink. They wouldn't buy season tickets for thirty-five games a year knowing that they had to take fifteen or twenty lousy games. Two more bad teams would make ten more bad games."

Smythe and Norris invariably were seconded by the most important *unimportant* member of the NHL Establishment, league president Clarence Sutherland Campbell. A Rhodes scholar, lawyer, and former NHL referee, Campbell was the third man to hold the presidency of hockey's only major league. The first was Frank Calder, a former newspaperman who reigned from 1917 until his death in 1943. Red Dutton, former owner of the New York Americans, succeeded Calder on an interim basis until Campbell was named president in 1946.

"Campbell," said one perceptive NHL critic, "has held his job by reflecting accurately the sentiments of the NHL owners."

When Smythe or Norris—or both—snapped their fingers Campbell invariably jumped. And when the Big Two said nix to expansion Campbell promptly and vigorously fell into step. "Expansion talk," said Campbell in 1965, "is newspaper talk. There's nobody who can create a new league faster than a columnist."

And as the columnists and the rest of the hockey world soon learned, nobody could do an about-face on an issue, when it was expedient, better than Clarence S. Campbell. Within months after he was denouncing expansion Campbell suddenly became one of its most outspoken advocates. What happened? Simple. The balance of power had shifted. A group of Young Turks had taken over the NHL, and expansion suddenly was "in."

The turnabout in the NHL power structure was hardly predictable, mostly because Jim Norris, Jr., and Conn Smythe both, despite advancing years, appeared destined for another decade of power. If Norris should step aside in Chicago, there was always his partner, Arthur Wirtz, to pursue the antiexpansionist policies. And if Conn Smythe seemed more interested in his horses than his hockey players, Stafford Smythe surely would continue Dad's policies. Or so it seemed.

But Conn Smythe did move out of the hockey picture, and son Stafford did *not* second his dad's motions. Instead, he decided that expansion would be good for the NHL. So did young J. David Molson, president of the Montreal Canadiens. Soon Norris found himself bucking William Jennings, the graying attorney who had become president of the New York Rangers.

Clarence Campbell began to waver. Jim Norris' power base was crumbling. The fence-riders—Weston Adams, Sr., in Boston and Bruce Norris in Detroit—began leaning toward the Young Turks led by Jennings. Suddenly "expansion" ceased to be a dirty word. Like Arabs acknowledging Israelis in their Middle Eastern midst, the NHL at last recognized that expansion was not a complete impossibility.

By the end of 1965 a corner had been turned. The NHL held what it billed as "an expansion" meeting in New York. There, while Jim Norris cringed in conservative horror, a blueprint was presented in which the NHL suggested a second division of six more teams to face the established six.

It was, of course, only a blueprint, and the Old Guard regrouped for one last propaganda assault against the young rebels. Leading the counterattack was the "Little Major" himself, Conn Smythe, who delivered his most eloquent antiexpansion speech to the governors.

"Look at it this way," said Smythe. "You still got Jimmy Durante and Jack Benny and Bob Hope and Danny Kaye, and there's two million every year trying to be comedians, and there isn't anybody coming along.

"Aren't there ten million politicians in the United States and how many Presidents are there among them? There's only room at the top for a few, isn't there? That is the biggest argument of all against expansion. You've got the best players in there now, and you've got a couple of weak teams as it is. What strength do you add by expanding to a league that's already pretty proud of itself?"

"Hear, hear!" snapped Jim Norris.

Clarence Campbell put his finger to the wind. "I'm not antiexpansionist, but I'm solid for the economics, and I think that's my primary responsibility."

The economics were being redefined by William Jennings, David Molson, and Stafford Smythe. "Expansion wouldn't dilute interest," said Molson, "it would increase it."

Within a year Big Jim Norris was dead, and Conn Smythe was given a distinctly noninfluential chair in Maple Leaf Gardens. The old Establishment was out, and the Young Turks were in.

Early in 1966 the NHL voted to expand from six to twelve teams. Clarence Campbell said he thought it was a wonderful idea.

9
The NHL Establishment:
The Expansionists

THE RENAISSANCE of big-league hockey, as far as Bill Jennings is concerned, occurred the day that Philadelphia, Pittsburgh, Oakland, Minnesota, St. Louis, and Los Angeles were accepted into the NHL as the West Division.

Whether it was a renaissance or a decline-and-fall remains debatable to this day, but there was no question that the power balance had perceptibly shifted. Jennings, because of his active role as an archexpansionist, emerged as a key power broker. He immediately exerted his influence and saw to it that an American office of the NHL—as opposed to the Canadian office in Montreal—was established in New York City. His first appointee, golf promoter Fred Corcoran, was found wanting and was soon succeeded by Don V. Ruck, a Connecticut newspaperman who quietly developed designs upon Clarence Campbell's presidency.

Unfortunately—and perhaps ironically—for Ruck, expansion turned out to be a boon for president Campbell, who heretofore had been regarded by insiders as the league buffoon, his credentials notwithstanding.

"Campbell," wrote Jack Olsen in *Sports Illustrated*, "in his tenure as NHL President has sat like the man dunked by baseballs at the carnival, absorbing shot after shot by critics who mistakenly assume that he is setting policy.

"But, Campbell realizes better than his critics that he is not the grand emperor of pro hockey, but simply the agent for the owners of commercial enterprises known as hockey teams."

Six of these owners—bosses of the new West Division teams—did *not* exactly realize that. They were new to hockey and for the moment looked to Campbell for guidance.

"Before expansion," said one NHL governor, "Clarence was nothing but a parliamentary clerk. Then came expansion, and Clarence was, all of a sudden, the world's self-deputized authority on hockey. He began injecting himself into the operations of expansion teams, and the owners would call him for advice."

This heady situation for Campbell lasted until the six new owners began feeling their oats. Soon, Sid Salomon, Jr., and his son, Sid III, in St. Louis moved to the fore along with Ed Snider in Philadelphia and Jack Kent Cooke in Los Angeles. Once again another power play was in the works.

Jennings' move to the top awakened Bruce Norris and Bill Wirtz, son of Chicago Black Hawks owner Arthur Wirtz. When Norris flexed his muscles it was just like old times; he had enough clout to command the votes.

"Bruce became the strongest single governor in the NHL," said one of his colleagues on the Board of Governors. "He was on top because the others realized that he and his family have given twenty-five times as much to the NHL as they ever asked in return.

"Now Bruce has people that he can count on, even if he says we're going to vote against soap in the men's room. He'll get Billy Wirtz, Harold Ballard [Toronto], Gordie Ritz [Minnesota], and Jack Kent Cooke. Bruce lifted Jack Kent Cooke right out of his chair once and sent him to the floor. I don't think anyone's ever done that with Cooke before. As a result they've become good friends."

The opposing clique, headed by Jennings, featured St. Louis, Philadelphia, and sometimes the Pittsburgh representative. Stafford Smythe liked to refer to them as the "Conspirators." One governor described their cloak-and-dagger style this way:

"Stafford Smythe discovered that the 'Conspirators' were having rump meetings among themselves before they came to the other meeting, the main meeting. Stafford would slam the table at the official meeting and say: 'Look, for Christ's sake, if you haven't got enough guts to come to this table and tell me what you think, then go —— yourselves.'"

According to one governor the "Conspirators" made a key mistake when they invited Minnesota governor Gordon Ritz to their rump meeting. "Gordie would go to the clandestine meetings," said another governor, "and then tell us what they were all talking about. We had an excellent pipeline."

Because of such duplicity and what amounted to an endless war among the many factions, unanimity was impossible at most governors' meetings. "I could take a broad," explained one governor, "strip her, and put her on the governors' table, and everybody would think of something different to do. One guy would want to stick it in her ear. Another guy would want to stick it in her tail, and then there'd be one who'd say, 'The hell with this, I want to go out and jump the bellboy.' "

From time to time, smaller battles percolated, especially after Buffalo and Vancouver were granted franchises. Stafford Smythe resented the Buffalo organization because its general manager, Punch Imlach, had once worked for him and the two had parted bitter enemies.

Once, the Buffalo club made a simple request before the Board of Governors, which seemed to be eminently passable. As soon as Buffalo's request was made, Stafford Smythe jumped to his feet and addressed the league president. "Mr. Campbell," said Smythe, "does the Buffalo request require a unanimous vote?"

Campbell said that it did.

"Good," snapped Smythe, "then I vote against it. Now let's get on to the next subject."

Of all the power brokers in the NHL Establishment the most reasonable and calm was David Molson, a member of the Canadian brewing family and one of the most—if not *the* most—distinguished members of the high command. Molson was knocked out of the NHL box, curiously enough, by the proletariat in predominantly French-speaking Quebec. He was too much the WASP in an area of strong French-Canadian political ferment. A few days after he sold the Canadiens Molson explained the circumstances to another governor.

"I told David," said the governor, "not to give me any bullshit about selling the club because he needed the money or for capital gains. He said, 'No, I'll tell you exactly why I did it.

" 'You don't know the intimidation I've been going through since we took over the Canadiens. I've had six threats on my life. I've had threats about my house being blown up, my kids being kidnapped.

" 'The French-Canadian militant radical element put out some sort of sheet with six names on it, six people who were doomed to death. There in the corner of it was the name David Molson.'

"I asked Molson just what the rap was against him in the province of Quebec. He said they were down for exploitation of French-Canadian athletes. 'After seeing that, when I went to sleep at night I'd wonder to myself whether this was the night when they'd blow up the house and kidnap the kids. My wife would wake up crying and say, "David, we don't need this." '

"Molson told me that for the last year he'd been carrying a gun. Now, when you have to carry a gun to own a hockey team . . . ! He put it all together and finally got out because he felt he owed it to his family."

Molson's exit did nothing to enhance the NHL's image; nor did the arrival of Charles Finley do anything for the league's perennial quest for a positive image. In fact Finley's acceptance in the lodge was perhaps the stupidest move the league ever has made.

The Oakland franchise, more than any other NHL operation, was pockmarked with failure from the very day the Seals opened their doors in October, 1967. A series of ownership fiascos finally resulted in the Seals' being put on the market. There were two potential bidders, Finley and Roller Derby entrepreneur Jerry Seltzer.

Actually, Finley would have had the field to himself if it had not been for an insult he had delivered to United States Senator Stuart Symington of Missouri when Finley obtained permission to move his Kansas City baseball franchise to Oakland.

"Finley and Symington hated each other," said an NHL governor. "When Finley finally got permission to leave Kansas City he went over to Symington and said: 'You can take Missouri and shove it up your ass!' Naturally, that infuriated Symington, and when Finley wanted to get into the NHL, Salomon led the fight against Charlie."

Tragically, in terms of the NHL's good and welfare, the Salomon-Symington plot against Finley failed. In no time at all, the Missouri "block-Finley" leaders lined up a substantial group of backers for Jerry Seltzer, including Wayne Valley, Ed McGah, and Lamar Hunt, wealthy and responsible men who had turned the American Football League from a farce into a prosperous business.

Had the NHL Establishment shown even the slightest bit of wisdom or even bothered to check with their baseball brethren, they would have been well-fortified against the Finley plague. The major-league baseball owners at least had the good sense to turn down Finley the first three times he tried to buy into their monopoly.

"The fact that they ultimately weakened and let him have the Kansas City Athletics doesn't take away from their original skepticism," said columnist Wells Twombly of the *San Francisco Sunday Examiner and Chronicle*. "They sensed that Finley probably wouldn't be good for their game. In a way their inability to keep saying 'no' is understandable. They had the mistaken notion that the best way to control him was to take him in and then try to outvote him. The Weimar Republic made the same blunder in 1933."

In what appeared to be a rush of masochistic glee, the NHL Establishment convened at a Long Island motel in the spring of 1970 to hear Seltzer and Finley bid for the Seals' franchise. Never was a deck more heavily stacked against one man than were the NHL governors—with the precious exception of Sid Salomon, III—against Jerry Seltzer. The ice barons betrayed the subtlety of a Sherman tank as they steamrollered Finley, their eventual tormentor, into power.

"Finley came in with a single piece of paper outlining what he planned to do if he got the Seals," said Seltzer. "We had a detailed report. They paid no attention to us. Why, Bruce Norris of Detroit even went to sleep."

So, the era of Charlie O. Finley—one of the true disasters of NHL history—had begun in Oakland, and as one observer noted, "Bruce Norris suddenly began wishing he had gotten more sleep the night before the league meeting when Finley was voted in."

Then, boorishly unaware of their utter contumely, the governors, months later, came hat in hand to Seltzer, asking him if he'd like to buy and bail out their sinking Pittsburgh franchise. His secretary took the message and was instructed to tell the NHL Establishment that Mr. Seltzer was "out of his office and wasn't expected back *until March 23, 1984!*"

By the time the offer to Seltzer was made—and rejected—several NHL owners were beginning to get weary of Finley's deportment, as if they had no forewarning about his heavy-fisted promotions, his humorless gags, and his habit of beheading front-office personnel. Clarence Campbell nearly fell out of his office in Montreal's Sun Life Building when he learned that before each home game Finley had two guys skating around the Seals' rink in a mule suit.

"That stunt went out thirty years ago," griped an NHL owner. "Why, it's so bad the Ice Capades hate to use it. What's the man thinking of with things like that?"

One by one—Bob Bester, the publicist, Frank Selke, Jr., the general manager—Finley's hired help beat it out of Oakland. Flying home from Detroit one day, a newsman took out a copy of *Inside the Third Reich*. An Oakland athlete came down the aisle, bent over, read the title, and asked: "Which one of Finley's ex-managers wrote that?"

At first the NHL barons did everything possible to help Finley, who, admittedly, knew nothing about hockey. Bruce Norris suggested that his good friend, the hockey-wise Munson Campbell, move to Oakland and help Finley. Campbell did and soon lured Garry Young as general manager. Despite Finley, the nucleus of a solid organization now existed.

But Munson Campbell, who grew up with Bruce Norris in the Detroit Red Wings organization, found Finley more and more intolerable and ultimately threw up his hands in desperation and left.

"Finley," said Campbell, "could never have a happy organization. For example, he would put a call through to the Seals' trainer and get a piece of information from him. Then he would play that back against the coach and then play *that* back against the manager, Garry Young. Then he'd play the sum total of it back against me. He second-guessed and totally destroyed any type of *esprit de corps* within the organization."

One of the many straws that broke Munson Campbell's back occurred just after Garry Young had been brought in as manager. Apparently, Clarence Campbell, who now fancied himself the titular adviser for Finley, suggested that Scotty Bowman be hired as the Seals' manager. Finley then phoned Munson Campbell and asked him what he thought about Bowman as a potential manager. He told Finley that the Seals already *had* a manager, Garry Young. This is how Munson Campbell recalled the conversation:

"The moment I had told Finley we were already committed to Young he said: 'Well, that doesn't make any difference. Forget about him. We haven't signed anything with him.'

"I told Finley that I wouldn't be a part of such a deal. 'If you do this,' I told him, 'You do it yourself.' So, he said, 'Well, I'm going to do it myself.' He then called Bowman and told him to come to Chicago. He and Bowman spent two days together.

"Every so often Finley would call me and say, 'I think I got him, I think I got him.' Finley was naive. He didn't realize that there's a pipeline in hockey. He didn't know that Bowman and Jim Bishop of the Red Wings have been pals for years. Jim had already been in touch with Scotty to find out if he wanted to come to the Detroit organization. Scotty said he was going back to Montreal. Scotty was talking to Finley trying to find his pal, Cliff Fletcher, a job.

"Here was the scene: Finley would call on one phone and tell me he thought he had Bowman. Then, Bishop would ring me on the other phone and tell me that Bowman had just called *him* and said he'd never talked to such a crazy son of a bitch like Finley in his life. It was like a two-bit comic opera. I knew all along that Bowman would never work for Finley, and he never did."

Garry Young eventually *was* hired by Finley, but he was warned by friends not to make any long-range mortgage commitments in Oakland. Meanwhile, word seeped up and down the NHL grapevine that Finley was running the Seals into the ground. First-rate scouts such as Aldo Guidolin quit and sought other jobs.

"Player development to Finley," said one NHL governor, "meant dropping off a couple of watermelons at some Black high school in Louisiana and saying, 'Charlie sends his best.' "

From time to time Finley's escapades reached print and caused still further embarrassment to the NHL. One such episode involved Bernie

"Boom Boom" Geoffrion, now coach of the Atlanta Flames, who then was scouting for the Rangers. Young had recommended that Finley hire Geoffrion, and Charlie O apparently agreed.

"Finley," said Munson Campbell, "went to Montreal to meet Boom Boom. They discussed the terms, shook hands, and agreed it was a deal. Geoffrion called his boss at the Rangers, Emile Francis, and resigned. Francis accepted, wished the Boomer luck, and that was it. But eight hours later Finley called Young and said the deal was off. Garry said, '*What!* You shook hands with the guy. You gave him your word. You hired him.'

"Finley said, 'Well, that doesn't make any difference.' So Garry said, 'Look, Charlie, you made the deal with him. If you want to break it, you call him.' Finley then used an expression that he employed quite a bit: '*I order you!!*'

"Well, Geoffrion was staggered by this. He had to call Francis again, and Francis agreed to hire him back with the Rangers. But there were repercussions. The Seals had been after young Mike Murphy of the Rangers, and Francis had agreed to 'loan' him to the Seals for a season. But after the Geoffrion incident Francis said, 'No deal. With that crazy son of a bitch Finley, how do I know I'll get Murphy back again?' And we told him he was absolutely right."

Owner sentiment against Finley congealed rapidly. Within a year after the NHL bosses had welcomed him to their club, they were trying to devise means of expelling him. "We got to hate his guts," said one governor. "Despise him is another way of putting it."

Once it was obvious to Finley that the Seals were drawing flies in Oakland, he decided it would be best to move the franchise elsewhere. At this time, the governors were considering another expansion, and Finley thought he held the trump card over his colleagues—a veto.

"Finley," said one governor, "wanted the right to move his franchise anytime and anyplace he wanted to in exchange for his vote in favor of expansion. He mistakenly believed that a unanimous vote was needed to approve such expansion, and he was not going to give his vote unless he got his way."

But Finley had so grated the governors they finally went for revenge. "They reworded a memorandum," said one owner, "so that a 12–2 vote could get approval for expansion. And they got it. This was later called the 'anti-Finley' vote. Afterwards I told him that if he wanted to get back into the NHL again he'd get one vote—his own."

A month later, Munson Campbell resigned from the Seals, and it was downhill all the way for Finley after that. Even the easygoing members of the NHL Establishment such as Harold Ballard of Toronto began turning against him, and eventually Charlie O got the message, and after four years of tossing mud at the NHL, Finley sold the Seals back to the league and quit hockey.

"Can you imagine," wrote Wells Twombly, "the NHL volunteered to take him in? The ice barons have no right to complain."

Finley had proved to be just one of several headaches brought on by the myopic NHL Establishment. Its callous treatment of respectable bidders such as Jerry Seltzer enraged many of those who had also been rejected by the NHL. What's more, a select few of the enlightened owners realized that they were courting danger from another source.

"If we keep matters as they are," said David Molson before he left the NHL, "a new league could start on its own, and we'd have a lot of headaches. You just can't tell people forever and ever that they're going to be minor league and there's nothing they can do about it, because there *is* something they can do about it. They can say, 'Well, why shouldn't we class ourselves as major-league hockey? We'll start our own league. We'll raid the NHL. We'll sign their players. We'll offer these guys *x* hundred thousand.' There's nothing to stop them. Then you get into lawsuits, antitrust actions, and everything else. This is all a definite possibility."

Nobody was more prophetic than Molson. At times it seems as though his rhetoric had been prepared by an agent of the World Hockey Association, the new organization that was being formed to challenge the venerable NHL. In September, 1971, the WHA held its first meeting, and as Molson had warned, by April, 1972, it was stealing players left and right from the NHL.

Invigorating characters permeated the new league from top to bottom. Instead of the conservative, stiff-necked old Campbell, who always gives the impression of having just stepped out of the shower, the WHA presented a youthful, tieless president, Gary Davidson, a young California lawyer with limitless energy. His sidekick, Dennis Murphy, enchanted audiences with his wild Irish hyperbole and boundless charm.

Overwhelmed with self-importance and terribly shortsighted, the NHL owners at first professed to be unconcerned about the WHA. Delivering one of his typically boomerang-laden statements, Clarence Campbell assured the world that "the WHA will never get off the ground."

A few members of the Establishment took the WHA seriously. One of them was Ed Snider, the dapper president of the Philadelphia Flyers, as well as his lieutenant, Keith Allen, the Flyers manager. "We believed right off the bat that the WHA was for real," said Allen. "We battled them buck for buck. A lot of NHL teams were skeptical. They took a look at where the WHA was putting franchises and shook their heads. 'No way the WHA can make it,' they said. They took the same approach when dealing with their players. Now those players are over in the WHA."

Within two months the NHL had lost such stars as Gerry Cheevers, J. C. Tremblay, Wayne Carleton, Johnny McKenzie, Derek Sanderson, and Ted Green to the new league. Then word circulated that the WHA was pursuing Bobby Hull. No question, Hull was the one super-duper Mr. Clean of hockey who would give any league the kind of credibility it needed to challenge the established NHL.

"At this point [May, 1972] the NHL still could easily have torpedoed the WHA and kept the hockey world in its palm," said respected sports agent Marty Blackman of New York. "But the Old Guard was too cocky. If they had given Bobby Hull what he wanted, and paid off some of the other players who were threatening to jump, the WHA couldn't have survived."

But the NHL didn't, and in June, 1972, Hull signed a $2,750,000 contract to play and coach the Winnipeg Jets. When that happened, the WHA knew it was in business and so did many NHL owners—especially when more and more reputable promoters turned to the WHA.

One of them was Nick Mileti, the gregarious Cleveland sports entrepreneur. Mileti had come to NHL expansion meetings certain that he would gain an NHL franchise for Cleveland. "Instead," said one of Mileti's friends, "he was rudely treated and promptly turned to the WHA."

Mileti was to the WHA on the ownership level what Hull was in the player realm. His entrance meant that the WHA would have a spanking new arena in Cleveland by 1975 and helped round out the new league geographically and monetarily; all because the NHL had been obtuse in dealing with Mileti. "Really," said Mileti's associate, "all the NHL had to do was guarantee him a franchise the next time around, and he would have thought twice about it. But after all the work he had gone through in preparing the new stadium plans and all the hopes he had had, this NHL rejection was too much."

In spite of Clarence Campbell and an assortment of lawsuits launched by the NHL, the WHA *did* get off the ground, although its first flight was rather shaky. But just seeing the new league in operation both infuriated and frightened the NHL Establishment and created new and deeper ruptures within the warring factions.

Much of the antipathy was generated against Bill Jennings, the Rangers president. Two separate decisions by Jennings inspired the anger from Bill Wirtz, Bruce Norris, and Jack Kent Cooke, in particular. The first was approval given the WHA's New York team to play in Madison Square Garden, home of Jennings' Rangers. "We felt," said one NHL boss, "that he was stabbing us in the back by doing business with them."

Jennings further angered his colleagues by signing such stars as Brad Park, Vic Hadfield, Walter Tkaczuk, Jean Ratelle, and Rod Gilbert to exorbitantly high contracts—even exorbitant by WHA standards—while the other NHL teams tried to hold the line.

When by the middle of the 1972–73 season, the NHL governors realized that the WHA would not collapse, a daring move purportedly was engineered by Jennings. A top-secret meeting between a rump Jennings' group and a select few WHA leaders led by Winnipeg's Ben Hatskin was held in New York. Somehow the story leaked out, and less than six months after the WHA began operation it *appeared* to be in the act of courtship with its older and supposedly wiser rival.

Just the idea of the NHL's seeking peace with the WHA, however true it might have been, detonated a chain reaction of explosive headlines across the continent. If Bobby Hull provided the first major stone in the WHA base, the rump meeting with the NHL was the firm foundation. Now, there was no turning back.

Unfortunately for Jennings, many of his NHL brothers felt betrayed by the meeting, however unofficial it might have been. "Bill got hell from the other governors," said one NHL boss, "but especially from Norris, Wirtz, and Cooke. After that, Jennings never enjoyed the same power in the inner sanctum. He still had his little act, but not much influence."

Another influential figure moving into the shadows was Weston Adams, Sr., son of the Boston Bruins' original owner, Charles Adams. According to his colleagues the secretive Adams was known as the "Howard Hughes of Hockey."

Munson Campbell recalled: "I would be sitting in Boston Garden watching a game, and someone would come over and say, 'Mr. Adams wants to see you.' Then I'd follow him upstairs, behind some hot-dog stand, where the great man would be, and we'd do our business."

When Adams, Sr., died in 1973, his son, Weston, Jr., took over management of the club, but his influence was minimal compared with his father's. Whatever his faults, Weston, Sr., was revered as an honest and reliable member of the NHL Establishment. Then there was Harold Ballard who was reviled even by his predecessor as boss of the Maple Leafs, Conn Smythe.

"Hal Ballard," says Conn Smythe, "is like one of those old pirates who would go to sea and battle and board each other and take whatever was there. If they had to walk the gangplank they didn't holler. That's his way of living."

Smythe, who has known Ballard since Harold managed one of the minor amateur teams in Maple Leaf Gardens, has also labeled Ballard one of hockey's "fast-buck" operators.

"Ballard has been a friend of mine," says Smythe, "for a lifetime, but I wouldn't give him a job at ten cents a week around here. I wouldn't have him around because I don't like his way of doing business."

Others have questioned Ballard's technique, especially since he received a three-year sentence in October, 1972, for theft and fraud involving $205,000 from Maple Leaf Gardens.

"I was totally surprised when the judge convicted me," said Ballard, who upon his release seemed more powerful in Canadian sports circles than ever. "I just didn't think it would happen. Not once did I ever feel guilty. Most of the people who knew me and a lot of people who didn't know me were very sympathetic to my case. I think they realized that what actually happened was an everyday occurrence in business today. I thought I was tried by the news media and convicted by the news media."

Ballard generated a flood of unfavorable publicity in July, 1973, when out on a temporary absence pass from Millhaven. He described it as more like a motel than a penal institution, with tenderloin steak served regularly to the inmates. He later claimed that he was playing a hoax on the media.

"I simply didn't want anybody to feel sorry for me," he explained. "I don't ask for any quarter and I don't give any. I also wanted to take a little shot at all those people who wanted to see me hung up by the nails, sadistic types who would like nothing more than to see you get a beating twice a day. What amazed me was that I should have been taken seriously by newspapermen who had known me for so many years. I thought they would say there's that old —— Ballard going again, but only Jack Dennett [of radio station CFRB] knew it was a gag."

Running the Maple Leafs (and the Gardens) was no gag for Ballard even in prison where he worked out the details for coach Red Kelly's signing. "People from the Gardens would come and visit," said Ballard. "The biggest inspiration was King Clancy [vice-president of the Leafs]. He never missed a week and often he would come twice a week."

Ballard's release from prison in October, 1973, did not end the spate of negative publicity for the NHL.

The Leafs' boss, despite his outwardly affable appearance, was hardly the NHL press agent's dream, particularly after Ballard revealed that he keeps a pet piranha in his office. "My sons, Bill and Harold, bought me two of them as a Christmas present," he said. "Thought the old man would get a charge out of something different.

"Then one piranha ate the other, just like they eat the live goldfish you feed them on. It's the same as human beings in business ways. A fellow has to live, so he eats his brother.

"This is a tough world."

It is tough, even for the most firmly entrenched members of the NHL

Establishment such as Bruce Norris. Distracted by his many other businesses, Norris moved his base of operations from Detroit to Homosassa, Florida, where he owns extensive property. The care and feeding of the Red Wings was placed in the uncertain hands of Jim Bishop, a lacrosse expert from Oshawa, Ontario, and Ned Harkness, a college hockey coach from Cornell. "While Bruce was away," said one former member of the Red Wings family, "Bishop and Harkness ruined the organization."

Once an NHL powerhouse, the Red Wings plummeted to the bottom of the league thanks to Harkness' blunders and Bishop's tacit approval. The most egregious mistake of all surrounded the handling of super-superstar Gordie Howe—Mr. Red Wing.

Disgusted with the Harkness system, Howe retired as a Red Wing in the summer of 1971 after setting NHL records for most goals, most assists, and most total points, among many others. Gordie was given a front-office position with the club with the understanding that he would be an active administrator. Instead, he was boxed out of the picture by Bishop and Harkness.

Occasionally, Norris would get wind of the rancor up north in Detroit and fly from Florida to restore peace and at least temporary harmony. But Howe was restless and unhappy. From time to time, he'd feel the urge to play again, and watching his two sons, Mark and Marty, excel in the best junior league whet his appetite still more. When the WHA made its astonishing offer to the Howes—Gordie, Mark, and Marty—and presented a Houston Aeros contract, few observers believed they would accept. Gordie Howe's joining the WHA was as unlikely as Anwar Sadat becoming premier of Israel.

"Gordie splitting with the NHL," said one critic, "would be as unthinkable as Damon splitting with Pythias or Edgar Bergen with Charlie McCarthy."

Once again the NHL Establishment was on the spot. Would it act with dispatch and ensure Howe's happiness and continued allegiance to the NHL or would it be embarrassed again by the baby WHA?

The wheels of negotiation began grinding more and more rapidly as the WHA anted its offers. Gordie, Mark, and Marty were offered contracts with Houston totaling more than $2 million. Meanwhile, the NHL brass sat on its hands. A counteroffer, preferred by Clarence Campbell, was too little and too late.

This time the mud on the face of the NHL Establishment's face had the distinct odor of manure. Howe scathed the NHL, and the Detroit Red Wings organization in particular, for its loathsome treatment. "Do you know," said Howe, "that in my scoring-title years and my Stanley Cup years I couldn't live on my hockey salary? I had to take a summer job.

Here I was, the star of the world, and I watched my neighbor, a salesman, take his family and his boat every Friday night for the weekend at their cottage. There I was, supposedly the star of everything, working a second job to get along."

The Howes signed with the WHA team and brought millions of dollars of credibility, publicity, and integrity to the new league. The defection stunned Bruce Norris to the core and left the NHL without its two most glorious veterans—Bobby Hull and Gordie Howe.

If Norris was guilty of uninterest and distance from his club, another member of the Establishment was guilty of too much interference, St. Louis Blues president Sid Salomon, III, who fancied himself a hockey expert and began meddling in team affairs normally handled by the general manager and coach.

The Blues once appeared to be the strongest of the expansion teams under the baton of Scotty Bowman and his aide, Cliff Fletcher. Then Salomon began involving himself in player trades and on-ice strategy. He fired Bowman and Fletcher after the 1970–71 season and has since employed four general managers and five coaches in three seasons. In April, 1974, the Blues finished out of the play-offs for the first time in the club's history, and Sid the Third, as he prefers being called, was ridiculed by players throughout the organization. "Thanks to his trades," said one St. Louis player, "we wound up with seven kids on the team who should be down in the minors learning how to play the game."

Such episodes as Salomon's blundering or the jailing of Harold Ballard have deflated the NHL Establishment, to be sure. But nothing has done more to destroy the league's intimations of immortality than its miscalculation of the WHA.

In July, 1972, Clarence Campbell, without blinking his steel-gray eyes, triumphantly asserted: "The World Hockey Association? It's my opinion that they won't make it."

Less than two years later, the WHA had brought the NHL to its knees, forcing it to sign an agreement of recognition that presaged an eventual merger of the two organizations.

"The NHL," said Bob Verdi, the respected hockey writer for the *Chicago Tribune*, "has surrendered. The NHL, which promised to destroy the WHA, instead crawled to the infant league with wallets in hand."

How could such an astonishing turnabout occur? Those who are familiar with the NHL Establishment had the answer—NHL duplicity, cupidity, and of course, stupidity.

"We beat the NHL," concluded a WHA owner, "only because everywhere we turned, the NHL bungled around, making another stupid move. We have come far, but *we owe it all to the NHL Establishment!*"

10

The Fat Cats and Their Agents

Hockey was a great game before Alan Eagleson and the flock of attorneys, agents, and other salary scavengers came along. Players thought of their teams first and themselves last. Money was a secondary concern. Finishing first and winning the Stanley Cup was primary.

"We played hockey because we loved it," said Maurice "Rocket" Richard. "Anything we got paid was considered a bonus."

The coach and manager were bosses, and pity the stickhandler who dared talk back. "If you fought them," said Los Angeles Kings coach Bob Pulford, "you could be sent to the minors forever."

As a result a big-league hockey player knew that he had to claw and continue clawing if he wanted to stay in the NHL. He made a decent salary if he was a journeyman. If he was a superstar, he might make $20,000 or $25,000 a year and consider himself the luckiest guy in the world.

The arrival of Alan Eagleson changed all that. At one time or another, and sometimes simultaneously, the "Eagle" has been boss of the NHL Players' Association, president of the Ontario Progressive-Conservative Association, and personal attorney for hundreds of hockey players, including Bobby Orr.

When Eagleson intruded his black horn-rim glasses and well-groomed hair onto the NHL scene in 1966, attorneys were *personae non gratae* with the Establishment, and the idea of a players' trade union was regarded as unadulterated heresy.

The NHL had a method of handling troublemakers. Once, in the early sixties, aces Doug Harvey and Ted Lindsay tried to organize such a union for hockey players. Both were immediately traded—Harvey from Montreal to New York and Lindsay from Detroit to Chicago—and everybody else, quick, got the message.

Eagleson just happened to come along at the right time and in the right place. Having budding league-savior Bobby Orr as a client helped. In September, 1966, he signed Orr to a $150,000 two-year contract with the Boston Bruins—although Bruins manager Hap Emms had vainly objected to the Eagle's presence—and in November he compelled the NHL to give Toronto defenseman Carl Brewer his release so that he could be reinstated as an amateur.

By this time Eagleson was a man in motion, and the motion was upward. The turning point developed in December, 1966. A minor-league team in Springfield, Massachusetts, was suffering through a winter of discontent with its owner, Hall of Famer Eddie Shore.

When the Springfield Indians voted to revolt against Shore they were advised to engage Eagleson as counsel. The Eagle promptly visited NHL president Clarence Campbell and was told the Springfield case was out of the NHL's jurisdiction, since the Indians played in the American League.

"That's ridiculous," snapped Eagleson, mounting a typically high dudgeon.

The Eagle realized he needed widespread support among the rank-and-file players if he was to win the Springfield strike. Fortunately, he had Orr's backing and with that he had the support of the entire Boston team. The Bruins invited Eagleson to confer with them during one of their stopovers in Montreal.

"When I walked into their room," Eagleson recalled, "the whole Boston team was there. They told me they wanted to support the guys at Springfield with cash donations and then they asked me if I would start a players' association. I agreed and settled for twenty-five hundred dollars for expenses. It was a gamble but it was exciting."

So was the campaign against Shore. At first it appeared that Eagleson was up against insuperable odds. Shore, who owned and managed the Indians, was ruthlessly frugal and bizarre in his treatment of players. "As an owner," said Eagleson, "Shore was a crackpot. The stories the players told me about him were so preposterous that I wouldn't believe them until they swore out affidavits on them. Bill White [Chicago defenseman], for instance, lost five top years of his career working in Shore's concentration camp."

Shore's intransigence, despite the horrific disclosures by his players, produced enormously bad publicity for pro hockey, and the strike further worried the NHL Establishment. Pressure impinged on Shore from within his own league as well as the NHL. Finally, he was brought to his knees.

Shore eventually sold the Indians to Los Angeles Kings owner Jack Kent Cooke, who made Springfield a Kings farm club, and Eagleson emerged as hockey's latter-day Joan of Arc—a fact that did not elude the Eagle.

He immediately embarked on an intercontinental expedition from December, 1966, to May, 1967. When he returned, all but two players from the NHL, American League, Western League, and Central League had signed up with Eagleson's new association.

Recognition from the NHL Establishment was another story. Antiunion members of the Establishment such as Toronto manager Punch Imlach bitterly fought against acknowledgment of the union. Most of the governors supported Imlach.

"On the owners' part," said Eagleson, "it was a case of bullheadedness more than greed. They had everything their own way for fifty years, and they refused to accept the fact that times were changing."

But the owners soon saw the handwriting on the wall. If they failed to recognize the union, every single professional hockey player in North America was likely to go out on strike. In June, 1967, the governors, overcome with depression, recognized Eagleson and his NHL Players' Association.

They also killed hockey in the process. They made hockey players rich beyond all reason, so rich that many of them no longer regard hockey-playing as their prime priority. They have made hockey players so busy doing other things that hockey players hardly can find the time to play hockey.

Typical of this breed is Vic Hadfield of the Pittsburgh Penguins, who earns $175,000 a year (he earned $8,000 in his preunion rookie season) and has so many businesses it's a wonder he ever has time to think about hockey. Hadfield is a partner in a golf course, operates two truck- and car-rental franchises, owns part of a hockey equipment company, and endorses various products. He also authored one of the worst books—any category—ever written.

Hadfield's affluence typifies the *nouveau riche* mediocre hockey player. Eagleson laid the golden egg for players such as Darryl Sittler of the Toronto Maple Leafs ($750,000 for five years), Syl Apps of the Pittsburgh Penguins ($750,000 for five years), and Mike Walton of the Minnesota Fighting Saints ($440,000 for three years), to name a few.

It wasn't so much a case of the balance of power shifting from owner to player; *all* the clout now resides with the skater and his attorney. The result has been catastrophic for the fabric of pro hockey. "The tragedy," John MacFarlane wrote in *The Death of Hockey*, "is that the player-businessman is an anti-sportsman. He mocks the effort of the duffer and the serious competitive athlete alike.

"The hockey player, the most influential athlete in Canada, could encourage more people to discover how good it feels to participate in sport. Instead, he reinforces the belief that sport has no intrinsic worth. He does not play the game for fun, he plays it for money. . . . He does not have the time or the inclination to be the best in the world—he is too busy making money."

And nobody helped them make it better than the Eagle. From his Toronto office he dictated terms to NHL and WHA owners. Thanks to the intrusion of the WHA, Eagleson—and others—were able to play one league off against the other.

In its December, 1973 issue, *Maclean's* magazine of Canada recounted an episode that underlines the Eagle's style. He had phoned Toronto Maple Leafs manager Jim Gregory to discuss a new contract for his client Paul Henderson, an average—at best—forward who happened to score a couple of dramatic goals in a 1972 exhibition series between Team Canada and the Russian National Team.

"If you want Paul to play for you," said Eagleson, "come up with a five-year package. We're already holding an offer from the Toronto Toros for between eight hundred thousand and a million. See you."

And so it goes; left and right the Eagle wheels and deals, setting a trend that since has been emulated by Bob Woolf (Boston), Gerry Patterson (Montreal), and Howard Casper (Philadelphia), to name a few. But it was Eagleson who fought and won the good battle against the NHL Establishment with his pal and client Bobby Orr providing the wedge. It was Eagleson who predicted that it would take him five years to make Orr a millionaire, and it was the Eagle who later conceded that he had failed—it took five years and a few months!

Orr made his million on ability. Others are making theirs purely as a result of the competition provided by the WHA. In fact, one man—Cleveland Crusaders owner Nick Mileti—inadvertently made several Rangers very wealthy men after he obtained his WHA franchise in the spring of 1972 and immediately bid for NHL talent.

With a budget of approximately $4 million, Mileti zeroed in on those players whose contracts were expiring. The best of them were on the Rangers—Brad Park, Vic Hadfield, and Rod Gilbert.

As soon as Mileti made his pitch, the Rangers had to decide whether to pass—the way the Black Hawks did with Bobby Hull—or whether to engage Mileti in some serious bidding. "It was apparent," said Rangers president William Jennings, "that Mileti was going for the Rangers' throat in three directions.

"We had to make a fast decision. Did we want to be a contending team? Or be struggling again at the bottom? We knew we could not give our fans a winner if we lost Park, Hadfield, and Gilbert."

In Park's case, the Rangers were fortunate. His attorney, former minor-league baseball player Larry Rauch, was an ardent Rangers fan and a pal of many of the New York hockey players. A few who knew Rauch well were betting that he'd never let one of his Rangers clients defect to the WHA no matter how high the salary.

But Jennings didn't know that for certain and approved a $250,000 salary for Park, making him the highest-paid NHL player at the time and far in excess of his true worth (about $75,000). "I'm not saying that I'm worth what they're paying me," said Park in a gross understatement. "Still, I'm getting it, and I don't feel guilty."

Word of Park's payroll shot up and down the Rangers roster in a matter of hours (attorneys always announce their kills in suitably vague yet extravagant terms), a fact that had not eluded Jennings.

"We were well aware," said Jennings, "that once we signed Park everyone else on the team had to be appropriately increased, too."

The Rangers payroll climbed and climbed from its previous level of $750,000 to nearly $1,750,000, and nearly every member of the club grinned like a big, fat Cheshire. "This is a very happy club," said forward Pete Stemkowski. "Even the goons like me make eighty thousand dollars."

As for poor little rich man Nick Mileti, he was able to make a millionaire out of only one player, Bruins goaltender Gerry Cheevers. And the Rangers never even sent him a thank-you note. None of the other NHL owners did, either. To a man, they felt betrayed on the grounds that Jennings peeled off many, too many greenbacks in his pursuit of a championship. "The Rangers," said Toronto owner Harold Ballard, "are trying to buy the Stanley Cup."

The Rangers failed miserably despite their vast outlay of cash. Rich players like Hadfield turned into skating pumpkins overnight, and in the spring of 1973 the Rangers were unceremoniously wiped out of the Stanley Cup semifinal round by the underpaid Chicago Black Hawks in only five games.

When Rangers general manager–coach Emile Francis resigned as coach and appointed Larry Popein as his successor, the fat-cat New York skaters immediately took a dislike to the rookie. Popein, whose salary couldn't have been more than $30,000, immediately clashed with Gilbert ($130,000), Hadfield, and a few other members of Broadway's golden sextet. Within weeks, rumblings of a mutiny against Popein were heard around Madison Square Garden, and by February, 1974, Popein had been fired and Francis had replaced him.

Such is the power and ruthlessness of the million-dollar hockey player. The player has become king—his attorney is prince-knave—and he doesn't give a damn about anyone but himself, least of all his team, his coach, or his manager, let alone his league.

"With few exceptions," said critic John MacFarlane, "the hockey player is a complacent performer who prefers the racetrack to the training room."

He is getting paid more money and generating less effort than any athlete in any sport, with full knowledge that neither manager nor owner can do a thing about it. Here are a few examples:

Exhibit A

The Detroit Red Wings opened the 1973–74 season with several high-priced "stars." One of them was center Marcel Dionne, represented by Eagleson and receiving approximately $100,000 a year. Another was Mickey Redmond, represented by Bob Woolf and receiving close to $200,000 a year. Ted Garvin, Detroit's coach at the time, was paid about $15,000.

Thus it was hardly surprising that the overpaid Red Wings ignored their grossly underpaid coach. They were the regals. They skated when the spirit moved them and goofed off when they wanted to—which was often.

On October 30, 1973, Detroit played a game against Toronto at Maple Leaf Gardens. The Red Wings were beaten, 7–0. Dionne and Redmond, the so-called leaders, weren't worth a plugged nickel.

"I told them," said Garvin, "that pride should force them to try and earn their fat salaries, that they were taking money out of their teammates' pockets."

But pride seems to be foreign to these adult ice brats. Pride has been replaced by greed. Redmond and Dionne remained with the Red Wings. Garvin was fired. His replacement, Alex Delvecchio, promised to be more lenient with the troops. He was, but it didn't help—the Red Wings still finished miles from a play-off berth.

Exhibit B

An NHL defenseman, who shall go nameless, was traded by the Red Wings to the New York Islanders during the 1972–73 season. At the time of the deal he was being paid $65,000 (worth no more than $15,000) by the Red Wings, yet he demanded that his contract be renegotiated before he would skate for the Islanders.

His attorney contacted Islanders manager Bill Torrey, who was desperate for defensemen at the time. Torrey decided to sign the defenseman for $90,000. The player then stunk out the joint in Long Island and was traded again. Once again, he demanded more money from the new club and by God he got it.

"We had no choice," said an official of the new club. "Manpower has become so scarce that you take whatever shit they throw at you and like it. Otherwise you don't operate."

Exhibit C

When the Philadelphia Blazers entered the WHA in 1972, management believed that the key to a money-making franchise was an exciting personality, who also played center, named Derek Sanderson. Sort of the Joe Namath of hockey. The Blazers signed Sanderson to a $2.5 million contract and *then* began wondering what in hell they had done.

They began asking themselves: Can a twenty-six-year-old high-school dropout be worth *all* that money? Trucking magnate Bernie Brown, who bankrolled the Blazers, tried to rationalize the obviously expensive blunder. "Signing Derek," said Brown, "was like buying an insurance policy. We were in the thing so deep we needed some insurance that we'd have some money coming in. We figured Derek would sell tickets."

The hell he did. Instead of flocking to see Sanderson, the people stayed away by the hundreds of thousands. At first Derek gloated: "All this money, man, it's just unreal. I can do whatever the hell I want now. I might just buy myself the whole damn city."

But Sanderson failed to fulfill his basic responsibilities as an athlete and couldn't even buy himself a goal, let alone the entire city. He was overweight, out of shape, and absolutely useless to the Blazers. Instead of leading the Blazers he enraged his teammates. Before two months had passed, he had been hospitalized, and soon Bernie Brown wished he had never seen Sanderson in the first place.

By midseason the Blazers' management had huddled with attorney Woolf and paid Sanderson a substantial sum for Derek *not* to play any more games for the Blazers. Shortly thereafter, Woolf negotiated with the Boston Bruins, and lo and behold, Derek finished the season in the NHL.

But Sanderson had become so rich he was uncontrollable no matter where he parked. Midway in the 1973–74 season he got into a fistfight with teammate Terry O'Reilly and soon was suspended by coach Bep Guidolin. The Bruins soon made Sanderson a free agent, and Woolf once more went to the marketplace to find another sucker for Sanderson. Eventually Derek was traded to the Rangers, who previously had unloaded Hadfield on Pittsburgh.

Exhibit D

Of all the NHL players, none has a more positive *image* than center Dave Keon of the Maple Leafs. He is the Scoutmaster on skates, Mr. Nice Guy who would run a mile to return a dime to an old lady who dropped it on the street. Keon has tried so hard to elicit a positive response from the public that he hired a voice and image coach to work on his style. In this way Dave Keon would be that much more salable.

At a reception for more than a hundred advertising and industry executives in Toronto held in March, 1971, Keon was introduced by his image coach, Ron Hewat, in this way: "This is to introduce you to Dave Keon the man. What we call the total package. The name Dave Keon generates excitement."

Well, that it did, both on and off the ice. Keon played capable hockey for Toronto and became a prime target for the Ottawa Nationals when the WHA team was organized. The Nationals' president, Doug Michel, not only pitched for Keon's contract, he thought he actually had it.

He didn't, of course, as things turned out; but what burns Michel is that in the process, the Scoutmaster himself, Dave Keon, kept the large bonus Michel had paid him. At least that's the way Michel tells it. In fact Michel was so disillusioned by Keon's behavior that Doug devoted a whole chapter to an analysis of it in his book *Left Wing and a Prayer*.

According to Michel, he gave $50,000 to Keon for what Doug believed would be an *advance on salary*. Based on his conversations with Keon, Michel nurtured high hopes of signing him to an Ottawa contract. "Mike Elik [Keon's business partner] and Keon reaffirmed our deal," said Michel, "and they told me it was just a case of letting the lawyers work it out."

The lawyers never did work it out. Keon's lawyer, Jim Stevens, sent Michel *another* contract treating the $50,000 *as a bonus*. "The biggest hurdle, though," said Michel, "was a brand-new wrinkle Stevens had added. If we [Ottawa] didn't play our first league game by December 13th, Keon could pick up the entire million dollars and just walk away."

Michel couldn't accept the terms, and much as he wanted Keon and believed that he needed him to launch the new franchise, the terms were impossible. He told Stevens thanks-but-no-thanks and actually felt a sense of relief about the whole ugly mess—except for one thing. "The only trouble," said Michel, "was I was out $50,000 along with the time and effort, and they wouldn't give it back."

Michel was prepared to go to court for the $50,000 but made one last attempt to communicate with his adversaries. "I asked Elik and Keon if they would come in to see me," said Michel. "I still wanted to make an attempt to get my $50,000 back without going to court. The answer was that they'd give me back part of it, but not the entire amount. I figured I had it all coming, so we couldn't agree.

"But after we got through that, Elik brought up the subject of coming to work for me. I almost laughed. How can you hire someone you're about to sue? Anyway, Mike never got hired. But I also didn't get my $50,000."

A further list of fat-cat–agent duplicity would stretch from here to Hades and back, but these should underline the point. Attorneys and agents, despite their endless pieties and homilies, are primarily after their 10-percent cut. They care not one puck for the good of hockey, or the product dispensed by their overweight clients to the overcharged fans, or for the financial structure of the teams they are raping. If they did, the Sandersons and Keons wouldn't be carrying on as they have.

But Eagleson has made life beautiful for hockey agents. Once these scavengers realized that the Eagle had a bankroll by the beak, they all jumped in like vultures to tear off a piece of meat.

That they have succeeded is amply proved by the fact that every fourth-rate stickhandler is represented by an attorney-agent who dictates terms to beleaguered managers and owners. But, nobody but nobody dictates like Eagleson.

In his role as head of the players' union he has the NHL owners dancing to his tambourines. As attorney for superstars like Orr and Dionne he merely has to suggest a jump to the *other* league and they cringe in fear.

It was Eagleson who had the clout to keep Bobby Hull, Gerry Cheevers, and Derek Sanderson *off* Team Canada in September, 1972—although they had been invited—because they had signed with the WHA.

By September, 1972, Eagleson had become so ubiquitous and seemingly omnipotent in the NHL that newspapermen would cringe before his wrath—some newspapermen, that is. Of course when the Eagle got angry his fury was like the wrath of God, and nobody knew that better than Trent Frayne, one of Canada's most respected writers.

Frayne encountered Eagleson during the Team Canada expedition to Moscow in September, 1972. That was after the Russians had won three, tied one, and lost one in the series. Before the series began, Eagleson had cockily predicted that Team Canada would win eight straight games. Now it appeared that the Eagle's skating birds would be lucky if they won another game.

This was not easy for the prideful Eagleson to digest; and when he met Frayne and asked the *Toronto Star* writer what he thought of the Russians, the Eagle must have expected the kind of sycophantish reply he might receive from one of the many hacks he usually meets.

Instead, Frayne told the Eagle that he had never seen a team pass the puck as impressively as the Russians. Eagleson reacted as though he had been stabbed in the back.

"Jesus," said Eagleson, "you must be a Communist."

Frayne, noticing that the Eagle's face was pale and drawn, reiterated that the Russians' style delighted him.

"We lost, you know," snapped Eagleson.

"Yeah," Frayne replied, "I know we lost."

"We lost, and you're telling me you like their passing."

"That's right."

By now Eagleson had reached the boiling point. "Anybody," he bubbled, "who thinks like you do has to be a bloody Communist."

The Eagle had succeeded in antagonizing one of the mellowest journalists in Canada.

"What is this?" Frayne shouted, "I tell you I like their passing, and you give me all this ideological gobbledygook. What the hell has. . . ."

But Eagleson wasn't finished either. "Are you calling what I have to say gobbledygook? If that's what you're saying, our friendship ends right here."

Frayne, who later recounted the incident in *Maclean's*, admitted that Eagleson had left him dumbfounded. The two were near blows when they parted, with Frayne delivering the final shot. "Friendship," he said, "is worth more than that."

Friendship between attorney-agent and hockey writer always is a touchy subject. Ever since the blossoming of Eagleson, attorney-agents have used the media as middleman to help strengthen their negotiating power.

Philadelphia attorney Howard Casper frequently would plant stories with me when he was negotiating Bernie Parent's contract with the stillborn Miami Screaming Eagles of the World Hockey Association. Casper believed that such stories appearing in the *Toronto Star* would inspire Toronto Maple Leafs manager Jim Gregory to sweeten the pot and thereby force Miami to up *its* ante until Casper obtained the best possible deal.

Such machinations help the writer because he frequently can get a *beat* on a story. And obviously they help the attorney-agent, who not only improves his bargaining position but obtains reams of free publicity.

By June, 1973, Casper had collected so much publicity and so many clients on the Philadelphia Flyers he was regarded as the second most powerful figure in Philadelphia's hockey scene. "Flyers owner Ed Snider has the power to sell his team and shut down the operation," said Jack Chevalier of the *Philadelphia Bulletin.* "Casper controls enough players to cause a revolt or sit-down strike."

Casper's power basically has been confined to Philadelphia. Attorneys such as Bob Woolf, Eagleson, and Rauch have been in positions where they could break if not make a league—the WHA in particular.

When the new league was organized it hired Steve Arnold, a sharp athletes' representative from New York, to sign players. It was Arnold's job to negotiate with the Eaglesons, *et al.* If he failed, there would be no players, and hence, no WHA.

Eagleson's ties with the NHL were too close to allow him to deliver any significant players to the WHA. If others followed the Eagle's policy, the WHA was dead. Wherever a WHA owner turned, he seemed to find Eagleson causing a headache.

"He created our league's biggest headache," said Michel, "when he invented what came to be known as 'front money.' Very early Eagleson distributed a newsletter warning players who might be thinking of jumping that they should make sure to have at least their first year's salary secured either by having the money placed 'up front' in their bank account or by some other ironbound means. 'Front money' became the keystone of most negotiations, and it made things that much tougher."

If Eagleson snubbed the WHA, other attorney-agents blessed the new league and immediately dealt with it. Woolf delivered Derek Sanderson and promising young defenseman Ron Plumb to the Philadelphia Blazers. Chuck Abrahams, an ebullient representative from Los Angeles, came through handsomely with several clients, as did Casper. They were enough to compensate for Eagleson's NHL bent.

Many owners were wounded by the epidemic of agent-attorneys. "There were no uniforms or programs to tell the good guys from the bad guys. After a while, you got so you could smell out the phonies, but in the beginning there was no way to tell."

One such phony was an "agent" who managed to obtain a secret WHA player list through a relative who had planned to operate a team. The relative had no knowledge of the insidious act until months later. By this time the "agent" had contacted several of the players, become their representative, and signed them—with NHL teams.

An aura of unscrupulousness seems to pervade many dealings conducted by hockey agent-attorneys. Their concern always seems to be riveted on the buck and not on the puck. Once they obtain the big, fat contract for their big, fat cats they seem to abdicate all responsibility to inspire their client to *earn* his money. As a result the client, once signed, just doesn't seem to give a damn.

"There's been an influx of guys who don't put out every night," said Bobby Hull. "A terrible complacency on the players' part has set in. There's no incentive left. Or at least there doesn't seem to be anything driving the players anymore."

Heaven forbid, an owner should suggest that a player is *not* earning his salary. Pfft! Just like that, the player is on the phone calling Daddy-agent for help. Yes, the relationship is that close. Ask Howard Casper.

One night he was asleep at home when the phone rang. It was 3:30 A.M., and one of his hockey player-clients was on the wire from Vancouver, calling collect. The guy was cockeyed drunk but insisted upon talking to his attorney.

"Hey, Howard," he pleaded, "you've got to talk to this broad I've got in my room. She wants a hundred bucks. Here, honey, this is Howard, my lawyer."

Oozing with sex appeal, the woman took the phone. "What's this hundred-buck shit?" Casper barked. "We'll give you fifty and not a penny more. That's our final offer. Take it or leave it. You're not the only dame in town, you know!"

11

The Rules Imbroglio

MANY YEARS AGO, when Gordie Howe was mustering one of his many assaults on Maurice "Rocket" Richard's record of fifty goals in a season, several critics suggested that a special dispensation be given the Rocket if Howe broke the record.

"The least that should be done," offered one analyst, "is provide an asterisk next to Richard's name. Remember, the Rocket's fifty goals were scored in only fifty games. Nobody has equaled that average."

Howe never reached the once-revered fifty-goal plateau, but in time, as the quality of the goal cheapened with the quality of play, everybody and his brother seemed capable of eclipsing Richard's record. Such mediocrities as Mickey Redmond (who couldn't carry Richard's laces, let alone his skates), Rick MacLeish, and Ken Hodge all have become fifty-goal men. And so today Richard's truly Promethean feat has been all but forgotten in the tidal wave of goal inflation encouraged by inept goaltending—there hasn't been a first-rate goaltender in the NHL since Glenn Hall—and disappearing defenses.

Richard's case is important because it symbolizes the grossly unfair scoring system that permeates the NHL. A player who scores fifty goals in fifty games certainly deserves more credit than a player who scores fifty goals in seventy-eight games.

If justice is to prevail in the NHL statistical department, scoring leaders will in the future be judged by the percentage system. A player would be required to participate in a minimum of fifty-five games. His total points, based on goals and assists, would be divided by his number of games played to produce his scoring average.

This average system would be infinitely more equitable because it would never deprive a player of the championship and prizes that go with scoring leadership simply because he missed games because of injury.

The percentage system is a must, but not the only one that would make hockey's scoring policies more equitable. The time has come for a reevaluation of the quality of goals and assists. The ancient system of giving equal value to each must be discarded for a more realistic approach. When all is said and done, the goal is infinitely more valuable than the assist and should be so recognized. Assists not only are cheap, they are further cheapened by a system in which they are distributed as indiscriminately as ticker tape in a parade.

Official scorers who sit on the fringe of competency dispense assists to players who barely handle the puck on a play that ultimately results in a goal. And there have been cases where players received assists *even though they were not even on the ice when the goal was actually scored.*

Since the name of the game is "score" it is axiomatic that the goal have a higher value than the assist. Therefore a goal should be afforded a higher standing. I believe it would be more equitable to award the goal-scorer two points for his effort while limiting assists to one point apiece. With one exception:

A player who makes an especially excellent effort in setting up a goal should receive more than the one-point assist. In special cases he should receive a point and a half. Here is an example:

Let us say that Yvan Cournoyer of the Canadiens carries the puck from his own blue line past several defenders, and just as he is being knocked down in his opponents' zone, skims a perfect pass to Jacques Lemaire in front of the net. Lemaire then slaps the puck into the net for a goal.

On such a play the scorer deserves two points because he produced the essential item, the goal. But the orchestrator, because he made an extraspecial effort, rates a little extra; hence the point and a half instead of a point.

Which brings us to a vital question: How can such a determination be made? The answer lies in giving the official scorer discretionary powers to award a point-and-a-half assist when he believes such an award is justified. Certainly, an effort such as the Cournoyer play is worth more than just a point, more than the single point given to a player who just happens to touch a puck in a melee that eventually results in a goal.

Naturally, the proposed system has a built-in inequity—cheap goals. Should, for example, a shot that bounces off a player's leg and into the net be counted as a two-point goal, just as would an artistic wrist shot from twenty feet out that catches the far side of the net a foot off the ice?

If the new system is to be honest, it must place cheap goals in perspective. These, too, must be evaluated by the official scorer. If the scorer determines that such a goal is not worth two points, the scorer should award either one point or half a point (on shots that occasionally are put into the net by the enemy and credited to the skater nearest the puck). Scoring, therefore, must become an art, and similarly, artistry on ice should be rewarded by the scorer. All of this, however, is contingent upon use of the video playback and a reasonable amount of time for the scorer to intelligently analyze the play.

It is unfair and stupid to credit a player with two points for a goal if he does nothing more in "scoring" it than happen to have his body in the vicinity of the goal crease when the rubber bounces his way.

Pro hockey's frenetic pace has made changes in the scoring system imperative. More than ever scrambles develop around the goal crease; long slap shots bound into the net off unsuspecting teammates, and the origin and final disposition of the puck on a scoring play is becoming more and more obscure.

Official scorers often have been criticized for their failure to diagnose a play correctly. Quite often the criticism is justified simply because the scorers are incompetent. And one of the best reasons they are incompetent is that the NHL encourages such incompetency. The league does so by its abjectly cheap attitude toward their minor officials.

Hard as it may be to believe, NHL minor officials are considered *minor* in every sense of the word and especially in the monetary arena. They are not paid one penny but rather are bought off by a pair of house seats to home games and in effect are manipulated by the home club. For starters, all official scorers should receive regular salaries from the league, just as referees and linesmen do.

As for improving the technology of the scoring system itself, modern science should be employed. Before awarding *any* points on a goal or an assist, the official scorer should first study the play on a videotape instant replay—*if necessary, after the game.* Then and only then will the scorer be in a position to determine calmly and intelligently exactly who was involved in the score and precisely how much value should be placed on the assists.

By utilizing the televised instant replay, the scorer no longer will rely on primitive techniques to determine what has become an important aspect of a major-league hockey game—the statistics.

Under the new scoring system proposed here, the videotape replay would be the decisive element. But what about the beleaguered goal judge who must make instant decisions during the course of a game and more and more often is finding it difficult to determine whether a puck flew in and out of the cage in a split second or hit one of the steel posts?

Unfortunately, science has yet to discover an adequate replacement for the human eyes of the goal judge. The answer, if science can come up with such a contraption, would be an electric eye sensitive only to the rubber puck. Thus, when the puck flew over the red goal line—and past the electric eye—the goal light automatically would flash on.

A similar arrangement is now used in tennis. Foot faults are detected by an electronic monitor placed along the baseline. When a player's sneaker crosses or touches the line, it activates the electrical circuit, which, in turn, relays a signal to the umpire.

It has been argued that few of the other major sports use any more sophisticated equipment than hockey; that baseball relies on the eyes of the umpire behind home plate, football uses no more, no less than human beings on the gridiron, and basketball does likewise.

Whether these sports do or do not adjust to different conditions of the seventies is their problem. It is not hockey's concern that Roger Maris' sixty-one home runs were accomplished under more favorable conditions than Babe Ruth's sixty home runs. Or that Hank Aaron required more games to hit his record-breaking number of home runs than Ruth.

Besides, hockey is infinitely faster than its big-league counterparts, and the puck is infinitely smaller than the football or basketball. It therefore stands to reason that hockey requires a much more sophisticated approach to its scoring, and it is about time the NHL escaped from the nineteenth century and recognized the need for change.

12

Expansion and the World Hockey Association

IF THE OLD GUARD of the NHL Establishment, led by Conn Smythe and Jim Norris, had had its way, the league would forever have remained a private six-team operation with a huge NO ADMITTANCE! posted in front of the governors' meeting room.

"We're selling out now," said NHL president Clarence Campbell in 1965. "Increasing our league wouldn't increase our revenue five cents per club."

Typically provincial, Campbell was ignoring two essential factors that would increase the league's treasury by millions more than "five cents per club." One was a network television contract and the other was a lucrative entrance fee—which eventually climbed to $6 million per club—to join the NHL club.

Young Turks in the NHL, led by Rangers president William Jennings, saw the gold at the end of the tunnel before Campbell realized it might be there. Jennings knew that no TV sponsor was interested in backing a network hockey telecast that included just four American cities.

If the NHL was to reap the big television money being raked in by baseball and football, it would have to expand. And when it did, the new clubs would have to be located, wherever possible, in new markets for televised hockey.

In 1966, when the first dramatic change was made in the NHL fabric,

100

these markets included Oakland, Los Angeles, Philadelphia, Pittsburgh, St. Louis, and Minnesota (Minneapolis–St. Paul). Curiously, Vancouver had bid for an NHL franchise at the same time as the other cities and appeared a sure bet to obtain one on the basis of its long hockey history. But the governors summarily rejected the British Columbia city at the time only because of the TV factor. Vancouver *already* was receiving televised hockey on the Canadian Broadcasting Corporation's "Hockey Night in Canada" Saturday programs. Vancouver, therefore, would not be a new television market. At least temporarily. In 1969, when it was apparent that the CBS network telecasts were obtaining low ratings, Vancouver and Buffalo were admitted to the NHL lodge principally because they promised to be instant box-office successes. Which they were.

In one sense, expansion was a boon to hockey. It provided hundreds of jobs to players who ordinarily would have been consigned to the minor leagues for life. And it gave hundreds of thousands of fans in such distant precincts as southern California and northwestern New York an opportunity to see Bobby Orr, Phil Esposito, and Frank Mahovlich *live* for the first time.

But for the fans in the six established NHL cities and for hockey purists elsewhere, expansion was an abject and utter disaster. "The price for television was expansion," said hockey critic John MacFarlane, "and expansion has done more damage to the game than anything else."

Expansion destroyed the quality of hockey to such an extent that even such an NHL partisan as Clarence Campbell was moved to admit as much. "You can't take half a bottle of whiskey," said Campbell, "fill it with water, and still have the same drink."

What made the drink so putrid was the manner in which NHL bosses distilled the new product. Instead of accenting quality they were smitten by greed. Established owners, although taking millions from the new clubs, gave them the absolute dregs from the player barrel. An imbalance of power was created in 1967 that continues to haunt the NHL to this very day.

"Maybe we could have developed a tolerance for whiskey," said critic-fan John MacFarlane, "if it had been watered down with care, but the NHL was sloppy."

The established clubs were so infinitely stronger than the new clubs that games between the East (established) and West (expansion) divisions were monuments to boredom. Without a shot at the best players the new teams could never expect to beat the old clubs. The resulting imbalance infuriated the fans, who suddenly found themselves paying major-league prices for a distinctly minor-league product.

Even worse, the mediocre expansion players contaminated the play of quality teams. "We played *down* to their level," said All-Star defenseman Brad Park of the Rangers, "because they couldn't play up to ours."

Most embarrassing was the defacement of the NHL's showcase, the Stanley Cup play-off finals. Up until expansion the finals invariably moved hockey fans to the highest pitch of excitement and generated the most interest from the media. But the arrival of expansion teams turned that all around.

In 1968 the St. Louis Blues were wiped out of the finals in four consecutive games, each outranking the last for colossal tedium. As Park had pointed out, the superior, established club goofed its way through the series, lowering itself to the expansion club's level. As a result, Montreal merely outscored St. Louis, 11–7, over the four games.

A year later the same clubs met in the finals while critics ridiculed Stanley Cup play as a "burlesque of hockey." They were right. Montreal once again shellacked St. Louis in four straight games and this time outscored the Blues, 12–3. At that, the Canadiens were taking it easy.

"On most nights," said John MacFarlane, "it's sheer nostalgia to call it hockey."

Normally, one might have expected the situation to improve rather than deteriorate, especially since the Blues were the wealthiest and at the time the best-run of the expansion clubs. Instead, the situation deteriorated. When the Blues reached the finals in 1970 against Boston, they were so thoroughly smitten by the Bruins that Derek Sanderson, Boston's outspoken center, suggested that it was a waste of time even to play the series.

Between stifling yawns, the Bruins won four straight matches and outshot the Blues, 20–7. The series was such an abomination from an artistic viewpoint that even the most sanguine NHL owners became jumpy. Their concern was translated into a highly secret investigation conducted by NHL President Campbell into the state of the NHL since expansion.

Completed in 1971, the report was delivered to all NHL bosses, one of whom leaked a copy to the *Montreal Star*. When *Star* columnist Red Fisher printed excerpts of the confidential message the NHL's embarrassment over expansion was, at the very least, quadrupled. (A source at the *Star*, not Fisher, indicated that the report had been leaked by a St. Louis Blues official.)

In the report Campbell made no bones about what he considered the NHL's "number-one problem"; it was expansion—or the lack of parity between the established teams and the expansion clubs. "Progress toward parity," Campbell told his bosses, "has been very scanty. Indeed . . . the trend has been in the opposite direction!"

Publication of the report had the impact on hockey circles that revelation of the Pentagon Papers had in Washington, D.C. For the first time hockey fans had the complete truth about what really happens in the smoke-filled rooms where the governors hold their secret meetings.

More important, the secret documents betrayed the fear Campbell and other governors shared about their cockeyed expansion and the manner in which the established clubs were decimating the expansionists.

"In the end," Campbell concluded, "there is only one way to ensure a steady demand for tickets for all games—the quality of entertainment provided. This is dependent entirely upon balanced competition—another expression meaning parity."

Ironically, that parity for which Campbell so ardently longed would eventually be obtained—to a minor degree, of course—by the very organization that the NHL had attempted to exterminate at birth.

It was the World Hockey Association and not the NHL that provided the NHL with a degree of parity; and the WHA achieved this delightful state for the NHL simply by siphoning off some of the superstars from NHL clubs such as the Black Hawks, Bruins, and Canadiens.

The Bruins, for example, were to lose All-Star goalie Gerry Cheevers, renowned forwards Derek Sanderson and Johnny McKenzie, as well as defenseman Ted Green. "When those four left the Bruins," said one Boston hockey writer, "the guts of the team was gone."

True enough, but the NHL also was that much closer to achieving parity. And it continued to move still closer as the WHA continued its early policy of raiding the NHL.

On the other hand, the WHA's intrusion meant that Clarence Campbell's "bottle of whiskey" now was so watery it tasted more like H$_2$O than Scotch. The man to credit—or blame—for this extravagant state of hockey expansion was a roly-poly Irishman named Dennis Murphy who had previously had a hand in creating the American Basketball Association. Murphy's achievement must go down in sports history as one of the biggest long-shots-turned-winners since the floating of Noah's Ark.

It was early 1967 when Murphy first indicated hockey would follow his basketball escapade.

"The idea of the ABA was just beginning to take hold when Dennis and I had breakfast together one morning in 1967," said Lee Meade, then sports editor of the *Denver Post* and later public-relations director of the WHA.

"Dennis drove me back to my office, and as I was leaving I remember him telling me, 'How about you and I getting together sometime and forming a pro hockey league?' I remember my answer, half in jest: 'Sure, Dennis, sure. Just call me.'"

Four years later, when Murphy returned to California, he had already laid some of the groundwork for his hockey scheme. A young Santa Ana lawyer, Gary Davidson, had been a founding partner in the ABA experiment, and Murphy recalled telling him of his eagerness to start the hockey project.

"If my basketball contract doesn't come through, I still have it in the back of my mind that the National Hockey League has had the run of things and we should make a run at them," Murphy told Davidson during a Christmas break in Los Angeles.

The thought had probably crossed a thousand and one minds. For most people the conversation never left the bar, but Murphy and Davidson, buoyed by the ABA experience, put their plan into action in the first week of April, 1971, only days after Murphy's return to California.

Together they formed the World Hockey Association, establishing the legal base from which to operate. Then they hit the road. For three months Murphy and Davidson combed the major cities of America, sniffing out enterprising sportsmen who had the money, guts, and commitment to challenge one of sports' most hallowed institutions—the fifty-five-year-old NHL.

Word spread quickly. By May, 1971, Los Angeles tax expert Charles Abrahams, a negotiator for more than a hundred hockey players, was advising his clients to sign only one-year contracts because "an alternate league may be emerging for your benefit."

Hardly a month had passed when Murphy and Davidson, gleaning the knowledge of their travels, came to the conclusion that Canadian cities would add a necessary new dimension to their fetus-stage league. Walt Marlow of the *Los Angeles Herald-Examiner* knew a few hockey people in Canada, and one day he suggested the name of Bill Hunter of Edmonton, Alberta.

Hunter, a fiery redhead, answered an invitation to fly south to meet two total strangers with the staggering new idea. For Hunter, the conditions sounded inviting. He loves a fight, and for a lifetime he had been fighting the NHL for a better deal for his junior Oil Kings, not to mention his belief that Edmonton, an oil-rich city of 500,000, was more entitled to big-league hockey than Pittsburgh, for example. Hunter left impressed. He had men in mind back home who might be receptive, too.

Now hockey blood began filtering into the veins of the WHA. Hunter recruited two associates in junior hockey. He found Scotty Munro in Calgary, who produced a millionaire backer in Bob Brownridge. From Winnipeg, there was another millionaire who made hockey his business, Ben Hatskin.

"If we hadn't got those three fellows [Hunter, Munro, and Hatskin] at that stage of the game, it would have been very unlikely the league would have survived beyond that point," said Murphy.

Hunter produced a list of more than two thousand professional and highly regarded amateur hockey players from Europe to North America. Hatskin spearheaded a pension scheme that would absorb players after their first season. But the biggest attraction of all was the prospect of establishing major-league franchises without the cumbersome expense of $6-million and $7.2-million expansion fees charged by the NHL.

The money that might otherwise be spent for a franchise and everybody's culls in the NHL's proliferation of a widening talent gap could be spent, they insisted, on competing for the best players in an open market.

Public opinion was wary that any upstart hockey league could actually carry out that battle plan. How could a Detroit Red Wing possibly be serious about dumping the security of the NHL for an untried team in a city only a fraction the size of Motown?

Sportswriters scoffed at the idea. They referred to the WHA as the "Wishful Hockey Association." But the germ of thought continued to multiply.

"I remember going to our first meeting in Los Angeles," said Hatskin. "I took one suit, thinking we'd be on our way back the day after we arrived. Instead, we stayed four days and I looked like a grub among all those prominent people."

Out of the Los Angeles meeting came eleven "definites"—Dayton, Miami, Los Angeles, San Francisco, St. Paul, New York, Chicago, Milwaukee, Winnipeg, Calgary, and Edmonton.

But even the so-called definites were insecure in time. As the meetings followed in New York, Chicago, Tampa, Anaheim, Ottawa, Quebec City, and Houston, the league drew closer to reality.

Finding adequate facilities was a major problem. Those who could afford to construct their own buildings needed land in a hurry, and land meant political expediency. There were untold problems to unravel.

The problems scared some.

Paul Deneau, a hotel executive, grew exasperated with civic stumbling blocks in Dayton and quickly shuffled his franchise to Houston.

San Francisco, owned by Davidson, experienced problems and finally ended up in Quebec City.

Milwaukee dropped out to chase an NHL franchise in the next fit of expansion. Miami was building an arena that would have been the WHA's showpiece, but president Herb Martin failed to provide ample parking space and the local zoning committee shot down the Screaming Eagles.

In the Eagles' healthier days, however, they created news by announcing the first major signing. The hockey world was aghast when goaltender Bernie Parent left the Toronto Maple Leafs one Sunday afternoon to pose in a Screaming Eagles uniform, confirming that he had signed a five-year contract for $750,000, a house, and a car.

Ultimately, Parent and the remaining Miami drafts were absorbed by the Philadelphia Blazers, a late arrival owned by Jim Cooper, a lawyer and chairman of five banks.

Miami had company on the sidelines. In a shocking announcement in March, Calgary bowed out. The sudden exit of a Canadian cornerstone sent tremors through the new league. But the Calgary demise had tragic overtones, never fully understood. Munro, typical of most hockey people, banked heavily on someone else's financing. Only in his case, Bob Brownridge, the oil executive who had led Calgary's charge into the WHA, was stricken by a terminal disease and quietly, sadly withdrew his support.

As late as mid-June the Calgary franchise was absorbed by Cleveland sports baron Nick Mileti, rebounding from a last-minute jilting by the NHL's expansion committee. And so, Cleveland became the twelfth franchise.

What had emerged as basically a league full of lawyers was gradually showing concrete signs of becoming inundated with successful entrepreneurs of the business world.

The New England Whalers, backed by fortunes, rose out of the Boston area as a potential alternative for legions of hockey-hungry Beantown fans, many of whom could not buy a ticket to see the Bruins.

The Minnesota Fighting Saints showed positive signs of health. A new arena in St. Paul, as beautiful as the crosstown home of the North Stars, had every prospect of absorbing the hockey madness in Minnesota behind the bankroll of scrap-iron tycoon Lou Kaplan. The Fighting Saints supposedly were a lead-pipe cinch.

Turbulence in New York, where original franchise holder Neil Shayne fought a legal battle for the use of the new Nassau County Coliseum, soon diminished with the takeover of the franchise by two lawyers, Dick Wood and Sy Siegel.

The Chicago Cougars and Ottawa Nationals joined the fight, flexing their muscles and flashing their bankrolls at the prospect of wooing major-league hockey. The size of their muscles and anxiety to succeed were more apparent than the scope of their wealth.

As each cornerstone of the WHA was fitted into place, the howls of derision could be heard bouncing up and down the corridors of NHL offices. The jibes of sportswriters were just as potent, but the WHA kept moving forward.

One by one, name NHL players signed WHA contracts—Jim Dorey,

Brad Selwood, Rick Ley, J. C. Tremblay, and Larry Pleau. Hardly any NHL team was immune from a raid. Nevertheless, even the most optimistic WHA owners believed that the new league required a major superstar to gain instant credibility and salability. When it was learned that Bobby Hull's contract was up for renewal the WHA zeroed in on him and conducted a long romance, which, if it had failed, would have killed the WHA at its inception.

"If we hadn't been able to deliver Hull," said Doug Michel, the original owner of the WHA's Ottawa Nationals, "if the NHL had stepped in to steal him back, we might as well have all cut our throats. Everybody in the WHA was aware of that."

The WHA–Hull romance began in November, 1971, in Vancouver, where the Hawks were playing the Canucks. In a coffee shop, Hull visited with Ben "Fats" Hatskin, the rotund, jovial fifty-four-year-old boss of the Winnipeg Jets who had drawn Hull's name in a draft of NHL flesh. Hatskin, rebuffed before by the NHL, wanted a franchise dearly and wanted Hull even more. The offer: $1 million for five years.

Hull reported to his financial representative Harvey Wineberg, who expressed interest but cautioned: "Let's wait on it. If they're really serious, they'll call again."

They did, and the negotiations commenced in earnest. Wineberg informed Hatskin that the million-dollar booty wasn't all that awesome, because Hull was earning about $150,000 a year from the Hawks. Wineberg wanted to know precisely the top WHA offer; he didn't want to conduct a bidding war with the Black Hawks, and neither did Hull. Fine, said everybody, and by February, 1972, the figure was around $2 million.

Just about this time, Hull began to wonder about his Chicago bosses—chairman of the board Arthur Wirtz and team president William Wirtz. He had met with them early in the season and confirmed that he wanted to be a Black Hawk for sometime to come. There was vague discussion of Bobby's next pact, and a figure of $1 million for five years was bandied about for starters.

But that was it, and soon Hull was saying: "I'd like to stay in Chicago, but I don't expect the Wirtzes to match the offer Winnipeg is making. The new league might need me a lot more than the Black Hawks will. But I don't want to discuss it until the season is over."

Neither, apparently, did the Wirtzes. After the season, according to Hull, he waited and waited for a meaningful message, but there was none. According to Bill Wirtz the two sides were constantly talking. One can only surmise that what the Hawk brass considered as definitive discussions were construed by Hull to be mere chitchat.

Meanwhile, the colloquy between Wineberg and Hatskin assumed the opposite path—it grew and grew. Soon WHA president Gary Davidson joined the conferences; it was he who would guarantee the $1 million "up front" from the league to get the most historic of Hull's thousands of autographs.

By mid-May Hull had become so impatient and puzzled by the Hawks' mysterious passivity and so flattered by Winnipeg's aggressiveness that he proclaimed in print: "I've made a verbal deal with Winnipeg, and if they make good on it, I'm gone. They've got themselves a hockey player!"

This was the beginning of the end for Chicago. Wineberg accelerated his schedule of meetings with WHA honchos, and every detail of the voluminous forty-page contract was hashed over and rehashed: $1 million for Hull to sign, $250,000 a year for five years as player—or if he wished, as player-coach—$100,000 a year for another five years as a Jets front-office executive. There were numerous clauses in case of injury to Hull, in case the Jets folded but the league didn't, in case both collapsed, in case the Black Hawks sued and won, in case of everything short of World War III.

"It's a fantastic contract, but it should be," Wineberg said proudly. "In any situation Bobby will be well taken care of."

The Wirtzes were not quite surrendering. Not yet! They offered Hull $1 million for five years—ironically, the figure that Hatskin had first used to tease Hull, and the figure that Hull and Wineberg had tossed out at the Hawks. But now it was June, and the Black Hawks had made their first concrete proposal, according to Hull. But it was too little, too late.

And so dawned the day of June 27, 1972. Hull rode a Rolls-Royce through St. Paul, Minnesota, to autograph the WHA portion of his contract and pocket the $1 million. Then the motorcade headed for the airport, where a chartered airliner waited to take Hull and family, Hatskin, and Wineberg to Winnipeg, along with a bevy of WHA officials and media folks.

The city of Winnipeg was wide-eyed and tumultuous, as befitting an end-of-war celebration. Hull was his always charming self, the exuberant, conquering hero. He signed the Jets contract, honored every possible request of interviewers, and of course obliged every little kid's autograph pad. Then it was off to the city's busiest intersection where, in front of thousands, Hull donned the Number 9 jersey—Winnipeg version—for the first time. The throng screeched, Hatskin sighed in relief, Wineberg sniffled a bit, and a tear came to the eye of Hull's wife Joanne.

"I have no regrets about leaving Chicago," said Hull when the day was done. "The whole thing has made me wonder what the hell they [the Wirtzes] were thinking. They must have thought I was bluffing, or they must have been gambling that the Winnipeg offer would fall through.

"If anything, I made the Wirtzes' job easier by saying right at the start of all this that I wanted to stay in Chicago and that I didn't expect them to come close to matching the Winnipeg offer. But they never took any serious steps to offer me a contract until two weeks before I signed with Winnipeg. Not even sit down and talk and start negotiating.

"If the Wirtzes had made me any kind of offer, that would have given us a starting point to talk, and I'm sure we could have worked something out and I would have ended up staying in Chicago. What man in his right mind would want to pick up a wife and five children from a place he's played in for fifteen years and move away? Maybe that's what they thought. They talked about me being a National Leaguer forever. Well, I'm not anymore."

Hull emphasized that his decision was just good business. He stressed that nothing else had influenced him, not even the notorious episode of three years earlier when Bobby was coerced by the Black Hawks into a public apology after missing a month of the season over a contract hassle. Now, he said, he had no axes to grind, but it appeared that any distress he harbored was directed at Arthur Wirtz, not Bill, and at general manager Tommy Ivan, not coach Billy Reay.

There were times during Bobby's long tenure in Chicago when Hull felt hurt by his employers. Little hurts like the sphinxlike manager Ivan's walking right past the Golden Jet's locker the night after he'd scored his six-hundredth goal. No handshake, no congratulations! There were deeper wounds, like the Chicago contract that Hull claims the Hawks never lived up to, the episode that prompted the great apologia of 1969. But nothing bloodied Bobby's sense of pride more than the Wirtzes' posture during the Winnipeg negotiations. In this respect, it was pride that swept Hull to the other network as much as the dollars.

"The Wirtzes are signing other Hawks," Hull would say, "why aren't they trying to sign me?"

Wirtz couldn't answer that question, because he said the Hawks were, indeed, trying to sign Hull. "We will not touch the Winnipeg offer," Bill Wirtz said, "because that would create a dangerous precedent for the team and league." What would the Black Hawks pay Tony Esposito, what would Buffalo pay Gil Perreault, if the Hawks paid Hull that kind of money? Of course Hull never asked the Wirtzes for that kind of money.

With Hull in the bag, the WHA bosses began smiling broadly and breathing easily. "I think we're really going to make it," said Murphy moments after Hull had signed his contract.

The WHA has made it, but their expansion has hardly been easy. Financial troubles beset the New York and Ottawa franchises in the first season. The Ottawa club was moved to Toronto in 1973–74, while the New York operation folded two months into its second year and moved to

Cherry Hill, New Jersey. Other franchises showed signs of weakness, but overall the outlook was rosy, mostly because of the armistice agreement signed with the NHL in February, 1974.

"In reality," said Bob Verdi of the *Chicago Tribune*, "the armistice, in effect, is a merger which guarantees the future good health of the WHA."

By the autumn of 1974 the complexion of big-league hockey had been so drastically altered that old Jim Norris would never have recognized it if he had returned to this earth. The NHL had expanded to eighteen teams and struck gold in Atlanta, Georgia, while the WHA iced fourteen clubs with an eye toward eventually including Miami as a fifteenth.

As for the "whiskey," it hardly was recognizable anymore. Quality was the first victim of expansion, and as a result veteran spectators in the six established NHL cities began staying away from the arenas in droves.

But somehow the NHL managed to replace the empties. In new hockey cities such as Atlanta, the league was catering to a fan whose only previous connection with ice had been in highballs. The question remained: Just how much expansion-dilution could big-league hockey sustain before even nonsavvy fans began turning away?

"The outlook," said *Toronto Star* sports editor Jim Proudfoot, "is dreadful. More dull, meaningless contests can be expected in the immediate future than ever before."

But an NHL official countered that the hockey boom would continue for at least two decades. "Who said you have to serve the people whiskey in the first place?" he said. "Let them drink water!"

Part Three

How to Improve Hockey

13

How to Make It a Better Game

In the Spring of 1974 panic struck the corridors of the NHL and the offices of the National Broadcasting Company simultaneously and with the impact of a thunderclap. After spending millions of dollars promoting big-league hockey for television consumption the league and the network learned that ratings—which were low to begin with—had fallen *below* ratings of the previous season.

Hockey, despite the seventy-six-trombone trumpeting of NHL flacks, was bombing on the network and Madison Avenue. The "fastest game on earth" just couldn't cut the ice against its natural TV rivals—basketball, football, and of course ABC's ubiquitous "Wide World of Sports."

There are some very good reasons for this state of affairs, and the best reason is that most Americans—and about twenty million out of twenty-one million Canadians—are almost totally ignorant of the whys and wherefores of hockey. They simply don't know what the blue line is for, let alone the red line and game-misconduct penalties.

As a salesperson, hockey is its own worst enemy. One of its major assets, speed, is the one factor that has made hockey too difficult for the average fan—and coveted TV viewer—to watch. Sad to say, but *hockey has become too fast for its own good.*

The smallness of the puck combined with the speed of play has made the game almost impossible for the average viewer to follow and absolutely impossible for the newcomer to comprehend.

Hockey rules, if followed diligently, are so complicated an Einstein would give up in disgust and return to his physics book. Of course hockey promoters have tried to simplify the game by telling new fans, "All you have to do is put the puck into the net, that's what hockey is all about."

Sounds easy, right? But try following the puck during an actual game. Author Ed Linn once did during a season in which he attempted to diagnose hockey styles and gave up in total frustration. "Nobody ever actually sees a goal being scored," said Linn. "The goalie doesn't see it, so why should the paying customer? Ninety-nine percent of the goals come out of a driving contest in front of the net or off a rebound after the goalie has made a save.

"A player fires the puck through a forest of legs and arms—and occasionally bodies—and if he's lucky, it gets through to the net. If the player is real lucky, the goalie doesn't see it through the arms, legs, etc., and he's got himself a goal."

Linn's analysis is very important because it reflects a basic problem for hockey and its promoters. If the game is to sell, the buyer must know what the hell is going on. And with each year hockey becomes a little faster, a little more illogical, and a lot more incomprehensible. What has happened to hockey is that there is so much action that there is no action at all. The rink has become an icy pinball machine with players aimlessly bouncing off boards, off each other, and occasionally off rubber pucks.

If NBC-TV is wondering why its potential mass of fans happens to be watching basketball—easier to follow because of the larger ball and smaller court—it should consider the hockey players' aimless marauding up and down the ice, producing the pinball effect of a bright, gaudy, splendidly staged blur.

Naturally, such nonsense appeals to the cretin instincts of some people. But an intelligent spectator like Ed Linn is turned off by the contemporary banality of big-league hockey.

"Under current conditions," said Linn in his analysis, "hockey can't be played. The once intricate, balanced game has disintegrated into a mass mugging on skates."

That, of course, is an understatement. Contemporary hockey is an obscenity compared to what it was meant to be and what it once was. Today's game is to the pre–World War II variety what New York subway graffitti are to the "Mona Lisa."

Big-league hockey once was as artistic as the "Mona Lisa." Stickhandlers abounded like a hundred Houdinis; intricate passing plays delighted audiences like a floating chess match on ice; and shooting was sensible. The slap shot, fortunately, had not yet been invented, and players accurately aimed either a wrist shot or a backhander at the goaltender.

Most important, the game didn't feature speed for the sake of speed. It was played at a more decorous pace, which allowed for cleverness and intrigue. Genuine bodychecking—as opposed to the modern, dumb boardchecking—was an absolute art in itself as defensemen braced themselves at the blue line and heaved enemy forwards over their hips and shoulders with awesome frequency.

The destruction of hockey as an art form occurred in two phases: the first with the introduction of the center red line by Frank Boucher in 1943 and the second with the invention of the slap shot by either Andy Bathgate or Bernie "Boom Boom" Geoffrion—the subject is debatable—in the midfifties.

Before Boucher introduced the center red line, forward-passing from one zone to the next was illegal. The red line changed all that, enabling players to pass the puck anywhere from the defensive zone all the way to center ice.

At first the change seemed to be for the better. It opened up the game and allowed for higher scores and more fluidity. But soon Boucher's best-laid plans were corrupted. He had hoped that once a player took a long pass at the center red line he would then stickhandle his way, or pass his way, into enemy territory.

But the rules allowed players simply to shoot the puck into the enemy zone once past the center red line. Within a few years the center red line became a crutch; rather than carry or pass his way into the opposition's zone, a player would simply dump the puck toward the end of the rink and hope that one of his teammates would get to it first.

Soon the "shoot-the-puck-in-and-hope-for-the-best" style of play became rampant, and style went out the window. By 1960 the beautiful hockey of the twenties, thirties, and early forties was totally unrecognizable compared with the new game. Intricate pass patterns were forgotten as players milled around, cutting up the ice, hacking at the puck and each other.

If that weren't dreadful enough, the slap shot came along and totally destroyed the game. Prior to the slap shot's arrival, players employed two distinct techniques for firing the puck. The most common, the wrist shot, was deadly accurate because the puck was cradled at the stick blade until its release. This enabled the shooter to get a good "feel" for the rubber. When he released the shot with a sudden cracking of the wrists, the puck could achieve speeds of up to 95 MPH. Control was a hallmark of the wrist shot to the extent that an average shooter like Johnny Wilson, formerly of the Red Wings, could in a test bounce nine out of ten shots off a goalpost from fifteen feet out.

The backhand shot was utilized when the puck was away from the shooter's normal shooting side. Like the forehand wrist shot, it featured control because it was released after nestling at the side of the stick blade.

Then the slap shot screwed everything up.

Unlike its predecessors, the slap shot featured a golfer's-style windup in which the stick was drawn back behind and over the shooter's head. Then there was a follow-through with the stick striking—slapping—the puck and driving it, like a golf ball, goalward.

Only in rare cases could the slap shot be controlled, and rarely did a slap shot from farther than thirty feet out land in the net area. Why, then, did the slap shot become so popular?

"Even though it was inaccurate and wasteful, it *looked good and sounded good,*" said Atlanta Flames scout Aldo Guidolin, who played NHL hockey when the slap shot was born. "It also became a crutch for players with weak wrist shots. They would skate over the center red line and let one fly. And if a guy was a lousy stickhandler, it was a crutch for him, too. Instead of trying to fake his way around a defenseman, he just took a slap shot and then chased after the rebound when it missed the net."

Try as they might, coaches failed to curb the outbreak of slap shots—especially after the glamorous young Bobby Hull of the Black Hawks demonstrated that he could propel the puck at speeds of upwards of 130 MPH.

Between the slap shot and the center red line, hockey went completely to pot. The two brought about a radical change in defensive patterns—or what was left of the defense—goaltending, and stickhandling—or what was left of *that.*

Like the fans, goaltenders could no longer follow the trail of the puck because of the rat pack in front of the net and the blinding speed of the slapped puck. Goaltenders learned that when a puck seemed to be emerging from the milling throng before them, the most effective strategy was to fall down.

Suddenly, the art of goaltending went to hell. Instead of punting the puck, ballet-style, goalies began flopping on the ice the way peewees of six and seven do in outdoor pickup games. It was dreadful, and many former hockey-lovers, myself included, turned against the game.

Soon goaltenders became so frightened about the screaming pucks that they began donning grotesque-looking face masks, and the intimacy, which had been such a grand aspect of the sport, was gone. The goalie mask soon inspired defensemen and forwards to wear protective helmets, and still more intimacy disappeared from hockey.

On some teams helmeted players outnumber those without the head-gear. The result has been a dulling of interest. To a viewer of the Chicago

Black Hawks, for example, a helmeted Pit Martin looks like a helmeted Stan Mikita, looks like a helmeted Cliff Koroll.

Other changes were made to the detriment of hockey's basic appeal. Prior to World War II an overtime period was played after every tie game. But because of wartime railroad-scheduling problems overtime was eliminated "for the duration of the war." Except that the NHL never revived overtime.

When fans clamored for its return, NHL president Clarence Campbell insisted that tie games—except during the play-offs—were perfectly acceptable.

Acceptable, that is, to Campbell. Fans loathed the fact that the NHL was the only organized sport that did nothing to discourage ties. If, as was the NHL's case, one out of every four big-league baseball games failed to produce a winner, they'd be closing ballparks from Boston to St. Louis.

Soon it appeared that the NHL was doing everything to eliminate its most appealing features, such as the penalty shot. By far one of sports' most spectacular sights, the penalty shot is hockey's cobra versus the mongoose—the goaltender against the lone shooter on the great expanse of ice, one skater roaring toward the netminder, ready to release his shot at a time of his choosing.

By the early sixties referees seemed afraid to enforce the penalty-shot rule that says a man is entitled to one anytime he is fouled in the act of shooting. Officials claimed that the penalty shot was too drastic a punishment to fit the crime, and in its place, referees called hooking and tripping penalties that amounted to two minutes in the penalty box and nothing more.

"To me," said Ed Linn, "such moves indicated that the NHL was determined to cleanse the game of skill."

And by 1974 it appeared that the NHL had succeeded in doing just that. The wrist shot and backhander were virtually nonexistent; pattern passing had given way to shoot-and-run; the slap shot was king; and hockey had gone to the dogs.

Its ratings were low because (a) intelligent viewers realized that there was, in fact, a better way of playing the game as proved by the Russians, and (b) new fans found the game impossible to follow because the absurdly high speeds resulted in hockey defying execution. The game had become too fast for its own good.

"The speed became such a detriment," said an NBC television executive, "that it often became impossible to follow the puck *even in slow motion.*"

Which meant that the human eye certainly could not keep track of the blurring hunk of rubber. And if the human eye couldn't see it, what was the point of going to watch a hockey game? None, unless some very specific changes were made to make hockey a better game.

I have a grand plan for doing just that, and it goes like this:

1. Reduce the number of players from six to five—a goaltender, one defenseman, two forwards, and a rover.
2. Eliminate the center red line; move the blue lines ten feet closer together. The puck must be stickhandled over the enemy blue line.
3. Tie games will be settled by "designated shooters" taking two penalty shots each against the enemy goalie at the end of the game. If the tie persists, two more penalty shots will be taken, and that failing, a tie will be awarded.
4. Slap shots and curved sticks will be outlawed.
5. Helmets and face masks will be eliminated, with certain exceptions.
6. Any player who chooses to wear a helmet will not be paid more than $25,000 per season. Any goaltender who chooses to wear a face mask will not be paid more than $27,000 per season.
7. Two referees—each responsible for half the ice—will officiate. Linesmen will be placed in raised seats off the ice at each line. In case of a disputed call, the referee will decide on the basis of an instant replay.
8. Two points will be awarded for a goal deemed "cleanly scored" by the referee. One point will be credited for "cheap goals," such as shots that bounce in off another player, etc.
9. Reduce the length of periods from twenty to seventeen minutes.

I believe these changes would restore hockey to its "Golden Age of Artistic Excellence" and make it the most exciting spectacle of all sports. Here's why:

At present the hockey rink is too crowded. Crowds of players inspire disorganized plays. Skaters get in each other's way and ruin what might ordinarily be clever plays. The most sensible way to correct the problem is to eliminate one player. Thus, we would have one defenseman instead of two, a pair of forwards, and a rover who would play both defense and forward the way Bobby Orr and Brad Park do now.

By opening the ice, more stickhandling and pattern play would be possible as well as more skating room for the artists who ordinarily are hampered by crowds.

When the blue lines are moved closer together, it will be possible to retain the long breakaway pass (passes will be permitted to the far blue line) while bringing back first-rate stickhandling. By compelling players to stickhandle over the blue line you return old-time defensive bodychecking to its proper high priority.

Tie games are boring and unfair to the paying customers, especially at today's prices. It makes sense to settle them with the most exciting one-on-one in sports—the penalty shot. Having this showdown at the game's end would create the most exciting possible climax to a match.

The slap shot is the most ridiculous, overused, and relatively valueless weapon in hockey. It *is* a crutch that is used over and over again by players too lazy or incompetent to stickhandle a puck into enemy territory.

The wasteful maneuver damages the player's own team more than the enemy because invariably the slap shot not only rebounds wide of the net but winds up on an opponent's stick. Since puck control is a prime necessity in scoring a goal, and since the long slap shot almost automatically results in loss of the puck, it is more an asset to the defending team than to the attackers.

Apart from being a crutch for lazy, inept shooters, the slap shot disrupts the continuity and logic of a game. This happens when the puck ricochets off the boards and players from both teams madly pursue it like football players scrambling for a fumble. The result is instant chaos.

In football the chaos ends when the fumble is recovered and the referee's whistle blows, halting play. But in hockey the chaos is perpetuated indefinitely because the battle for the elusive puck continues as forechecking forwards madly pursue cornered defensemen for possession. These constant collisions make it virtually impossible for logical plays to develop.

One of the worst results of the slap shot is the fact that it has forced goaltenders to wear the grotesque face mask that makes goalies look more like Martians than Canadians. Fear of the crazy, uncontrollable slap shot is what has made almost every goaltender wear one. "If it weren't for the mask," said Cleveland goalie Gerry Cheevers, "I'd be a coward!"

Because of the mask it's no longer fun to watch goalies. I do not want to see Tony Esposito's mask, I want to see his expression-filled face as the enemy threatens; the convolutions of the cheeks, brow, and nose as he fidgets in his goal crease. These expressions are as important to the spectator's enjoyment as any emotions betrayed by forwards or defensemen. But if the slapshot were banned, along with curved sticks, masks would be unnecessary and it would be fun to look at goaltenders again.

The depersonalization of hockey players by use of masks and helmets could lead to the death of what should be a very personal game. Like the mask, the helmet would be unnecessary under my revised system.

I realize that some critics believe this to be a bloodthirsty approach to the game, but that is far from the truth. The revised system would put an accent on logical play, would create a fluidity of action that, in effect, would be a throwback to the thirties when hardly any players wore helmets.

There were few serious head injuries—at least very few that would have been prevented by a helmet—and never a clamor for protective headgear.

Why, then, if players choose to wear helmets, do I propose that they be abolished—bearing in mind, of course, that helmets would be worn if players accepted the special salary limitations?

While this may seem like a rather primitive position, it is predicated on the notion that hockey is a specialized brand of entertainment, selling *machismo* as one of its three prime products along with skill and speed. Those who promote the NHL in the big money markets of television, radio, and publishing stress the violent nature of the sport more than any other aspect of hockey. Its color and sense of adventure are all portrayed by these very same players.

"If I had my way," says one NHL owner, "I'd toss every helmet in the trash can. I want my fans to see each of my players as a different personality. Violence is one of our assets, but you can't promote it as well when too many guys are wearing headgear."

The big rush for helmets began when Minnesota North Stars rookie Bill Masterton was killed following a fall during a game against the Oakland Seals in 1968. While much was made of the fact that Masterton *might* have survived the fall had he been wearing a protective helmet, the fact remains that his death was the only one that came as a result of an accident during a big-league hockey game in the modern era. To this day there remains a question as to whether a helmet would have made a difference in Masterton's case.

Masterton's death was tragic, but no more tragic than the thousands of deaths that occur on highways, in automobiles, airplanes, trains, and in homes every year. The ratio of hockey accidents in the major leagues— among players without helmets—is almost nil compared with accidents in other aspects of our lives.

The point is simple—if big-league hockey players are so adventuresome, as they claim to be, and as tough as advertised, then a certain element of chance must be taken by them as part of their jobs. They must justify the image they portray and the image they allow portrayed of them in magazines, on television, and in the advertising media.

If a Stan Mikita is worth a million-dollar contract and supposedly is so brave, the least he could do for the fans is take off his helmet.

This is not to suggest that I'm against safety in its proper place. I believe in auto seat and shoulder belts for motorists and hard hats for construction workers and miners. Why not for hockey players? Because hard hats are not selling their brands of hazard for public consumption the way hockey players are.

The abolition of helmets and face masks would be a big step toward humanizing hockey. Elimination of slap shots would sensibly slow down a sport that has become too fast for its own good. What is needed is the reintroduction of the skillful aspects of the game, especially stickhandling.

Compelling players to *carry* the puck over the enemy blue line would automatically force them to revert to the lost art of stickhandling. It would slow down attackers enough for defensemen once again to employ the appealing and often devastating hip check, which now is virtually extinct.

Under the grand plan, the art of passing would remain a part of the game. Elimination of the center red line would mean that teams could pass the puck all the way from their own defensive zone to the enemy blue line, thereby creating new worlds of playmaking potential.

Ironically, one of the biggest hindrances to pure playmaking is provided by the NHL refereeing corps—the men who are supposed to enforce the rules. Referees operate on the theory that only a small fraction of the rules should be enforced, no doubt in an effort to retain a high degree of violence. The thinking among owners and their employees, the referees, is that blood is a wonderful thing for hockey because the spectator can glory in the violence without undergoing any of the discomforts of the wounds.

Unfortunately, the better players generally suffer because of such laxity in officiating. "There should be stricter adherence to the rules," said superstar Bobby Hull. "Individuals who have more talent and skating ability shouldn't have guys hooking and holding and interfering with them—and not be penalized."

The difficulty is that hockey, in its present form, is virtually impossible for one man to referee correctly. Too much goes on—especially behind a referee's back—for him to call a fair game. This accounts for the high degree of vindictiveness in a game. "What happens," said Aldo Guidolin, "is that a foul is committed, the referee misses it, and then the player who is offended takes the law into his own hands and retaliates. Soon, all hell breaks loose."

The remedy is a more comprehensive officiating system. Linesmen should be removed from the ice because they are an encumbrance and can do their jobs just as well from upraised seats on the sidelines. Their practice of negotiating fights can be handled by the two referees.

Each of the referees would be responsible for half the ice. This would enable them to remain on top of the play, would permit closer scrutiny, and therefore omit much of the unnecessary and cheap fouling that currently takes place. When play was in the "other" referee's zone, the second referee would station himself just outside that zone and back up the action in case any advice was needed from his partner.

Finally, there is the matter of quality goals as opposed to cheap goals. I believe that hockey would be improved if it rewarded quality. To me a shot that bounces accidentally off an opponent's leg and into the net should count for a goal but only be awarded one point as opposed to a cleanly executed shot that beats the goaltender, which would be worth two points.

And finally there is the matter of time. Hockey games take too long. The three twenty-minute periods should be shortened to three seventeen-minute periods, and of course in case of a tie, it would be settled with the showdown penalty shots.

The point of my grand plan is rather simple. The game, if it is to appeal to the American masses, must be streamlined and cleaned up. Otherwise, as Jimmy Cannon once said, "It would be a better game if it were played in mud."

14

The Fall and Rise of American Hockey

By SHEER WEIGHT of numbers Americans should obliterate Canadians in hockey warfare. There are more than 200 million people in the United States and less than 30 million in Canada. Americans have excelled at every sport in which they have participated and have enjoyed special success in contact games.

Yet up until recently the United States has lagged far behind Canada as an international hockey power. How come?

Adverse (for hockey) weather conditions has been the prime factor. Except for a handful of northerly states such as Minnesota and Massachusetts, natural ice on which youngsters can learn to skate, stickhandle, and shoot has been a rare commodity in the United States. Until the recent proliferation of artificial ice rinks American youngsters had few opportunities to learn to play a grade A brand of hockey. Those who did, however, became very good at it; a few such as Princeton University ace Hobey Baker, a World War I casualty, were inducted into the Hockey Hall of Fame.

The first United States hockey emperor to display complete faith in the American-born player was Major Frederic McLaughlin, the original president of the Chicago Black Hawks. While his Canadian colleagues mocked him McLaughlin insisted that it was possible to ice an NHL club composed of American-born skaters.

McLaughlin's noble experiment was launched in the 1931–32 season when he hired Emile Iverson to run his team. Being an American, Iverson qualified for the job, although he had never coached a day in his life. With Iverson at the helm, the Black Hawks headed for Toronto to open the brand-new Maple Leaf Gardens and test McLaughlin's theory. If they weren't the worst-prepared team ever to open an NHL season, they were very close. Their foes, finely honed to lift the curtain on their handsome new arena, were eagerly awaiting the arrival of the Chicago sextet. The date was November 12, 1931.

The largest crowd to witness an indoor event of any kind in Toronto turned out to see the Chicago massacre. All the trimmings were there, right down to the bands of the Forty-eighth Highlanders and the Royal Grenadiers playing "Happy Days Are Here Again." The opening ceremonies included the presentation of two floral horseshoes to the Maple Leafs. Eventually, the game started.

When it was over, Iverson's ill-trained, perplexed men were the most surprised people in the building. They had beaten the Maple Leafs, 2–1.

However, nothing the Black Hawks could do after that was right. They finished seven points behind the American Division leaders, the Rangers, and were rapidly eliminated by the New Yorkers in the opening play-off round.

Part One of the Major's all-American plan was a flop. But McLaughlin was patient and persistent, if nothing else.

In the 1935–36 season he began to plant the seeds for his all-American NHL team. He traded goalie Lorne Chabot to the Maroons and decided to go with Mike Karakas, a ruddy-faced goaltender from Eveleth, Minnesota. The Hawks finished third, six points out of first place. Then they lost to the New York Americans in the semifinal round.

Instead of improving, the Hawks deteriorated as the 1936–37 season progressed. As his team plumbed new depths of ineptness, the Major became more and more determined to fill his lineup with Americans. One of his leading forwards, Johnny Gottselig, expressed the sentiment of the team when he observed, "We thought it [the all-American plan] was pretty ridiculous."

McLaughlin's scouts eventually extracted Albert Suomi, Curly Brink, Bun LaPrairie, Butch Schaefer, and Ernest "Ike" Klingbeil from the Minnesota–Michigan hockey belt and imported them to Chicago undercover. The Major wasn't quite ready to spring the surprise on the unwitting public, nor did he want to risk a flop. His first project was to condition the athletes, so he sent them to none other than former coach Emil Iverson, who now bore the title of physical director of the Black Hawks.

When the Americans finally faced their Canadian teammates the more experienced veterans treated the newcomers with utter contempt. They refused to sit next to the Americans and ignored them as if they weren't there. When the two teams scrimmaged, the Canadians really laid on the lumber.

"It was awfully rough," said Klingbeil in an interview. "They came at us with the works—high sticks and everything."

To prevent a bloodbath, the Major agreed to sprinkle the Canadian lineup with Americans and vice versa. In this way Klingbeil and Schaefer played defense with a Canadian forward line. The integration proved a tonic all around. Suddenly the team's spirits were buoyed, and they began climbing in the standings.

Somehow this integrated lineup didn't appeal to the spectators, though. Despite the Americans, they weren't flocking to Chicago Stadium. The reason, the Major believed, was that all five Americans weren't on the ice at the same time. Yet he was stymied. The Black Hawks were right in the midst of a play-off race, and to put the Americans out all at once would bring almost certain defeat. His only hope, strangely enough, was for the team to be eliminated from contention. Then he could safely experiment with the American line.

It wasn't until the last weekend of the season that the Black Hawks cooperated and finally bowed out of the race. McLaughlin announced that the Yanks would be present in force for the last home game, against the Boston Bruins. As luck would have it the publicity did a boomerang turn on the Major. Hockey's most beloved star, Howie Morenz of the Montreal Canadiens, was dying in a hospital at the time, and the Black Hawks, though wrongfully, had been blamed because Morenz had been hurt tripping over a Chicago player.

When McLaughlin's scheme was made public the Canadian managers and coaches throughout the league were infuriated. They denounced the Major and demanded his expulsion from the NHL. Nevertheless, McLaughlin persisted with his plan, and when the Black Hawks met the Bruins they faced a Boston team determined to bludgeon them into the ice. Fortunately, Klingbeil and friends retaliated, but even though they held the Bruins to a draw in the department of fisticuffs, they lost the game, 6–2.

After a 3–2 loss in Toronto, Klingbeil's pals finally came out on top by edging Lester Patrick's New York Rangers, 4–3. It was a stirring triumph, because earlier Patrick had derided the Americans as "amateurs."

Although the Hawks were eventually whipped by both the New York Americans and the Bruins the idea of American-born skaters seemed good enough to be continued as far as the Major was concerned. When the following season began, more than half of his lineup consisted of United

States–born skaters. In addition he hired an American coach, baseball umpire Bill Stewart. McLaughlin knew Stewart not only for his superb baseball work but also for his hockey refereeing, which had elevated him to the job of chief arbiter in the NHL.

"This was the happiest club I ever saw in professional sport," Stewart has said. "And we had some pretty good talent, too. Players like Gottselig, 'Mush' March, Paul Thompson, Art Wiebe, and Doc Romnes. Lionel Conacher once told me he regarded Romnes as one of the finest centers he ever played with. The biggest reason we won, though, was that we had Earl Seibert on our defense. The big guy played about fifty-five minutes of every game."

The Americanized Black Hawks managed to plod along through the schedule at a slightly quicker pace than the Red Wings. The result was that Chicago finished third in the American Division, just two points ahead of its Detroit pursuers but a good thirty points behind division-leading Boston. Their chances for winning the Stanley Cup were considered no better than 100 to 1.

To begin with, the Hawks were the only one of the six qualifying teams to have less than a .500 record (14–25–9), and their first-round opponents were the Montreal Canadiens, who had a considerably more respectable 18–17–13 mark. Further complicating matters for Chicago was the fact that two of the three games would be played in the Montreal Forum.

The Black Hawks surprised everyone by winning in three. The final game, an overtime victory, was decided in Chicago's favor when Lou Trudel's long shot bounced off Paul Thompson and into the Montreal cage, although some observers insist that the puck was shot home by "Mush" March.

Now the Black Hawks were to face an equally aroused New York American sextet that had just routed its archrivals in Manhattan, the Rangers, in three games. Once again the Hawks would have the benefit of only one home game in the best-of-three series. The Americans opened with a 3–1 victory at Madison Square Garden. But when the series shifted to Chicago Karakas took over again and the teams battled to the end of regulation time without a score.

The game was settled in sudden-death overtime by none other than Cully Dahlstrom, the man McLaughlin had once lobbied against so vigorously. McLaughlin and Stewart had clashed over the merits of two young players, Cully Dahlstrom and Oscar Hanson. McLaughlin was more impressed by Hanson's minor league record, but coach Stewart "unequivo-cally" selected Dahlstrom.

Chicago clinched the series with a third-period goal by Doc Romnes in the third game. The final score was 3–2, and the Black Hawks advanced into the Stanley Cup finals against the Toronto Maple Leafs.

By now the betting odds had dropped considerably in Chicago's favor. But they soared again when it was learned that Karakas had suffered a broken big toe in the final game with the Americans. Karakas didn't realize the extent of the damage until he attempted to lace on his skates for the game with Toronto. He just couldn't make it, and the Hawks suddenly became desperate for a goaltender.

The Leafs were not in the least sympathetic to the Black Hawks' problem and summarily rejected requests for goaltending assistance. So the Chicago brass finally unearthed Alfie Moore, a minor league, free-agent goalie, who purportedly was quaffing liquid refreshment in a Toronto pub when he was drafted to play goal for the Chicagoans. Moore answered the call and went into the Chicago nets on April 5, 1938, defeating Toronto, 3–1, in the opening game of the series at Maple Leaf Gardens.

For the second game the Hawks tried their luck with Paul Goodman, another minor league goaltender. But this time Toronto rebounded, 5–1. It was obvious that if the Hawks were to win they urgently required Karakas; and they got him by constructing a special shoe to protect his broken toe. Chicago won the game before a record crowd of 18,496 at the stadium on goals by Romnes and Carl Voss, whom McLaughlin had wanted to discard. The score was 2–1.

By now the Leafs were reeling, and Chicago applied the *coup de grâce* with relative ease in the fourth game, routing Toronto, 4–1, on goals by Dahlstrom, Voss, Jack Shill, and March. After the game, when the ecstatic Chicago players sought out the Stanley Cup, they finally realized what an upset they had engineered.

"NHL president Calder had earlier caused the trophy to be shipped to Toronto," wrote Edward Burns in the *Chicago Tribune*, "reportedly on the assurance that a hockey team which harbored eight American-born players as did the Hawks couldn't possibly win the Stanley Cup."

The Black Hawks' triumph indicated that there *were*, in fact, American skaters capable of winning professional hockey's most coveted prize, and there were more aces pouring out of such hockey centers as Eveleth, St. Paul, Aurora, and Duluth, Minnesota. Frankie Brimsek, a goaltender from Eveleth, stunned the hockey world in 1939 by scoring ten shutouts in forty-four NHL games for the Boston Bruins. Another gifted American in the NHL was burly Johnny Mariucci, who joined the Chicago Black Hawks in 1941 and immediately became a favorite in Chicago Stadium.

These were not journeymen hockey players but the cream of the crop. "There are many," says hockey historian Kip Farrington, Jr., "who believe that Brimsek was the best who ever played goal. There is no doubt in my mind, he had the finest, quickest hands of any goaltender I ever saw."

Likewise, Massachusetts also was funneling players to the professional ranks. Bill Moe of Danvers, Massachusetts, eventually graduated to the New York Rangers defense, where he popularized the "submarine" body check.

What appeared to be an American hockey boom went bust with the first explosion at Pearl Harbor on December 7, 1941. When the United States entered World War II the advancement of hockey not only was braked, it eventually was set in reverse. The very best American skaters were drafted or enlisted in the armed forces, and all rink construction was abruptly halted, thereby eliminating the necessary training ice for most young skaters.

By 1946 the amateur ice hockey program—from which players graduated to the pros—was a shambles throughout the United States. Even the climate was against hockey. A generally warmer climate meant that natural ice was available only in the most northerly states, and even in these cases it was a chancy situation.

Artificial ice rinks were at a premium, and even when they were available, hockey players had to compete for playing time with figure skaters and racers. Clearly, it would take at least a decade to reconstruct the American hockey machine.

In 1947 the first concrete results began taking shape. The Minnesota Amateur Hockey Association was formed under the auspices of the Amateur Hockey Association of the United States, becoming one of the first state associations in the nation to become a member of the powerful AHA. The new group embraced seven leagues, and participation was statewide.

The most relevant aspect of these events was the fact that they signaled a rejuvenation of hockey interest on the playing level. "You could tell," said Gerry Cosby, who played on the 1933 U.S. world title–winning team, "that kids in the States wanted to play hockey. All they needed was the ice and the encouragement. The seeds had been planted for another hockey boom that would be bigger and better than any before."

Minnesota's new activity provided the impetus for an astonishing growth of hockey, and a flow of superior players gushed from those new leagues. Soon, such outstanding skaters as John Mayasich of Eveleth, Ken Yackel of St. Paul, Tom Williams of Duluth, Bill Christian of Warroad, and Jack McCartan of St. Paul burst on the international hockey scene. However, nobody took them especially seriously until February, 1960, when Uncle Sam dispatched a determined group of stickhandlers to Squaw Valley, California, for the Winter Olympic Games.

(Above) *One of the Greatest Games.* The Rangers halt a Red Wings drive in the first period of their final playoff game in Detroit on April 23, 1950. Battling for control of the puck are: Red Wing forward Jerry Couture (18); Ranger goalie Chuck Rayner; Ranger defenseman Gus Kyle; and Red Wing George Gee.

(Below) *Team Canada vs. U.S.S.R.* Here Paul Henderson is hugged by Yvan Cournoyer for his game-winning goal against the Russians in Moscow on September 28, 1972, during the Team Canada series.

(Opposite page, top) Ten months before his infamous, near-fatal fight with St. Louis' Wayne Maki on September 21, 1969, Ted Green (6) of the Bruins roughhouses with another Blues player, Bob Plager (5).

(Opposite page, bottom) Dave Schultz (8) of the Philadelphia Flyers doing what he does best—taking an opponent into the boards and out of play, allowing his teammates full possession of the puck.

(Top) The promise of a good fight often draws a larger crowd than any display of hockey skill. Here the Rangers and the Bruins indulge in a center ice free-for-all while the fans eagerly await the outcome.

(Top left) Gary Davidson, a California lawyer and cofounder, with Dennis Murphy, of the World Hockey Association. Davidson has also figured prominently in the establishment of the ABA and the WFL.

(Bottom left) Alan Eagleson (right) and Phil Esposito hoist Paul Henderson aloft at Team Canada's triumphant homecoming in October 1972. Eagleson, organizer of the NHL Players' Association, is also personal attorney for hundreds of hockey players, including Bobby Orr.

(Top) *One of the All-Time Worst Teams.* Chicago
Black Hawks' goalie Frank Brimsek manages to
deflect a Ranger shot in the third period of their game
on December 28, 1949. The Black Hawks just
couldn't seem to get it all together that season. The
Rangers, however, came from behind with a four-goal
rally in the last five minutes of play to defeat Chicago,
5–2.

(Left) Captain Bobby Clarke of the Flyers and New
York's Walt Tkaczuk have a slight collision. Tkaczuk,
one of the best all-round players in hockey, is often
overlooked in favor of the flashier players like Clarke
and Bobby Orr.

(Top) *Two Coaching Greats.* On February 21, 1946, Lester Patrick (center), the "Silver Fox" who built the New York Rangers' dynasty, passed the managerial reins to his successor, coach Frank Boucher (right), "one of the most innovative coaches in hockey." Joining in the three-way handshake in this photo is Tom Lockhart, who was named as the club's business manager.

(Left) Two charter members of the All-Nasty Team, Derek Sanderson, late of the Boston Bruins and now with the New York Rangers, and ex-Ranger captain Vic Hadfield (now with the Pittsburgh Penguins), are separated while it's still mostly words, not fists, that are flying.

(Opposite page) *The Most Perfect Team Possible.* Phil Myre, goaltender (top left); Bobby Orr, defenseman (middle left); Ed Van Impe, defenseman (bottom left); Walt Tkaczuk, center (top right), Bill Fairbairn, forward (middle right); Steve Vickers, forward (bottom right).

(Top) *A Couple of the All-Time Greatest Players*. Gordie Howe (left), who holds most of the important NHL scoring records, and Bobby Hull, the "Golden Jet" of hockey, here take time out for a somewhat less dangerous form of entertainment.

(Left) Maurice "The Rocket" Richard, with Boom Boom Geoffrion (right), exhibits the Montreal Canadiens' fourth consecutive Stanley Cup in April 1959. The only modern player to score 50 goals in 50 games, Richard led the Canadiens to eight Stanley Cup victories during his career.

(Top) The Flyers' Dave Schultz (8) lands a punch on the jaw of another well-known rowdy, Terry O'Reilly of the Bruins. Boston's André Savard looks on, while keeping a tight grip on Philadelphia's Terry Crisp.

(Left) Philadelphia's Bob Kelly aims a looping right to the head of former Penguin Shel Kannegiesser as Pittsburgh teammate Bob Blackburn (4) goes to the rescue.

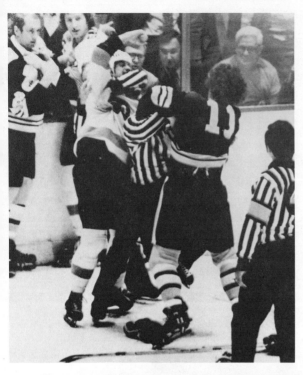

(Left) This time around, it's Orest Kindrachuck for the Flyers and André Savard (11) for the Bruins, while the official seems to be getting the worst of the battle, as the two most violent teams in hockey go at it again.

(Below) Violence is nothing new to hockey fans. This 1964 wrestling match started between Detroit Red Wing Ted Lindsay and Dickie Moore of the Toronto Maple Leafs—then everyone decided to get into the act.

(Opposite page) *A Sampling of the Unofficial NHL All-Nasty Team.* Jim Pappin (top left), Rick Foley (middle left), Vic Hadfield (bottom left), Marcel Dionne (top right), Paul Henderson (middle right), Peter Mahovlich (bottom right), Derek Sanderson (bottom center).

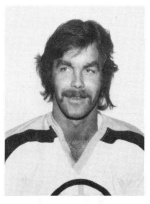

(Top) While hockey fights are nothing out of the ordinary, Bobby Orr (4) is seldom found in the center of them. Here the Golden Boy of the Boston Bruins struggles with Ranger Brad Park, a more seasoned combatant.

(Left) As the gloves fly and the bodies roll in this dispute between the St. Louis Blues and the California Golden Seals, violence-oriented fans gleefully cheer the players on.

"We were underdogs," said coach Jack Riley, who had been selected to head the U.S. club after guiding the U.S. Military Academy sextet at West Point. "We couldn't possibly win a gold medal. At least that's what they all said before we hit the ice."

Riley's 1960 Olympians were to do more to bolster the prestige of American hockey than any team since the 1938 Chicago Black Hawks.

Their most formidable opponents would be the Russians and the Canadians. It was not believed to be even remotely possible for the Americans to topple either of these power teams.

Riley's first challenge was against the Swedish National Team, traditionally a strong-skating, hard-shooting club. The favored Swedes were routed, 6–3. Murmurs about the American squad began filtering around Olympic Village. The murmuring got louder after the U.S. skaters demolished Germany, 9–1. Now the Americans were scheduled to meet Canada's National Team for the first time.

Almost incredibly, the Americans defeated the Canadians, 2–1, and then knocked off the Russians, 3–2, then Czechoslovakia, Sweden again, and West Germany. Suddenly, the Americans found themselves in the unlikely position of being in sight of a gold medal. They had three games—three obstacles—ahead of them: Canada, Russia, and Czechoslovakia.

The Canadians looked like the better team as they poured volley after volley at goalie McCartan. "All I could see," said McCartan, "were streaks of green Canadian jerseys."

McCartan made thirty-nine saves, most of them difficult, and allowed only one goal. "He made one incredible save after another," said Riley. The Americans scored twice and won the match, 2–1. On Saturday, February 27, the Americans faced-off against the Soviet team. More than ten thousand spectators jammed into Blyth Arena for the contest while millions watched the test on television.

After two periods the clubs had battled to a 2–2 draw, but more important, the Americans had proved that they could skate with the fleet Russians. For nearly fifteen minutes of the final period the rivals tested goalies McCartan and Nikolai Puchkov, and neither gave an inch—until 14:59 of the period.

Roger Christian and Tom Williams teamed up to feed Billy Christian who found himself one-on-one with goalie Puchkov. "When the goalie came out of his net to cut down the angle," recalled coach Riley, "Billy outsmarted him and slid it in. That was it because McCartan wasn't going to let the Russians score again."

The final score was United States 3, Soviet Union 2. Only one more opponent blocked America's bid for a gold medal, Czechoslovakia. And for a time it appeared that Riley's stickhandlers would blow it all on the final day of the championships. They tied the Czechs, 3–3, after the first period, but fell behind, 4–3, after the second. At that point a strange twist of luck helped the Americans. Nikolai Sologubov, a crack defenseman for the Russian National Team, visited the Americans' dressing room and offered Riley some advice. "He suggested that our players take some oxygen to restore their pep," Riley recalled. "As it turned out, some of our guys took his advice."

Whether the oxygen did the trick or not will remain a point of debate for hockey historians as long as the 1960 Olympics are discussed. Whatever it was, the Americans stormed out onto the ice and nearly knocked the Czechs off their skates.

Roger Christian, alone, accounted for three goals in the last period. He tied the score, 4–4, at 5:50 of the period. Then Bill Cleary put the Americans ahead, 5–4, and followed that with a power-play goal. Within a thirty-eight-second span Roger Christian and Billy Cleary scored, and then Roger closed the scoring at 17:56 for the sixth and final goal of the period for Uncle Sam's skaters. The final score was 9–4 for the United States. America had won its first Olympic gold medal in hockey.

"We had become a team of destiny," said Riley. "We won because of conditioning, spirit, and a real desire to bring home the gold medal. The players had a deep belief in the old adage: 'There's no substitute for victory'!"

America's Olympic victory shook the hockey world with the impact of a thunderclap. Overnight, Uncle Sam's native-born skaters were once again taken seriously. Murray Patrick, general manager of the National Hockey League's New York Rangers, immediately signed goalie Jack McCartan and brought him to Broadway.

In his first NHL game against the Detroit Red Wings the Olympic ace stopped superstar Gordie Howe cold, and overnight McCartan became a sensation. His play was so spectacular, in fact, that he bumped regular goalie Al Rollins—a former winner of the Hart Trophy as the NHL's most valuable player—off the regular roster. McCartan played four games, allowed only seven goals, and completed the season with a remarkable 1.75 goals-against average.

Not to be outdone, the Boston Bruins signed Tommy Williams off the U.S. Olympic squad. The tall blond right wing was shipped to Kingston of the old Eastern Professional League for grooming. After two seasons in the minors Williams graduated to the NHL and to this day has remained a major leaguer, most recently with the Washington Capitals.

The 1960 triumph at Squaw Valley marked the renaissance of hockey in America, although, in a way, it was deceptive. By any standard the victory was an upset and hardly reflected the growth of hockey at the grass-roots level. There still were not enough rinks to go around to meet the demand in universities, in high schools, and in the neighborhoods of Boston, Chicago, New York, and other potential hotbeds of hockey. But indications were clear that help was on the way.

"The Squaw Valley win in 1960 turned everything around for American hockey players," said Gerry Cosby. "From that point on, the U.S. hockey boom was under way. It would only be a matter of time before our kids caught up to the Canadians."

By 1967 America had caught Canada in one aspect of the hockey revolution. NHL expansion from six to twelve teams had switched the balance of power. With only two Canadian franchises against ten in the United States, Canada no longer was a factor in determining professional hockey policy.

NHL expansion caused repercussions on other levels, especially on the pipeline funneling talent from the minors to the major league. It was obvious that Canada, with its limited population, could not handle the demand for first-rate players. And that meant that the most obvious vein to be tapped was the rich American lode in Minnesota, northern Michigan, and New England.

Even that wasn't going to be enough, so NHL scouts began training their periscopes on American college hockey, hoping to pluck the cream of the crop for the NHL. When the NHL expanded from twelve to fourteen teams and again to sixteen clubs, the quality of major-league hockey was so thoroughly diluted that collegians, even with modest training, could make the leap to the majors. Then, the World Hockey Association arrived, and it became easier still for the Americans.

Major McLaughlin is long gone from hockey now, and in a way it's a shame he couldn't have stuck it out for another thirty-five years, for future hockey historians may someday look back on the 1972–73 season as the time the Major's dream began to be realized, the time these greedy Americans started to steal the Canadian national game right from under Canadian noses.

Item: The New England Whalers won the championship of the World Hockey Association in 1973 with no less than six native Americans on their roster, more than any other championship team of a major hockey league—and if the New York Islanders and the California Golden Seals can call themselves major league, why not the whole WHA?

The Whalers Americans were Larry Pleau of Lynn, Massachusetts; Tim Sheehy of International Falls, Minnesota; Kevin Ahearn of Milton, Massachusetts; Tommy Williams of Duluth, Minnesota; Paul Hurley of Melrose, Massachusetts; and John Cunniff of South Boston, Massachusetts.

"It was no promotional stunt, we wouldn't have put them on the ice if we didn't feel they were capable of playing up to the competition," says Jack Kelley, the Whalers' general manager, an American himself (Belmont, Massachusetts) whose NCAA championship teams at Boston University had a strong Canadian flavor.

Item: Tim Sheehy, whose birthplace is listed in the record books as Fort Frances, Ontario, simply because the hospital on the Canadian side of the border is shared with International Falls, was second to his teammate Terry Caffery for WHA rookie-of-the-year honors in 1973.

Sheehy was one of four Americans who scored more than thirty goals in the WHA's first season. He had thirty-three. Teammate Pleau had thirty-nine. Bobby Sheehan of the New York Raiders, who hails from Weymouth, Massachusetts, had thirty-five after scoring twenty in the NHL the year before. Billy Klatt of the Minnesota Fighting Saints had thirty-six.

Item: One of the most exciting rookies of the 1972–73 NHL season was Henry Boucha, the twenty-one-year-old Chippewa Indian from Warroad, Minnesota, whose bright red headband attracted more attention than the fourteen goals he scored for the Detroit Red Wings. Boucha came to the Wings right off the U.S. Olympic team.

Item: One of the best players in the WHA during 1973–74 was a nineteen-year-old American named Mark Howe, who originally came from Detroit with his brother Marty to help the Toronto Marlboros to the Memorial Cup. That their father was Canadian-born Hall of Famer Gordie Howe does not alter the fact that they began in a Michigan youth hockey program and graduated to the Detroit Junior Red Wings of the Southern Ontario Hockey Association. Both young Howes became instant stars in Houston.

Item: The two finalists in the 1973 NCAA hockey tournament, Denver and Wisconsin, were about equally divided between Americans and Canadians, but the only all-Canadian team in the tournament, Cornell, lost in the consolation final to Boston College, the only all-American team. And the tourney's MVP was Dean Talafous of Wisconsin, out of Hastings, Minnesota.

Final Item: The Boston Junior Braves, a group of eleven- and twelve-year-olds from suburban Middlesex County, was not only the first American team to win Quebec City's International Peewee Tournament in its fourteen-year history, but did so with ease, outscoring the all-Canadian opposition thirty-two goals to nine in six games.

"The future is there for the American kids," says John "Bucky" Kane, a scout on the American beat for the Buffalo Sabres. "And don't think they don't know it. I'll bet Minnesota kids alone outnumber Canadians in college hockey now."

(They don't, but it's closer than you might think.)

For another thing, there is what may be called the rink-building explosion. There are now more than six hundred skating rinks in all but one of the fifty United States (the exception is Arkansas). And there is the distinct feeling that if the enumerator had really been trying he might have found a rink tucked away deep in the Ozarks, complete with a passel of small boys in official Bobby Orr sweatshirts.

"Not only are there more arenas now, but the kids are getting top coaching in the youth hockey programs and in high schools right up through college," says the Whalers' Kelley. "That's what it boils down to—ice time and coaching."

"The average American player is much better than he was eight or ten years ago," says Don McKenney, the twelve-year NHL veteran who has run a summer hockey school in the Boston area since 1961.

"There are always good players and there are always great players, but the true measure of the caliber of hockey is the average player. And the average American player is much better. I could take a team of juniors from around here and be competitive in the OHA [Ontario Hockey Association]."

It is precisely at that point, the junior age group, where American hockey has traditionally come apart at the seams.

In the past ten or fifteen years, the three most intense hockey-playing areas of the United States—Minnesota, Michigan, and Massachusetts—have developed youth hockey programs that equal their Canadian counterparts at the age levels of mites (seven and eight), squirts (nine and ten), peewees (eleven and twelve), and bantams (thirteen and fourteen). The Boston peewee victory in the Quebec City tournament was not really as big an event as it would appear.

"Progress is good right up to bantam," says Don McKenney, "and then it's watered down so much that it's almost worthless. The good players are spread out so much that it lowers the competitive level."

The culprit, in Massachusetts at least, is high-school hockey, which snatches the best players out of the youth hockey programs at the midget (fifteen and sixteen) age level and then severely restricts their participation in the game.

"There's no way a boy can keep up with the Canadians abiding by the rules set up by the Massachusetts Headmasters Association," says Whalers manager Jack Kelley. "They limit the high-school player to twenty games, plus play-offs, and only allow twelve-minute periods, and they keep the boys from practicing until the Monday after Thanksgiving.

"As the boys become more pro-conscious, you're going to see more and more kids bypassing high-school hockey to compete in junior hockey programs where they can develop by skating twenty-minute periods for forty games a season."

In the spring of 1973 at least three Americans were drafted from OHA junior teams by the NHL—Walt Johnson of Omaha, Nebraska, by the Boston Bruins, and Max Hansen and Chris Ahrens, both of New York City and both by the Minnesota North Stars.

The Whalers' Paul Hurley had a chance to play junior hockey in Canada but he turned it down.

"When I was a junior at Melrose High the Bruins sent me to Niagara Falls to try out for their junior team," he says. "I was picked to stay, but my parents thought I should get an education first. So I decided to come back to the States. This was unheard of in Canada in those days [1962–63], passing up a chance to play junior hockey.

"The trouble is you have to forgo an education if you go to Canada. If you're lucky it works out well. If you're a first- or second-round draft choice you have good bargaining power. But the ones who don't make it wind up with nothing, not even an education. If you're a college boy, you can do something besides play hockey."

For a number of years now, a few top Canadian prospects like Ken Dryden and Keith Magnuson have been passing up Tier I junior hockey to go to American colleges on hockey scholarships. You can't do both. Tier I juniors in Canada are paid $60 a week, and the NCAA logically feels that that makes them professionals.

"The more intelligent boys are leaving junior hockey to play college hockey when they're seventeen or eighteen," says Jack Kelley, who lured a lot of them off the Canadian assembly line to play for his BU teams. "In fact since the NCAA banned players from the Tier I leagues from competing in NCAA schools, many Canadian boys are refusing to move up to the Tier I leagues."

Furthermore, young Canadians who don't go on to college are showing an interest in sports other than hockey now.

Twenty years ago, when Don McKenney was playing junior hockey, he used to pass the summer agreeably, playing shortstop for the Smith Falls, Ontario, senior baseball team. He was good enough to get contract offers from the Boston Red Sox and the New York Yankees, offers that included the promise to start him high in their farm chains. He turned them down without a second thought.

"If you were a Canadian kid and you had a chance to play NHL hockey, there was just nothing else," he says.

But now there is the example for Canadian boys set by pitcher Ferguson Jenkins of Chatham, Ontario, the Cy Young winner who is now with the

Texas Rangers, and the opportunities opened for Canadian boys by the Montreal Expos, the first major-league baseball team outside the borders of the United States. Two members of the Montreal team in the Quebec Junior League, goalie Michael Dion and defenseman Blair Mackasey, have already signed with the Expos and may pass up hockey altogether for baseball.

"Canadian baseball and football are becoming more popular," says the Sabres' Bucky Kane. "More and more Canadian kids are trying to make it in those sports. I don't think Canadians are working as hard at hockey as they used to. They seem to feel that the game is coming to them. But it is a challenge to an American boy to make it in a Canadian sport."

"Eight or ten years ago," says Jack Kelley, "a Canadian boy had only hockey on his mind, and he'd give up everything else for a career in hockey. Now he is more sophisticated. He's also interested in a career in football or baseball and he's more aware of what a college education can do for him."

Junior hockey is rising in the Northeast to challenge the high-school hold on hockey. One new league, the American Junior Hockey League, has seven teams in such widely scattered places as New York; Philadelphia; South Jersey; Baltimore; Marlboro, Massachusetts; Portland, Maine; and Nashua, New Hampshire.

Another league, the Major Junior A League of New England, features eight teams in Portland, Maine; Berlin, Manchester, and Nashua, New Hampshire; and Marlboro, Burlington, Beverly, and Worcester, all in Massachusetts.

Still a third league, a less ambitious venture called the New England Junior Hockey League, opened in October, 1973, with teams in North Smithfield, Rhode Island, and West Springfield, Fitchburg, Tyngsboro, Pembroke, Weymouth, Concord, Newton, and Millis, Massachusetts.

The New England Junior Hockey League plays under pro rules, a minimum of sixty games, including play-offs and exhibitions, and its president, Ed Dalton, owner of the Weymouth Arena and franchise, figures it will start out comparable to a Junior B league in Canada. At least he's inviting Junior B teams down for exhibition games.

"The most important thing," says Dalton, "is to develop junior hockey in a professional way. We are concerned with educational development, too. We'd like to develop players so that they can compete for the scholarships the colleges are giving to Canadians now."

There's little doubt that within the decade there will be as many Americans playing major-league hockey as there are Canadians. It's too bad, in a way, that Major McLaughlin couldn't be around to enjoy the last laugh.

15

International Pro Play

No SINGLE EVENT did more to damage the prestige of North American–style professional hockey than the notorious series between Team Canada (a collection of NHL stars and pseudostars) and the Russian National Team, held in September, 1972.

And no hockey tournament did more to revolutionize the sport. Overnight, hockey ceased being Canada's game. In the future it would be shared by the Russians, Czechs, and Swedes.

No longer would the NHL scoff at a genuine world series of hockey between the European champions and the Stanley Cup winners.

Within days after the Team Canada–Russia series had ended, NHL scouts were swarming over Europe like a plague of locusts, searching out the wonderful continental stylists who suddenly emerged after the Canadians were taught their bittersweet lesson in how to play the game.

Until the Team Canada series, NHL hockey was regarded as the definitive style of play. NHL players supposedly were the best in the world, and anyone who claimed otherwise was either a subversive or an impostor, or both.

From time to time, the Russians would challenge this theory. After all, the Soviet Union had developed a spate of good hockey teams. What's more, Russia had all the natural resources to produce champion hockey players—the climate was good and cold, the population was enormous, and interest was keen.

"After all," warned Dennis Braithwaite, highbrow page columnist for the *Toronto Star*, "the Russian population is 250,000,000 and Canada's 20,000,000-plus. Their climate is even better for ice-making than ours. Their young men are vigorous and rough, physical fitness being close to a religion in the Soviet Union.

"Most of all, the Soviet players and the country that backs them have the will to win. What our players and team managers have, primarily, is a yen to make money."

The NHL did *not* want to play the Russians for several reasons, most of all the fear of losing to the Soviet skaters. "We've got everything to lose," NHL president Clarence Campbell once said, "and nothing to gain. If we win, we'd just be reinforcing the claims we've made right along. But if we lose, it would be quite a blow to our prestige."

In a sense, the NHL was lucky because there were several superficially valid reasons to avoid a confrontation between the supreme hockey powers. Theoretically, the Russians were amateurs, according to the Olympic definition—athletes who had never received any material gain from sport and played only for pleasure.

But by 1970 the Russians had enough Olympic and amateur world championships to satisfy the collective Soviet ego. What they did not have was the satisfaction of playing against the best professional hockey players and beating them.

Soviet hockey leaders were prepared to do anything—even if it meant jeopardizing their amateur and Olympic standards—to arrange a series with the North American professionals. But the NHL wanted no part of it. Prestige was a factor, but there also was the matter of scheduling, since the regular NHL schedule runs from October through May, including the play-offs; and there also was the matter of rule differences between the North Americans and the Europeans. How could these be resolved?

Comfortable in this cocoon of alibis, the NHL was able to resist demands by the impatient and improving Russians to "put up or shut up!" Then, in the autumn of 1971, a surprise element emerged to alter completely NHL thinking.

On a November afternoon in 1971 the World Hockey Association was formally organized in New York City. It was designed to compete for the free-flowing American sports dollar with the NHL. But more than that, the WHA said it would be ready, willing, and able to play the Russians sometime in 1972.

That's all the NHL had to hear. The NHL governors realized that the WHA could mine a fortune by competing against the Russians; could gain instant credibility and perhaps permanently damage the prestige of the established pro league.

Almost overnight, all of the NHL's objections to a Russian series were forgotten, and the machinery was put in motion to activate the tournament. The professionals received a big boost from a group called Hockey Canada, created and financed by the Canadian government to promote and improve hockey by and for Canadians.

Cooperating with the NHL, Hockey Canada eventually created Team Canada in cooperation with the Canadian Amateur Hockey Association (CAHA), the official national governing body of amateur hockey in Canada. The CAHA played a vital role in overcoming the amateurism obstacle that had prevented the pros from legally playing the Russian "amateurs" in the past. In this case the CAHA obtained an agreement from the amateur hockey governing body in Russia and the International Ice Hockey Federation, the world amateur hockey organization, to stage the series. Thus, in a matter of a few months, the NHL in cooperation with key hockey organizations regained ground temporarily lost to the WHA, and a September series was scheduled.

But by August, 1972, several important NHL stars had "jumped" to the WHA, including Bobby Hull, Gerry Cheevers, and Derek Sanderson, each of whom would have been selected to play for Team Canada against the Russians. However, NHL officials and Alan Eagleson, executive director of the NHL Players' Association, vigorously opposed inclusion of the WHA aces in the Team Canada lineup.

The NHL stand was denounced from one end of Canada to another, but Eagleson and Team Canada officials stood by the decision on the grounds that a clause in the contract between Hockey Canada and the NHL stipulated that only players with NHL club contracts could be members of Team Canada.

Eagleson and the NHL prevailed against the storm of public opinion that raged throughout August, 1972. "To the NHL," said an editorial in the *Toronto Star*, "the series is obviously just a pawn to be used in its contest with the upstart World Hockey Association. It's an outrageous way to treat the home of the game."

But Eagleson and his pals in the NHL pulled off their coup. Eventually, the storm abated as the opening face-off of the series approached. Indignant as they may have been, both fans and writers were more interested in the tournament itself than the political sideshow.

The groundswell of enthusiasm over the eight-game series—of which the first four matches would be played in Canada and the next four in Russia—revolved around Canadians' conviction that, once and for all, they would prove their supremacy. "Hockey," wrote columnist Jim Kearney in the *Vancouver Sun*, "was the one form of human endeavor in which we prided ourselves as being the very best in the world."

Of course nobody expected shame to come to the NHL stars who comprised Team Canada. True, Bobby Hull, Gerry Cheevers, J. C. Tremblay, and Derek Sanderson were absent because of their leap to the WHA, but a glance at Team Canada's roster hardly could give comfort to the enemy:

Goaltenders—Ken Dryden and Tony Esposito; defensemen—Brad Park, Gary Bergman, Guy Lapointe, Pat Stapleton, Bill White, Serge Savard, and Rod Seiling; forwards—Frank and Peter Mahovlich, Phil Esposito, Yvan Cournoyer, Bobby Clarke, Ron Ellis, Paul Henderson, Mickey Redmond, Red Berenson, Rod Gilbert, Jean Ratelle, Stan Mikita, Gil Perreault, Wayne Cashman, Bill Goldsworthy, and Dennis Hull.

There were still others, but these were considered the cream of Canada's professionals available for the series, and they surely would give the Russians a few hockey lessons that the Soviets never thought possible. The question was not *whether* Team Canada would *win* the tournament but would it be an *eight-game sweep?*

Team Canada officials selected Harry Sinden and John Ferguson to be coach and associate coach, respectively, for the NHL squad. Sinden had led the Boston Bruins to a Stanley Cup in 1970 before abruptly retiring to become a business executive. Ferguson had long experience playing for Montreal Canadiens Stanley Cup winners until he eventually quit for private business.

Throughout August members of Team Canada took their own good time getting themselves ready for the tournament in Toronto. At first they seemed to be taking the series too frivolously. Many skaters were overweight and appeared unable to reach top form by the start of the series. If physical conditioning was one problem, mental conditioning would prove to be an even bigger dilemma for the Canadians. To a man, they took for granted the fact that they were superior to the Russians. This feeling was cultivated by most sportswriters, who freely predicted an eight-game sweep of the Soviet sextet.

"Canada to romp in eight," wrote Dick Beddoes, echoing the prevailing opinion. "It's a Russian team in decay."

American writers were no different: "8–0 Canada," wrote Fran Rosa in the *Boston Globe*. "And that's also the score of the first game." Only three journalists, John Robertson of the *Montreal Star*, Pierre Gobeil of *Montreal Matin*, and yours truly, thought the Russians would win more than two games.

As the teams prepared for the opening game on September 2, 1972, at the Forum in Montreal, there was considerable speculation about the strategic approach to be taken by the rival coaches. The Russians had extensively scouted NHL teams and Team Canada down to the minutest detail. Casual to a fault, the Canadian strategists had sent a two-man delegation to Russia for a look at the Soviet sextet. They stayed only briefly and filed a terribly cursory report that concluded with one major point—goaltending on the Russian team was weak, so weak as to be easily exploited. It was only one of many intelligence errors committed by the egomaniacal Canadians.

Sinden, who was notorious for developing a bashing style of hockey in Boston, was believed to be working on an aggressive campaign that would intimidate the Russians. Many of the NHL skaters favored this strategy, but some of them—especially those such as Red Berenson of the Red Wings who had played amateur hockey against the Russians—objected to this blueprint for victory.

"The European hockey teams have a different attitude toward sportsmanship," Berenson explained. "They're just as competitive as North Americans but more complete athletes. They take a hard-nosed approach to the game and play to win. But they never seem to lose sight of the fact that they're playing a game."

The atmosphere at Montreal's Forum was one of total tension as the teams lined up for the opening draw, later described as the "Face-off of the Century" or the "Death of a Legend." The legend, of course, was that Canadians were the best hockey players in the world.

After falling behind, 2–0, in the opening period, the Russians systematically destroyed the Canadian defenses and emerged 7–3 victors before a thoroughly stunned crowd of 18,818. "Explanations, excuses, apologies," said French-Canadian writer Gilles Terroux, "nothing will do."

Alibis gushed like water tumbling over Niagara Falls. Canadians were humiliated as never before. To them the defeat was taken as a national castration, "as if the male population of this land suddenly had been sterilized by some diabolical secret plan," as one observer put it.

It wasn't simply a matter of the Canadians losing by four goals. As Berenson had feared, Team Canada reacted bitterly as the score mounted. NHL players became annoyed with the more skilled Russians and began a series of illegal attacks against individual Soviet skaters that infuriated fair-minded Canadians.

"The thing that shamed me, and I guess many of us," said columnist Scott Young of the *Toronto Globe and Mail*, "was not the loss. That was nothing—one team playing hockey at its best and deserving to win. But when grown Canadians wearing their nation's name on their backs get chippy, cheaply chippy, I feel badly for us. The night when we show that we can't dish it out, we show that we can't take it either."

To the average Canadian and American viewer the chippiness of Team

Canada was less relevant than its impotence. For no matter what happened for the remainder of the series, the crunching damage had been done on September 2, 1972. "Our invincible image," said Ted Blackman, "now lies bare, a myth."

The image hardly improved in days to come, although Team Canada did manage to win one game—the second, 4–1, at Maple Leaf Gardens in Toronto—out of the four on its home turf.

But the Russians rallied to tie the third game, 4–4, at Winnipeg and sent Team Canada off the ice with a chorus of boos on September 8, 1972, at Vancouver after whipping the NHL stickhandlers, 5–3. By now Harry Sinden's skaters were executing a disorderly retreat to Moscow. They were disgraced not only on the ice but off the ice as well.

Ever since the third game, reports had circulated that several NHL skaters were prepared to mutiny against Sinden. A few even threatened to walk right out on the team and not make the trip to Russia. Denials issued by Sinden and his band of lackeys sounded hollow to those privy to the facts, and the facts were that players such as Vic Hadfield (Rangers), Rick Martin (Buffalo), Gil Perreault (Buffalo), and Josh Guevremont (Vancouver), among other dissidents, were prepared to jump ship.

Another fact was that the Soviets had devised a brilliant game plan for each match while the Canadians were illogically bouncing around the ice like pinballs on a crazed amusement-park machine. The Russians deliberately ignored the cheap-shot artists on Team Canada and methodically went about their business of scoring and defending. The Soviet approach reminded one observer of psychologist Dr. Kurt Adler's analysis of the Russian style: "In collective societies such as Russia, the player plays the board rather than his opponent."

The Soviets dazzled Team Canada with chessboard passing, accurate wrist-shooting—as opposed to the idiotic slap shot employed almost exclusively by Team Canada—and a cool that enabled them to brush off body checks as one would sweep a piece of dust off a sleeve.

When Vancouver fans hooted Team Canada off the ice, they were expressing a multifaceted displeasure with their erstwhile heroes. The boos, according to Eric Whitehead of the *Vancouver Province*, were for the "fat-and-happy NHL Establishment that has been content to sit back and just rake in the money while the skills of the game have gone to pot. After this long week of humiliation it is already plain that the upstart Soviets play a sounder, better and more exciting hockey than is seen in the NHL."

Team Canada jetted to Sweden for a week of recuperation and practice, including some games against Swedish teams. Instead of providing the Canadians with a welcome respite, the exhibition games in Sweden further disgraced many of the NHL stars. The games were idiotically bloody, yet those Canadians who lived by the high stick were hurt by the high stick, especially bruising Wayne Cashman.

Cashman collided with a Swedish player and suffered a devastating facial wound that made it impossible for him to take nourishment. He had to be taken to a hospital and fed intravenously, and in less than a week, lost eighteen pounds. The Canadians seemed ill-prepared for the first game of the series in Moscow on September 22, 1972.

Meanwhile, the mutineers who had gone underground temporarily surfaced again, and this time all hell broke loose. Vic Hadfield, Josh Guevremont, and Rick Martin quit Team Canada because coach Sinden was not treating them in the manner that they had hoped he would. Except for Hadfield, there was a tendency to dismiss the departure as the impulsive act of immature young players. But Hadfield was a veteran, captain of the New York Rangers and one player who had his attorney, Robert Woolf of Boston, along with him.

"I decided to leave," Hadfield explained, "because I felt I didn't want to be treated the way Sinden was treating me [he rarely gave Hadfield ice time and often ignored him at practice]. I didn't deserve that treatment and I wasn't about to take it."

Sinden argued that Hadfield was being rejected because his play had been inferior to that of most other forwards on Team Canada.

"Hadfield," said Sinden, "wasn't playing well enough to make the squad that dressed for the games."

Shock waves reverberated throughout the NHL camp when Hadfield's exit became known. "I was stunned," said attorney Woolf. "As soon as I heard about Vic's decision I tried to locate him and calm the guy. But I couldn't find him and when I finally did learn where he had been, he was on the plane home. If I could have reached him in time, I never would have let him go back to Canada. I knew what kind of damage it was going to bring on him."

Hadfield's rationales for walking out on his mates were dismissed by respected critics, including Jim Proudfoot, sports editor of the *Toronto Star*, who was in Moscow at the time. "The suggestion that Hadfield was unjustly dropped from the starting lineup was simply ridiculous," said Proudfoot. "He played miserably in Stockholm, at a time when the team was supposed to be getting ready for its final four matches against the Soviets. And, in any event, reserve strength was a continuing necessity."

Some members of Team Canada regarded Hadfield's departure as a good omen, as if the club had been purged of its loser. Sinden was understandably bitter, especially with Hadfield but with Martin and Guevremont as well. "I'd like to make them walk back to Canada myself,"

Sinden snapped after the players took a flight home from Moscow. "They aren't man enough to stand up and say they wanted out on the moral commitment they made to Team Canada because things looked gloomy."

Without Hadfield, Team Canada lost the opener in Moscow, 5–4, but the NHL skaters had not quit. They rallied to win the sixth, seventh, and eighth games of the series. Mathematically, Team Canada had "won" the tournament four games to three with one tie. But the so-called victory was only by the margin of a single goal in the 480th minute of play. Serious observers scoffed at Canadian chauvinists such as Alan Eagleson who continued to proclaim, "We're Number One!" Actually, the Russians had taught Team Canada several lessons, but apparently many of them never sank in.

"Our capability for self-delusion," wrote Jim Kearney in the *Vancouver Sun*, "seems limitless."

While the cretins rejoiced over what appeared to be a noble victory—the expression "great victory" was sounded every minute on the minute—more rational reporters X-rayed Team Canada's performance for what it was, an artistic and cultural fiasco in terms of what had been promised. The boorishness of the players was one matter that could not be overlooked.

Soviet critics had a word for Team Canada and Eagleson—*nekulturny*. Liberally defined, it means "yahoo," "boor," or "pain in the ass." Canadian columnists used different words to say the same thing but none said it more emphatically than the *Montreal Star*'s John Robertson:

"We didn't really win anything! We merely salvaged something from the wreckage—something to cling to; so we can say to the world: Well, we may be obnoxious barbarians; we may have come across as the most grotesque, uncouth people ever turned loose in an international athletic forum; we may have undone just about everything our diplomats abroad have been able to do for Canada's image; we may have shown the world we have absolutely no respect for game officials, opposing coaches, or the laws and customs in countries in which we are guests; we may lead the league in both menacing and obscene gestures; but at least we won the damned hockey game."

The Russians had actually outscored Team Canada, 32–31, and in the hearts of hockey fans around the world—if not throughout Canada—had won the series. The NHL, its system, and its player leader, Eagleson, had lost. In sober moments many Canadians regarding the episode equated the event with the loss of their national manhood. After hockey, was there *anything* at which Canadians could be best in the world?

"Sweet are the uses of adversity." So wrote William Shakespeare, and so hoped many sincere admirers of the Canadian (NHL) hockey system.

Perhaps, they thought, the adversity of Team Canada's experience would produce some sweet changes. After all, the Russians didn't invent hockey, Canadians did. All the Soviet skaters did was mimic the best of the old NHL style when passing, wrist-shooting, and intelligent play was supreme.

"The way the Russians played," said Foster Hewitt, the voice of Canadian hockey, "reminded me of the old New York Rangers, especially the line of Frank Boucher and Bill and Bun Cook. If anything, the Rangers were a little better. It always seemed to me they had the puck on a string."

Just the idea that so respected an authority as Foster Hewitt would compare the Russians with the best the NHL has ever produced was staggering. As a result it was believed that *some* efforts would be made to retool the Canadian (NHL) style along Russian hockey lines. Experts such as Howie Meeker, a former Toronto Maple Leafs star in the forties and more recently a commentator and instructor, pleaded with the NHL teams to study the Russian system. Which was another way of saying: Study the old NHL system of the Cooks and Boucher.

A few token gestures were made. The Buffalo Sabres hired a special physical-fitness instructor to exercise the team. In Philadelphia, the Flyers hired Mike Nykoluk, a former minor leaguer, to act as assistant coach, as if this were the height of all insight. But for the most part, the NHL reacted as if the Team Canada debacle hadn't happened at all.

"Nothing changed," said Jim Kearney of the *Vancouver Sun.* "The basic fire-and-fall-back, show-biz NHL style remained the same. If anything new was learned from the eight-game series with the Russians it was never made evident by the NHL."

But it *was* made evident by NHL fans. They were impressed by the Russians and depressed by the so-called big-league product. "Hockey Night in Canada," the network telecast of NHL games, suffered a serious drop in its ratings following the Russian series. Attendance began to slip in NHL arenas where packed houses had been traditional. The awful aftertaste of the series didn't disappear as many thought it would. In October, 1973, for the first time in 192 consecutive home games, Boston Garden was not filled to capacity for a Bruins game. As avid a fan as Canadian Senator Keith Davey, who conceded that "I always organize my life around hockey," admitted that he went to "a lot fewer games last year."

Nobody summed up the results of September, 1972, Canadian hockey's month of infamy, better than authors John MacFarlane and Bruce Kidd. Shortly after the Team Canada–Russia tournament they produced a book about their favorite sport.

It was called *The Death of Hockey.*

Canadian poet Irving Layton said he was happy, for the sake of the nation's hospitals, that Team Canada had won the final game of the series even if it was only by a single goal. "I refrain from asking what would have happened had Team Canada lost," said Layton. "Mass suicides across the country . . ."

Time magazine (Canadian edition) underlined its literary blast at Team Canada with the headline: ADOLESCENTS ON THE LAST FRONTIER.

Apart from shaking up the foundations of North American pro hockey the Team Canada series demonstrated that the NHL no longer could, nor would, ignore the Russians. "We're interested in eventually playing a world championship series with them," said NHL president Clarence Campbell. "Let's face it, the Russians are here, and we're going to have to live with them. To rest on your laurels is to sit on your ass! There's no way you can live unto yourself. No, the NHL can't be an island."

The essential question is: How and when will the North American pros couple their schedule and play-offs with the Europeans to produce intercontinental competition?

An amalgamation of the best European hockey teams and the finest North American professionals is as inevitable as 1984. The National Hockey League leaders are afraid of the Russians—and, to a lesser degree, the Swedes and Czechs—but they also are fascinated by them. They realize that there is money to be made in bringing a superstar from the Soviet Union to North America, provided the timing is right in the eyes of NHL and WHA barons and the American sports public.

An annual transatlantic series cannot be ignored because nobody knows better than members of Team Canada that the Russians have provided a new dimension to contemporary hockey. Eventually the fear of losing to the Soviets and the potential humiliation that would go with it will become dissipated and the games will take place.

Gradually, steps are being taken in preparation for a European-NHL-WHA link. In September 1974 a second Team Canada outfit comprising WHA stars played another series against the Russians. This was believed to be the predecessor to a regular annual series between the best European teams and the best North American sextets.

More likely than not the Russians eventually will play against NHL or WHA clubs along with the Czechs, Swedes, and Finns. Of the European teams the Russians have generally been the best. The question remains—just how good will the Russians become?

"Our plan," said a Russian hockey technician, "will be to make the maximum use of the individual styles of the players."

The Russian who figures to be the star will be the same one who starred in 1972 against Team Canada, twenty-eight-year-old Valery Kharlamov, a brilliant though smallish forward.

In his book *Hockey Showdown*, Team Canada's coach Sinden vividly described one of Kharlamov's goals against Team Canada:

> His first goal was magnificent. He came into our zone alone against Rod Seiling [Rangers] and Don Awrey [Bruins]. As he came across the blue line he dipped his left shoulder like he was going to bust to the inside and between them. When Awrey started to go with the move, Kharlamov just blew by him to the outside, and then swooped back in front of the net, still in complete control. As he swept in front of Dryden, Kharlamov made a move as if he was going to switch the puck to his backhand, but all of a sudden he gave it a quick forehand flip into the far corner of the net. Our players were stunned. I looked down the bench and I caught two of our great offensive players, Phil Esposito [Boston] and Frank Mahovlich [Montreal], looking at each other and just shrugging their shoulders as if to say, "Can you believe that?"

Nor could NHL types believe the superb condition of the Soviet skaters. "We can say," explained Anatoli Tarasov, the former Russian coach, "that the players in a single hockey match skate around four miles. So, we must then skate eight miles. Our players have to work twice as hard with the result that, after four miles, the NHL players will be tired and we will still be skating."

Tarasov conceded that goaltending will also be a problem for the Russians. "We must assist our goalies," he asserted. "The Canadians shoot fast. Their shots have to be blocked by defenders as often as possible."

Then, a pause and a summary of what the Soviets must do in their inevitable clashes with the NHL. "Instead of the wild, we must become the hunters. We have to skate three or four times more than the NHL players. We have to hunt in groups—one bodychecks, the other takes the puck."

Unfortunately for the North American teams, more and more neutral observers are beginning to believe that sooner or later the Russians are going to surpass completely the best hockey playing to be produced in Canada and the United States. And they offer very good reasons for this turnabout that received its first bit of international exposure when the Russian National Team won three games in September, 1972.

One such esteemed critic is Toronto Toros coach Billy Harris, the former NHLer (Toronto Maple Leafs) who played against the Russians, who coached the Swedish National Team in 1971–72, who is a student of Russian hockey styles, and who directed Team Canada 1974 (the WHA All-Stars) against the Russian team.

Harris sees the decline and fall of the Canadian style as rooted in modern hockey history. "We learned to play hockey by accident," said

Harris. "It evolved on lakes and rivers. The Russians learned scientifically, by studying every available piece of material. The whole European approach is that way."

Himself a center during his major-league days, Harris has been impressed with several Russian forwards who bear watching when the Soviets play the North American clubs.

"Aleksandr Yakushev, for one, will take the puck behind his net," said Harris, "and make his own play, through an opening. The centers, mainly Vladimir Vikulov, Valery Kharlamov, and Aleksandr Maltsev, forecheck strongly, and Maltsev particularly will swing over behind the defense when it moves up, to cut off passouts along the boards."

A segment of NHL-WHA–watchers believe that the Russians may be intimidated by the bloodthirsty American crowds and a few headhunters on each big-league club. Harris disagrees.

"That's nonsense," he said. "The Russians don't fight because the penalties are so severe, but don't think they can't. It will be interesting to see what would happen if a North American decided to get into a one-on-one fight and the Russians decided to fight back."

No matter what transpires, the inevitable North America–Russia series is nothing but good news for North American hockey fans because they will see a brilliant, although different, brand of major-league hockey.

The Canadians believe they will win because they are convinced—prop-aganda is very effective in a democracy—they are the biggest and the best.

The Russians believe they will win because they have analyzed the game more intensively than the Canadians and they are more flexible in their approach to it than the North American pros, who too often accent beef over brains.

"Size," said Soviet ace Aleksandr Yakushev, "does not make the Canadians strong or give them ability. I think it's better to have players of all sizes because then you have players who can do many things well.

"If you have too many big players then your team is too slow. You need variety. I think there is a place for a Phil Esposito and a Valery Kharlamov on any team. No, I'm wrong, there's not a *place*, there is a *need* for both."

There is also a *need* for resumption of the North American–European major-league hockey rivalry, not on a one-shot basis as it was in 1972 or 1974, but as a permanent tournament. When that happens, hockey will replace soccer as the foremost international professional sport.

16

What a Hockey Player Should Really Get Paid

SOMETIMES I GET THE FEELING that hockey players, in all their infinite greed, do not want the sport to continue and flourish in what should be the ice boom of the Seventies.

Their insatiable thirst for the dollar got out of hand when the National Hockey League expanded from six to twelve, then to fourteen and sixteen teams. But the monetary mania reached the realm of complete madness when the World Hockey Association came along and skating clowns began demanding what heretofore had been superstar salaries.

Granted that expansion has converted big-league hockey from an owners' to a players' market, the problem is that avaricious stickhandlers have lost all sense of propriety. They seem not to care a damn about the fan who has to ante up the dough to pay the inflated ticket prices; nor do they seem to have concern about club owners, who, after all, can make or break the game.

I normally take the side of the players against management almost by reflex action, but the money-mad behavior of players in the past few years has teed me off no end.

One example involves the late New York Raiders, a team that finished out of the play-offs during the WHA's first season.

An especially terrible Raider happened to be a defenseman who had never played big-league hockey until the WHA came along. Because of his pseudointense appearance and his burly physique, he suggested the role of a "policeman" and had the overt trappings of a charismatic skater. But in reality, he wasn't.

In fact he was a bum. Plain and simple. He may have been skating in a major league but he was not, in any sense, a major leaguer, and everybody, from fans to his coach, knew it.

Do you know what this joker did at the end of the 1972–73 season? He audaciously went to the front office and warned management that he wouldn't be back for 1973–74 *unless he received a healthy raise.*

That would be a funny story if it were an isolated case, but unfortunately it is more the rule than the exception. I'll give you another for instance:

The Winnipeg Jets had a forward named Norm Beaudin. Beaudin had been a journeyman American Leaguer in pre–WHA days. But in 1972–73 he had the good fortune to be available when the new league was forming, and the even greater good fortune to be placed on a line with Bobby Hull.

As a result, Beaudin scored 103 points—which may or may not be impressive, depending on your perspective. When columnist Jim Taylor of the *Vancouver Sun* was appraised of Beaudin's accomplishment he remarked that on the Hull line *his mother could get fifty points!*

What made *L'affaire* Beaudin so absurd was the fact that this hitherto unknown skater was being paid $38,000 by Winnipeg owner Ben Hatskin for the regular season and the play-offs. That's a lot of money for a nobody.

Beaudin decided he wanted to renegotiate his contract. (You never hear of a player who had a lousy season come to the boss and say he wants to renegotiate his contract downward.) Hatskin told Beaudin he could go jump in Lake Winnipegosis, or if he didn't like *that* one, he could try Lake of the Woods.

Then Hatskin turned soft. He decided to reward Beaudin with a $5,000 bonus, but no new contract. Beaudin said nix.

Taylor is right. Hatskin is right. The players are crazy.

Crazy mad with power and crazy mad for money.

Would you believe that Bobby Orr, who never finished high school and whose articulation can best be described as postgraduate Mortimer Snerd, commands $2,500 *for a single speaking engagement?* And that, apparently, isn't enough.

The absurdity of all this money mania in hockey will not end until there is a merger or some sort of unspoken agreement between the NHL and WHA to put a freeze on salaries before everybody is priced out of business by the likes of the Orrs and Beaudins.

What makes matters even more annoying is the quite obvious fact that these mortals are not worth the immortal salaries they are commanding. The interleague war did it and ruined it for everyone but the greedy skaters.

Let's for a moment consider what it might be like during more sane conditions, the conditions that prevailed before the advent of the WHA, and going a decade further back, before expansion of the NHL. Just for the sake of argument I am going to present six player's names. The names will be followed by their representative, an appraisal of them, and their *estimated salaries* (bearing in mind that these figures almost never are accurate). These will be followed by what I believe they would make if this were a pre–WHA year and a pre–NHL expansion year.

Vic Hadfield, Pittsburgh Penguins (represented by Bob Woolf)

Hadfield is getting old, has a hard shot, is pseudotough, picks his spots with rough stuff, and is less useful without Jean Ratelle and Rod Gilbert. SALARY: Now—$170,000. If this were a PRE–WHA year—$40,000. If this were a PREEXPANSION year—$21,000.

Bobby Hull, Winnipeg Jets (represented by Harvey Wineberg)

Hull is aging but retains the magnetic personality; truly the glamour skater among the veterans and by far the best drawing card of the WHA, as he was in the NHL. SALARY: Now—$200,000-plus. PRE–WHA—$150,000. PREEXPANSION—$75,000.

Gordie Howe, Houston Aeros (represented by Gerry Patterson)

Howe is Mr. Hockey, a living legend, Paul Bunyan on ice skates. SALARY: Now—$200,000. If it were PRE–WHA—He would not be playing. PREEXPANSION—Same.

Mickey Redmond, Detroit Red Wings (represented by Bob Woolf)

Has good legs and a good shot; lacks leadership qualities but gets star treatment because of the sagging nature of the Detroit franchise in recent seasons. SALARY: NOW—$200,000. PRE–WHA—$65,000. PREEXPANSION—$25,000.

Lanny McDonald, Toronto Maple Leafs (represented by Dick Sorkin)

Only two years out of the juniors, fourth draft pick; completely unknown quality as a pro, let alone an NHLer. SALARY: NOW—$150,000. PRE–WHA—$30,000. PREEXPANSION—$8,500.

Red Berenson, Detroit Red Wings (represented by Alan Eagleson)

Good technique, good head; doesn't like to hit or be hit; superb stickhandler and skater; terrific in practices. SALARY: NOW—$90,000. PRE–WHA—$60,000. PREEXPANSION—Wouldn't make the NHL.

Part Four

Fischler's Best

17

Molding the Perfect Hockey Player

It has been said, with some justification, that Bobby Orr comes closest to fitting the mold as the "Perfect Hockey Player." He plays defense well enough to have been awarded the Norris Trophy almost every year since he was signed by the Boston Bruins in 1966. Offensively, Orr was so awesome that he led the NHL in scoring in 1970, winning the Ross Trophy.

"And," says former NHL defenseman and now Atlanta Flames scout Aldo Guidolin, "if Bobby Orr played goal, he'd surely win the Vezina Trophy!"

For all Orr's awards, the Boston superstar has several chinks in his armor. He actually has many defensive weaknesses and rarely throws body checks. Orr wins the Norris Trophy more because of his offensive accomplishments than his defensive play. He is a grand hockey player, to be sure, but perfect? Hardly.

The fact is that the perfect hockey player does not exist. Bobby Hull, for example, owns a mighty shot but always has been weak as a stickhandler. Stan Mikita is a deft stickhandler with an accurate shot, but his light physique has rendered him vulnerable to injury.

Thus if one were to design the perfect hockey player, the architect obviously would have to borrow "parts" from each of several superstars. Harry Sinden, managing director of the Boston Bruins, once tried this and surprised everyone by shying away from several aces.

"Frankly," said Sinden, "I would probably pick only half of the players on any official All-Star team. Why? Because I'd be seeking a *team* rather than a collection of individual stars."

Sinden's ideal hockey player comprised sections of several NHL greats, past and present. It went as follows: the head of Bobby Orr, the torso of Bobby Hull, the right arm of Stan Mikita, the hips of Bob Plager, the legs of Bobby Orr, the elbows of Gordie Howe, the left arm of Red Berenson, and the heart of Jean Beliveau.

"I picked Orr's head," Sinden explained, "because he's in a class by himself when it comes to setting the pace of a game. Hull got the vote on torso because between the shoulders and waist he has the power."

Sinden explained that he chose Beliveau, the retired former captain of the Montreal Canadiens, for the heart because of Beliveau's inspirational qualities. He wanted Berenson's left arm because of the center's excellent backhand shot.

"I wanted Mikita as a right-handed shooter," he went on, "because there are three basics in forehand shooting—accuracy, deceptiveness, and hardness. Mikita gets a slight edge because of his accuracy.

"Plager has been the best hip-checker in the business—you get by him, but his hip knocks you off stride. The legs are Orr's for obvious reasons, and the elbows—at least the left one—belong to Howe."

However, Sinden's choices were hardly unanimous. Almost every NHL manager and coach had different selections, although Orr's name emerged most frequently. For example, Philadelphia Flyers coach Fred Shero preferred Mikita's head over Orr's. "Mikita," said Shero, "can read situations on the ice, and he knows how to react to them."

By contrast, New York Islanders manager Bill Torrey selected Gordie Howe for the head. "Howe," Torrey explained, "simply psychs people out, especially because of his toughness. After he beat up Lou Fontinato of the Rangers [1958–59]—and Fontinato was supposed to be the NHL tough guy—word got around to give Gordie plenty of room."

Instead of picking Orr's legs, Sid Abel, general manager of the NHL's new Kansas City team, preferred the legs of Yvan Cournoyer, the Montreal Canadiens' blurry right wing. Abel selected Orr's head, the arms of Phil Esposito of Boston, and the heart of Bobby Clarke, captain of the Philadelphia Flyers and a diabetic.

There are experts who believe that dealing with a composite superstar is absurdly unrealistic. In fact many reputable observers believe that All-Star teams selected by newspapermen are grossly inaccurate in terms of the true on-ice value of players. Only coaches, managers, and players themselves are able to perceive the nuances so necessary for an accurate All-Star selection.

Sinden once dramatized these differences a few years ago by taking the hockey writers' official All-Star picks and contrasting them with his own personal selections. The differences were extremely interesting to hockey students.

The official NHL All-Stars that year were as follows: goal, Tony Esposito; defense, Bobby Orr and Brad Park; center, Phil Esposito; right wing, Gordie Howe; left wing, Bobby Hull.

Sinden's All-Stars included: goal, Jacques Plante; defense, Bobby Orr and Jacques Laperrière; center, Phil Esposito; right wing, Ron Ellis; left wing, Bobby Hull.

"For raw goaltending ability," said Sinden, "I haven't seen anybody to equal Plante. Ellis was my right-wing selection because he is awfully hard to check and he hurts with his own checking. Ask the left wings who oppose him. I went with Laperrière because I considered him the matchless defensive defenseman—just by watching him on two-on-one and even three-on-one situations."

Still others intimately involved with the game believe that a player's "clutch-ability" is more often the key criterion for greatness. It's not how many goals a man scores, they say, as much as it is his ability to come through when it counts most. "A clutch player," explained Brad Park, the Rangers defenseman, "is a guy who's doing his job whenever the chips are down. He comes through in the tight spots all the time."

And whom do the experts rate as the better clutch players?

"Bobby Orr and Phil Esposito," said Park. "You can always count on them to come through in difficult situations. Henri Richard, captain of the Montreal Canadiens, was another. He didn't score as much as Esposito, but his club always seemed to get into the play-offs and won a lot of Stanley Cups."

Bill Chadwick, a member of Hockey's Hall of Fame and an NHL referee for sixteen years, offered another perspective on clutch-ability. "The clutch player does not have to have all the tools and ability of the so-called star, but he must have the *desire* and *pride*. Some examples of these players are Steve Vickers and Walt Tkaczuk of the Rangers; Guy Lapointe of Montreal; Stan Mikita, Pit Martin, and Tony Esposito of Chicago; and Dallas Smith and Bobby Orr of the Bruins."

Inevitably, a discussion of clutch playing results in play-off accomplishments. Hall of Famer Dickie Moore, who starred on several Canadiens Cup-winners, explained that clutch-ability had a special meaning to him. "When I talk about clutch hockey-playing," said Moore, "I usually think about what a man did in the Stanley Cup finals. This is where the clutch player is most often sighted.

"When the score is 2–2, or 2–1, and you're looking for that very special fellow from the bench who'll turn the game around, you're looking for the clutch player. When I played for the Canadiens that guy was Maurice 'Rocket' Richard. He was an exceptional clutch player and he had one attribute that other clutch scorers have—quickness around the net. He'd get rid of the puck without hesitating. Nowadays, Rick Martin of Buffalo is that way. He's always in position and will come through for you."

Camille Henry, an NHL star with the Rangers and more recently a coach and assistant general manager in the World Hockey Association, played against Richard and Gordie Howe. "Howe wasn't in Richard's class as a clutch player," said Henry. "The Rocket always was the one who lifted the Canadiens when they weren't doing too well. He'd go out and fire the team up by scoring, often while carrying two men on his back. Richard's counterpart today is Yvan Cournoyer of the Canadiens. He's in the right place at the right time. That's the most important factor in scoring clutch goals."

Clutch players are often skaters who play the game with little fuss and fanfare until their moment arrives. In 1967 Jim Pappin, who had had a hard time cracking the Toronto Maple Leafs' lineup, found himself the star of Toronto's upset Stanley Cup victory over the Montreal Canadiens. More recently, Pappin has played his best hockey for the Chicago Black Hawks in play-off games.

"Pappin," said John Ferguson, a former Canadiens ace and assistant coach of Team Canada, "is not a very fast skater or the best checker, but he can score goals at the right time. Speed is irrelevant as long as the man comes through. Which Pappin usually does. In the play-offs he just seems to give you a little bit more.

"Most clutch players have their own style and ways of treating a game. I attribute it all to the fact that if a player hates to lose he has to be a good clutch player. It's as simple as that."

The so-called official NHL All-Star selections are meaningless when it comes to a true evaluation of the aces because a majority of writers who pick the stars are ignorant of the game and see too few games to make a truly intelligent judgment.

The men most qualified to judge are the coaches who regularly see the skaters in person and constantly study their styles on film and video replay. In 1974, *Toronto Star* writer Frank Orr polled NHL coaches for an evaluation of special player skills.

Several runners-up are included in many of the categories, because only five selections received decisive support, and two were unanimous. There were also five ties.

Interestingly, the 1972–73 Most Valuable Player, Bobby Clarke, was the only player upon whose skills the coaches could agree. The Philadelphia

Flyers center was chosen "best checker" and "hardest worker" in the NHL by wide margins. He was also second to Chicago's Stan Mikita for "skill in face-offs" and tied with three players as "best penalty-killer."

Clarke also received votes as the "smartest player," the "best play-maker," and the "most dangerous near the goal."

These are the NHL coaches' choices:

1. *Most underrated player:* Walt Tkaczuk, New York Rangers. Chicago's Pit Martin was close behind.

2. *Best shot:* Boston's Phil Esposito and Buffalo's Rick Martin, tie. Boston's Bobby Orr and Detroit's Mickey Redmond followed.

3. *Hardest shot:* Chicago's Dennis Hull by a wide margin over Redmond, Orr, and Martin.

4. *Best penalty-killer:* Tie among Tkaczuk, Clarke, Buffalo's Craig Ramsay, and Montreal's Peter Mahovlich.

5. *Best skater:* Orr by a slim margin over Montreal's Yvan Cournoyer.

6. *Best checker:* Clarke, nearly unanimous. Also mentioned were Montreal's Jim Roberts and Ed Westfall of the New York Islanders.

7. *Best referee:* Art Skov, with Lloyd Gilmour right behind, and Andy van Hellemond getting a few votes.

8. *Best on face-offs:* Mikita. Clarke and Esposito tied for second.

9. *Best fighter:* Dan Maloney of Los Angeles over J. Bob Kelly of Pittsburgh and the Islanders' Garry Howatt.

10. *Most dangerous in goal area:* Phil Esposito, followed by Rick Martin. Highly rated were Boston's John Bucyk and Bob Schmautz; also, Jim Pappin of Chicago.

11. *Best coach:* A tie between Chicago's Billy Reay and Philadelphia's Fred Shero.

12. *Smartest player:* Mikita, with Orr a close second. Clarke and Esposito were also recognized.

13. *Best bodychecker:* Barclay Plager of St. Louis, followed by brother Bob, the Leafs' Brian Glennie, and Chicago's Doug Jarrett.

14. *Hardest worker:* Clarke was the top hustler, with Tkaczuk and Chicago's Chico Maki collecting a few votes.

15. *Best defensive defenseman:* Chicago's Bill White far ahead of the Leafs' Borje Salming and Montreal's Jacques Laperrière.

16. *Best goalie:* A tie between Philadelphia's Bernie Parent and Chicago's Tony Esposito. The only others mentioned were Atlanta's Dan Bouchard and Rogatien Vachon of Los Angeles.

17. *Best young player:* Gil Perreault, Buffalo Sabres, squeezed this out over gifted Tom Lysiak of Atlanta and Denis Potvin of the Islanders.

18. *Best playmaker:* Mikita was far ahead of Pittsburgh's Syl Apps, Clarke, and Orr.

19. *Most improved player:* Pittsburgh's Dave Burrows and Dick Redmond of Chicago shared this.

20. *Most colorful player:* The Leafs' Eddie Shack, with Perreault and Cournoyer on his heels.

Considering all the possibilities, the general managers—*not* the coaches—believe that they would narrow their choice of the perfect hockey player down to one—Bobby Orr. He's proved himself superb in the clutch, has played while injured, hates to lose, and appears to do more things better than most of his opponents.

Toronto Maple Leafs manager Jim Gregory crystallized the thinking on the ideal player when he was asked to select a composite player from all the big-leaguers.

"There are a lot of players in hockey to fit each category—head, torso, arms, hips, legs, and heart," said Gregory, "but I pick Orr for all of them. You watch him on the ice and you check his accomplishments in the record books. You talk to those who play against him and with him, and you can't argue with Bobby Orr as the perfect hockey player!"

POSTSCRIPT: A NOTE OF DISSENT
OVER THE "GREATNESS" OF BOBBY ORR:

The case for Bobby Orr as the world's best hockey player has been made so many times it has become as much of a bromide as declaring "Britannia Rules the Waves."

Yes, Britannia once did rule the waves. Great Britain did boast the biggest most powerful navy in the world. But that was once upon a time and long, long ago. Similarly, Bobby Orr once was the best major-league hockey player. His reign hardly was as long as Britannia's rule of the waves. In fact it lasted two seasons—1969–70 and 1971–72—when Orr not only led Boston's Bruins to the Stanley Cup but also led the National Hockey League in scoring (1970) and won the Hart Trophy as the game's most valuable player.

Stop!!

Let's get it straight here and now that I am not—repeat, *Not!*—putting down Orr as a superb hockey player. I admire his skills as much as a classical music lover would worship the fingers of Van Cliburn.

However, it is one thing to be a superb hockey player; it is quite another to be indiscriminately labeled the best in the world.

In 1971, 1973, and 1974 Phil Esposito was a better player than Orr and so was Bobby Clarke of the Philadelphia Flyers. At times it seemed Brad

Park of the New York Rangers was superior to Orr over an entire season.

It has *appeared* that Orr has been *the* greatest because we live in the era of image-building, and Bobby's has been better constructed by the media than most. When he was a mere sixteen-year-old stripling, skating for the Oshawa Generals, the name *Orr* was already a household word in Canada.

"The boy will save the Boston Bruins" was the promise generated by Boston Garden mimeograph machines.

By the time he *did* become a Bruin everybody who knows the difference between a stick and a puck had heard of Bobby Orr. The fact that Boston finished in last place in Bobby's rookie year never blemished his image. Rather it was enhanced as he won the Calder Trophy as rookie of the year and was toasted by hero-hungry NHL promoters preparing the world for expansion.

Obviously Orr was a gifted young man and proved it in the seasons to come. My point is that his image was created and reinforced well in advance of his abilities. It was only in 1969–70 that Orr genuinely fulfilled his notices. He did it again when Boston won the Stanley Cup in 1972, but by that time Phil Esposito had caught and passed Bobby as a truly great hockey player. Esposito proved it with his effort for Team Canada in September, 1972.

After Boston's 1972 Cup win, Orr was never the same, literally, figuratively, and physically. An endless succession of knee injuries was the principal cause of his slip from the pinnacle.

Orr's game is predicated on speed and strength, but mostly on speed. He's not a stickhandler in a class with Park nor is he a defensive defender in a class with Chicago's Bill White. The great Bobby Orr we once knew is the fellow who lugs the puck out of his own end and whirls his way past the enemy like a thunderbolt with what one observer described as "sixteen variations of fast."

That aspect of Orr's superiority ended during the 1972–73 campaign, when Boston tumbled in the opening play-off round to New York. Esposito was hurt, and Orr couldn't do it alone. It became quite clear that the "sixteen variations of fast" were no longer there, and Bobby could be stopped.

Greatness, as I define it, requires more than a barrelful of press clippings and a well-built image. It takes more than trophies won in seasons past and a legion of jock-sniffing hockey writers determined to perpetuate the idea of Superman Orr.

Greatness is what happens on the ice that is both seen by the average fan and appreciated by every player. This includes the obvious and the subtle, offense and defense, the nitty-gritty and the glorious. To me the Orr of today is basking in past glory. He lacks the total game that less-publicized skaters display, particularly Walter Tkaczuk, the New York Rangers' center.

"I don't think there's a player in the NHL, except maybe Bobby Clarke and Bobby Orr, who does as many things as well as Tkaczuk," commented one NHL coach.

Tkaczuk is more indestructible than Orr. He now is stronger than Orr as a skater and a body- and stickchecker. He is a smarter player than Orr, and he plays offense and defense with equal zeal and with no harm to either aspect of the game.

Don't confuse me with statistics or trophies. I am more than aware that Tkaczuk has won nothing. But that's old business; same as all of Orr's and Esposito's and Bobby Hull's silverware. I'm talking about the now and the future.

It is what you *don't* see Tkaczuk do that makes him a genius. Many of his talents are obvious, but he has more subtle assets than any skater in the game; and if you don't believe me, ask Phil Esposito or some of the other centers who have tried to cope with him.

Tkaczuk's balance is so firm he is able to withstand simultaneous body checks from both left and right without breaking stride. His wrist shot has a crispness and accuracy seen in few attackers, and his ability to contain high-scoring and highly emotional opponents while he himself remains inordinately cool has inspired Montreal's Ken Dryden to single him out as the best defensive forward of his kind in the game.

To me Walter Tkaczuk is the best-balanced player in the game— offensively, defensively, physically, mentally, and any other way you care to mention.

As for Bobby Orr, I'll take him on my team anytime—provided I can have Walt Tkaczuk first!!

18

The Twelve Greatest Players of All Time

DEFINING WHAT MAKES a genuinely great hockey player is as easy as visiting the Hockey Hall of Fame in Toronto. Just study the backgrounds of aces such as Maurice "Rocket" Richard, Howie Morenz, Ted Lindsay, and Gordie Howe, to name a few, and you have all the qualifications.

To the list we would add the names of such contemporary gems as Bobby Hull, Phil Esposito, Bobby Orr, and Bobby Clarke, among others. But then this great list suddenly becomes too long and cumbersome, almost without meaning.

I think it's time we narrowed the ever-widening category of supermen and selected the dandiest dozen—the twelve greatest players of all times, including those still in action. Here's my list, and the reasons behind the picks:

1. *Gordie Howe*

He not only holds all the important National Hockey League scoring records but has been as durable as a heavy tank, as creative as Albert Einstein, and most remarkable, has done what nobody else has—played long enough so that he now actually skates alongside his sons, Mark and Marty, in Houston with the WHA's Aeros. Gordie's the best, hands down.

2. Eddie Shore

Renowned as the "Edmonton Express," Shore literally saved and then made the Boston Bruins franchise in the late twenties and starred until the early forties. He was one of the toughest players who ever lived and could play defense both offensively and defensively equally well, and considerably better than Bobby Orr does today.

3. Red Kelly

He frequently was an All-Star defenseman for the Detroit Red Wings. Then, after more than a decade starring in Detroit, he went to Toronto where he became a crackerjack center and the man who made a star out of moody Frank Mahovlich. Nobody in the game's history has displayed such total brilliance at both positions for so long. In fact Kelly was the pioneer among the modern rushing defensemen.

4. Frank Boucher

The most creative center who ever lived, Boucher won the Lady Byng Trophy so many times (seven) that the NHL finally upped and gave him the darn thing permanently and struck a new trophy. Frank was responsible for three New York Rangers Stanley Cup victories, playing on two teams and coaching the third.

5. Maurice Richard

In Richard's time the Montreal Canadiens won the Stanley Cup eight times, and the Rocket was usually the reason why. He was the only man in modern times to score fifty goals in fifty games and to this day ranks as the most galvanic goal-scorer and singularly exciting player ever to lace on a pair of big-league skates.

6. Bobby Hull

Rocket Richard put the NHL on the international hockey map when it was a six-team league, but nobody glamorized the game and paved the way for today's grand and revolutionary expansion more than the "Golden Jet." The NHL owners should have paid him $1 million just for all the bullion he put into *their* pockets. Now he is the showpiece of the WHA in Winnipeg. Needless to say, he permanently altered the style of hockey by popularizing the slap shot. He also has done quite a bit of scoring and personally put the World Hockey Association on the map. Were he a playmaker and defensive ace, he'd have been atop this list.

7. *Howie Morenz*

The Maurice Richard–Bobby Hull of another era, Morenz of the Canadiens was known as the "Babe Ruth of Hockey," and for good reason. His flashing speed was precisely what enabled owners to sell big-league hockey as the "World's Fastest Sport." He was gifted, gallant, and the early heart of the Canadiens' heritage.

8. *Bobby Orr*

To some, the Boston superman-boy *is* the greatest of all players, but he misses the top on this list for several reasons: (a) He *still* has not fully stood the test of time—another year or two will tell if his damaged legs can last; (b) his achievements have been accomplished during a period of expansion and concomitant dilution of talent; and (c) as a defenseman he is not all that good defensively. However, his achievements speak for themselves, particularly his scoring and ability to sell the game without putting too many phrases back to back.

9. *Doug Harvey*

As defensive defensemen go, he was the best after Eddie Shore and very likely the best modern blueliner of all time. His ten elections as First All-Star confirm that fact. Superb as a playmaker, Harvey made a policy of rarely getting caught in the enemy's end—*à la* Orr—and helped make the Canadiens of the fifties one of the NHL's rare dynasties.

10. *Max Bentley*

Playing for the Chicago Black Hawks and then the Toronto Maple Leafs, Bentley more than anyone combined the gifts of stickhandling, shooting, skating, and playmaking to exquisite perfection. He survived, starred, and played on Stanley Cup winners (in Toronto) despite a frail physique and chronic hypochondria.

11. *Ted Lindsay*

Smallish like Bentley, Lindsay carried intimidation to its ultimate degree, and because of that, fighting frequently overshadowed his talents as a left wing on the Production Line with Gordie Howe and Sid Abel. He put the mustard into Jack Adams' first-rate Red Wing clubs from the late forties through the fifties.

12. *Syl Apps*

Described by some as "Hockey's Greatest Star," the father of Pittsburgh's Syl, Jr., was captain of Toronto's Cup winners in 1942, 1947, and 1948. A lyrical skater, Apps played center the way it was written in the book. Unfortunately, he retired in the prime of his career.

That's it, folks. Any arguments?

19

The Four Greatest Games

IN THE SPRING OF 1950 the New York Rangers met the Detroit Red Wings in the Stanley Cup finals. Experts predicted it would be no contest, and for good reason.

Detroit had finished in first place, twenty-one points ahead of the fourth-place Rangers. What's more, the Rangers were forced to play all of their home games on the road because a circus had forced the club out of Madison Square Garden. Hence, the New Yorkers played their two "home" games at Maple Leaf Gardens in Toronto.

Yet despite these and other obstacles, the Rangers came to within inches of winning the Stanley Cup. They led Detroit three games to two and were ahead of the Red Wings, 2–0, in the final game.

RANGERS VERSUS RED WINGS

APRIL 23, 1950

SEVENTH GAME OF THE FINALS

The Rangers prepared for the fifth game of the series tied two games apiece, but with the grim specter of injuries clouding their camp. Forward Nick Mickoski had suffered a dislocated shoulder, and Jack Gordon, another forward, was lost for the rest of the series with torn knee ligaments. And of course there was the problem of playing another game at unfriendly Olympia Stadium in Detroit.

No matter. Game five was on, and the Rangers went out to take a 1–0 lead on Dunc Fisher's goal at 7:44 of the second period, then saw the lead evaporate with less than two minutes remaining in the game when Ted Lindsay sank his own rebound. But the Rangers treated Lindsay's goal as an idle annoyance, particularly when Bones Raleigh, on a pass from Ed Slowinski, saved the game for the Blueshirts during overtime.

The speed of Raleigh's goal arrested the imagination of the 12,610 spectators. The play had evolved with only a minute and a half gone in overtime. Slowinski captured the puck behind the net and fed Raleigh, who unleashed a ten-foot shot that found an opening between goalie Harry Lumley's pads.

"Eddie did all the work," Raleigh insisted. "It was the best pass I've ever had." So now New York led the series, three games to two, and needed but one win in the next two games to take the Cup and the upset of all Cup upsets.

The sixth, and what Ranger followers believed would be the last, game of the series was held at Olympia on Saturday, April 22, 1950. To many observers it should have been the grand finale, and those who saw the game or heard New York broadcaster Bert Lee describe it on the radio still have difficulty believing that the Rangers ultimately lost.

The tragedy developed rather unexpectedly, for in the first period, before the Red Wings could find their groove, the Rangers had built a lead on goals by Allan Stanley and Dunc Fisher. Lindsay reduced the lead by one in the period's final minute, but Pentti Lund scored after three minutes of the second period to put New York ahead by two. Again the Red Wings retaliated, scoring late in the second period, and the Rangers went ahead again in the third on a goal by Tony Leswick.

But the fact was, there was too much Lindsay for the Rangers. The ubiquitous left wing stickhandled through three Rangers to score at 4:13. Then Sid Abel scored later in the game after snaring his own rebound in front of goalie Chuck Rayner.

After a disappointing loss for the Rangers it was time for the climactic event, the final game on April 23 at Olympia. For the first two periods it appeared that the Rangers had the Stanley Cup in the bag. Goals by Stanley and Leswick gave them a 2–0 lead after the first period. Detroit tied it in the second at 2–2, but Buddy O'Connor put New York ahead again at 11:42 of the middle period.

That was the Rangers' last moment to exult in a lead. Shortly thereafter, Jim McFadden beat Stanley to the puck and shot an "impossible" angled shot past goalie Chuck Rayner to tie the score. There was nothing left but excruciating overtime—the first goal deciding the game and the Cup winner. "You could see it coming," said Rangers coach Lynn Patrick.

"Once overtime started I figured we were through. The boys just had nothing left."

Well, not quite nothing. The Rangers traded blow for blow, shot for shot, with the Red Wings in the hostile Olympia Stadium for twenty minutes of the first sudden death and very nearly won the Cup. A shot by Mickoski had Lumley beaten, but the puck hit the goalpost and went in the wrong direction.

By the second overtime the Rangers were still there, but they were tiring fast and the end was near. "The Wings had carried the play to the fading Blueshirts," wrote Lew Walter in the *Detroit Times*, "and had missed goals by hairline margins."

Detroit's George Gee was one who barely missed scoring the winning goal. He was put in the clear by Pete Babando. Rayner moved slowly out of his cage, ten, twelve, fifteen feet. Gee shot. Rayner sprawled and smothered the puck. Referee Bill Chadwick (who later became the television "color" announcer for Rangers home games) whistled a face-off in deep Ranger zone, to the left of the net.

Patrick sent out Buddy O'Connor, Alex Kaleta, Nick Mickoski, Pat Egan, and Allan Stanley. Detroit's unit consisted of Gee, Babando, Doc Couture, Leo Reise, and Marcel Pronovost. Gee was to take the face-off against O'Connor. The Red Wing paused and skated back to Babando. "Move over behind me," Gee said. "You're too far to the left." His words proved to be insightful.

"I moved over," the American-born Babando said later. "I still wasn't far enough, because Gee beat O'Connor to the draw and whipped the puck back to my right. I had to reach for it to catch it on my backhand."

More than eight minutes had ticked away in the second sudden death when Gee won the draw. Rayner was at the near corner of the net as the puck moved toward Babando. The Ranger goalie's view was obscured by Stanley, his defenseman. "When the puck hit my stick," Babando recalled, "I just let fly through the scramble. I wasn't sure the shot was on the net." It was.

The puck took off along a straight line two feet off the ice. It flitted past Gee, past Stanley, and past Couture toward a three-foot opening at the right corner. Rayner knew the shot was coming, but he couldn't find the puck through the forest of bodies in front of him. "I never saw it coming," said Rayner. At the last second he fell to the ice, kicking out his left pad in a spread-eagle split. But he felt nothing hit his pads.

Intuitively, his head turned back to the left—toward the net. The puck was there in the corner, along with the Rangers' shattered dreams.

When the cheering subsided and the Rangers wiped away their tears,

Red Wing captain Sid Abel walked into the New York dressing room and gave the Blueshirts the finest testimonial they could receive, short of winning the Cup. Abel pumped Rayner's hand, looked around the room, and said to the other exhausted New Yorkers, "Don't you guys ever know when to quit?"

Prior to NHL expansion and the subsequent dilution of talent, Maurice "Rocket" Richard was the greatest goal scorer in hockey. Period.

Others may score more, but none will ever do it so flamboyantly and in such dramatic clutch situations as the Rocket.

It would take a catalog to list all of Richard's most spectacular goals. However, one that most observers agree is among his top ten occurred in April, 1952, against the Boston Bruins when the great Rocket was teetering on the edge of unconsciousness. Here's how it happened:

BOSTON VERSUS MONTREAL
APRIL 8, 1952
SEVENTH GAME OF THE SEMIFINALS

The final game of the semifinals was played at the Montreal Forum on April 8, 1952, and some consider it the most exciting hockey match ever played. This, of course, is debatable, but there was no doubt it was Maurice "Rocket" Richard's most courageous display of hockey ever.

Each team managed a goal in the first period and then settled down to vigorous end-to-end rushes, giving the ice the look of an endless stream of downhill ski racers. With one major exception the game was, as one reporter noted, "clean, hard-fought, and played with fine spirit." But that one exception played a vital role in the game's evolution.

With the score tied, 1–1, in the second period, Leo Labine, a Bruin forward with scant acquaintance of the rule book, took dead aim at Richard as the Rocket knifed through the Boston defense. Richard had already tripped and fallen to his knees when Labine ruthlessly charged him. Labine's stick thudded against Richard's head, and his knees rammed into Richard's stomach with the impact of a battering ram.

Already down, the Rocket keeled over on his back and from all appearances was dead. His legs spread out in an inverted V formation as trainer Hector Dubois, physiotherapist Bill Head, and teammate Bert Olmstead hovered over Richard's limp body, searching for signs of life. In time he responded to the waft of smelling salts, and his face smeared with blood, Richard lurched to his feet and groggily skated to the Forum first-aid room where the deep cut over his left eye was stitched and repaired. That completed, he returned to the bench.

"My legs felt fine," Richard recalled after the game, "but my head . . .

was I dizzy! I didn't remember anything after I got hit. They told me it was Labine. I don't know. I didn't even know the score when I went back to the bench."

Toe Blake, retired member of the Punch Line, was standing in the press box, high in the Forum rafters, when Richard returned to the bench. Blake immediately spotted his old buddy and turned to one of the reporters. "You watch," Blake said, "the Rocket will get one in the last five minutes of the game."

It became apparent as the third period moved along without a score that the next goal would decide the game. It was also obvious to most observers that Richard, of all people, would *not* score that goal. "After receiving his stitches," commented one Montreal newspaperman, "he was in partial coma for a while, his head fuzzed up from pain, his eyesight impaired, with dull noises ringing in his ears."

More than sixteen minutes had elapsed in the third period when Bruin veteran Woody Dumart carried the puck toward the Canadiens' zone. Butch Bouchard thrust out his stick with rapierlike speed, jabbing the puck away from Dumart. The Montreal defenseman looked up for a moment and spotted Richard near the blue line. The Rocket captured the pass as Dumart futilely tried to bat down the puck. Richard wheeled around Dumart like a speeding car skirting a disabled auto on the highway. First he reeled to center and then cut sharply to the right, jabbing the puck ahead of him with short pokes from his black-taped blade.

Blond Bill Quackenbush, one of the most experienced and intelligent defensemen in the NHL, skated backward on the Bruin defense, prepared to meet the ominous challenge, for Richard was now in full flight, his eyes blazing madly, his destination known to all. Quackenbush was traveling at about ten miles per hour in reverse as Richard bore down on him with more than twice that speed. Quackenbush hurled his black-shirted body at the Canadien ace, but it was as if he were checking a phantom.

Nevertheless, Quackenbush had done his job quite well, for he forced Richard to take so circuitous a route along the right side that the Rocket appeared to have been taken right out of play. "He looked too deep for a shot," said Baz O'Meara of the *Montreal Star*, "but then he suddenly did a deft cut to the left."

A right-handed shot playing right wing would have been cradling the puck too far to his right to release a threatening drive, but Richard, the anomaly, was a left-handed shooter. Thus the puck was on his left side, closer to the net, as he barreled past the flailing Quackenbush. "Sugar" Jim Henry, both eyes blackened from previous injuries and barely recovered from a broken nose, guarded the right corner of the net, allowing Richard nothing but the "impossible" angle shot to the far left corner.

Almost atop Henry's bulky goal pads, Richard finally released his drive. It was low and hard, and Henry never managed to touch, let alone see, the puck. "One minute I was facing him," said the Boston goalie, "waiting for the shot, the next he had whizzed by, and the puck was in the net."

The ovations that have traditionally greeted Richard goals have had the impact of a thunderclap. This time, however, the din shook the very foundations of the ancient Forum. "Richard has received ovations in his day," said O'Meara, "the likes of which have never been seen in the Forum, but the ensuing roar, which lasted fully four minutes followed by a paper shower, left all others in the also-ran class."

Reactions to the goal were as surprising as the score itself. Elmer Lach, sitting on the bench watching the Rocket in orbit, leaned forward onto the sideboards and fainted. Art Chapman, manager of the Buffalo club, was watching from the press box and simply stood, mouth agape, after the red light flashed. "Only Richard could score like that," he said later.

"He is like Babe Ruth was," said Montreal coach Dick Irvin. "He adds that little extra flourish to everything."

"That little flourish" provided Les Canadiens with the winning goal, although Billy Reay added another score into the open net with less than a minute remaining, and Montreal won the game, 3–1. When the final siren wailed, reporters searched their minds for the proper adjectives with which to describe Richard's feat. Baz O'Meara, who had seen more hockey games than nearly every other member of the press corps, summed it up this way:

"In all his storied, starry career, Richard has scored some of the most spectacular goals of hockey history. No player has ever matched him as a thrill-producer. No one has come close to him for versatility of execution. Of all the goals credited to him, none ever excelled that game-winner against Boston. . . . None ever drew a greater ovation, more gasps of admiration, because it was scored under the pressure of pain."

The pain had not entirely dissipated when the Rocket fell into the bench in Montreal's joy-filled dressing room. His father, Onésine Richard, walked in and put his right arm around the Rocket's shoulders and hugged his son. No longer able to control the emotion that welled within his battered frame, the Rocket broke down and cried.

Skeptics too often tend to minimize the accomplishments of contemporary hockey stars by labeling them "products of expansion." Granted, the facade of hockey has changed in the past decade, the fact remains that games often are as thrilling as they have ever been, and recent Stanley Cup play-offs are no exception.

What better proof than the seventh game of the 1971 Cup finals between Chicago and Montreal, when a young graduate of Cornell University became a household name.

The contest was not only one of the most thrilling ever played, it was also the making of Ken Dryden, professional goaltender.

MONTREAL VERSUS CHICAGO
MAY 18, 1971
SEVENTH GAME OF THE FINALS

After ninety-seven games for the Canadiens (seventy-eight during the regular season plus nineteen in the play-offs) and ninety-five for the Black Hawks, the whole 1970–71 campaign came down to one final match. The Hawks were favored, primarily because of the home-ice advantage, but also because of lingering doubts that the publicly aired rift between Hab coach Al MacNeil and veteran forward Henri Richard had indeed been healed. Publicly, the Canadiens were presenting a united front. Privately, well, no one could really tell.

When the teams took the ice for game number seven the temperature inside Chicago Stadium was in the low 80s. The ice was soft, the players obviously tense and tired. Happily for the National Hockey League, the game was being televised nationally in the United States by CBS. This, on a Tuesday night, meant tremendous prime-time exposure. What millions of television viewers and the twenty thousand fans in Chicago Stadium witnessed during sixty minutes of play was hockey at its most exciting.

From the opening face-off Chicago carried the play. Only rookie goalie Ken Dryden prevented a Hawk runaway in that first period. First, he stopped Stan Mikita at point-blank range with a kick save, then moments later smothered a close-in follow shot by Eric Nesterenko. Further into the period he snaked out his long right leg to deflect a screen shot from the point by Keith Magnuson. Montreal, meanwhile, was having trouble getting organized. Chicago goalie Tony Esposito was tested, but not severely.

At 17:35, Rejean Houle was detected holding Bobby Hull and sent to the penalty box for two minutes. With his team shorthanded, Dryden stopped Jim Pappin on a close-in shot. Seconds later, Bobby Hull fired a slap shot from the right point. Dryden used his stick to deflect it. When Hull's shot made contact with Dryden's stick it sounded like a rifle shot. Cliff Koroll captured the rebound and fed the puck back to Hull, still stationed at right point. He unloaded again. Dryden went flopping across the crease to make sure he had the left-hand corner covered.

Hull's shot went wide, but the puck rocketed off the boards behind the net and went straight to Dennis Hull, who was positioned in the left face-off circle. He shot as Dryden skidded back across the crease. The puck struck Dryden on the shoulder and glanced into the net. At 19:12 of the first period the Hawks had the lead.

Early in the second period, with the Hawks down two men and Montreal down one man, Jacques Lemaire of the Canadiens captured the puck five feet in front of Esposito and flipped a backhander for the corner. Somehow Esposito got his right leg out and blocked it. This inspired Chicago, and for the next few minutes the Hawks swarmed around the Montreal net. Finally, after a face-off deep in Montreal ice, Doug Jarrett shot the puck behind the net. Pit Martin outhustled two Canadiens for it and centered to Danny O'Shea. He fired from twenty-five feet out, and the Hawks had a 2–0 lead. That was at 7:33, and with Esposito seemingly in top form and the rest of the Hawks playing exceptionally well, it appeared that two goals would be enough for a Chicago win.

Then the roof fell in on the Black Hawks. Montreal got its first goal when Jacques Lemaire, skating leisurely toward the Chicago blue line, suddenly fired a slap shot toward the Chicago net from eighty feet out. Esposito flopped to his knees. But the puck kept rising and sailed over his right shoulder and into the net.

"I saw it all the way," Esposito said later. "I just missed it."

The goal stunned the Chicago crowd and the Chicago players as well. You could almost feel the confidence starting to drain out of them, as if someone had suddenly pulled the plug in a bathtub full of water. Lemaire's goal came at 14:18.

At 18:20 the Habs tied the score. Nesterenko and Lemaire chased the puck into the right corner of the Chicago zone. Nesterenko reached it first and shot it toward Bill White behind the Chicago goal. The puck hit the side of the net and bounced back to Lemaire. He centered to Henri Richard and the Pocket Rocket beat Esposito at point-blank range.

As the third period started, there again was that feeling of inevitability, the feeling that the Canadiens were not to be denied. At 2:34 Henri Richard scored what proved to be the winning goal. He flashed across the Chicago blue line on the left side. Then, after eluding Magnuson's frantic dive, Richard drew Esposito to the ice before flipping a shot over the sprawled goalie's shoulder. After that the game was in Dryden's hands. Ten minutes from the end of the game he made what has been described as the "Stop of the Season."

Jim Pappin took a pass that left him wide open eight feet in front of the Montreal net. Pappin shot, then raised his stick in celebration, so certain was he that the puck was in.

"I was moving across the net, following the course of the pass," Dryden explained. "I really wasn't moving toward Pappin's shot. Pappin's shot hit me low on the right pad. I was fortunate."

Ten minutes later it was all over. The Canadiens had won their sixteenth Stanley Cup since the formation of the National Hockey League in 1917. It may have been the most satisfying Stanley Cup of all, for the Canadiens had been underdogs throughout the play-offs.

In the Montreal dressing room there was unrestrained joy. Some players were laughing, others were crying. Three of the Canadiens had hoisted coach MacNeil onto their shoulders and carried him off the ice. In the dressing room MacNeil and Richard embraced. All was forgiven in the flush of victory.

A classic among classics, the 1951 Stanley Cup final between the Toronto Maple Leafs and Montreal Canadiens will forever be remembered as the "Sudden-Death Series."

Every one of the five matches was tied after regulation time and had to be settled by the pulsating sudden-death system.

Toronto won the first, third, and fourth matches on overtime scored by Sid Smith, Ted Kennedy, and Harry Watson, respectively. In the second match a shot by Maurice "Rocket" Richard decided the game for Montreal.

The fifth and final game was memorable for many reasons; but perhaps most of all because it was the last game ever played by "Bashin'" Bill Barilko, the marvelous Toronto defenseman who disappeared on a flying expedition in the summer of 1951. But before his misfortune Barilko had been hailed a superhero for his accomplishment in the biggest moment in the "Sudden-Death Series."

TORONTO VERSUS MONTREAL

APRIL 21, 1951

FIFTH GAME OF THE FINALS

As the teams prepared for the fifth game of the series, at Maple Leaf Gardens, experts wondered whether it was possible for there to be still another overtime. "There are two schools of thought on tonight's game," wrote Al Nickleson in the *Toronto Globe and Mail.* "One is that the Leafs will break out for a decisive win in regulation time after battering down an early Montreal drive.

"Another viewpoint is that the game will be just as close as the others, and there's fearful speculation among some followers that if it moves into overtime, that great opportunist Rocket Richard will do as he did a week ago. . . . There's a possibility, too, that neither team will triumph. Overtime could run into the Saturday night curfew and force replay of the game later, if necessary."

Feeling in the Montreal camp was remarkably confident under the circumstances. "Canadiens are so confident they're going to win in Toronto," wrote Dink Carroll in the *Montreal Gazette*, "that they've neglected to bring anything along with which to break training in case they lose."

The Canadiens reinforced their pregame confidence by taking the lead twice. First Rocket Richard scored one of his patented goals. He took a pass from Bud MacPherson and had only defenseman Jim Thomson between him and the goal. "Thomson may be an all-star defenseman," said Dink Carroll, "but they all look alike to the Rocket in those circumstances. He went around Thomson like a hoop around a barrel, pulled goalie Al Rollins out, and fired the puck into the empty net."

But Tod Sloan tied the score for Toronto less than four minutes later. With Eddie Mazur of the Canadiens harassing him all the way from center ice, Sloan managed to skate in on goalie Gerry McNeil and beat him with a hard shot. Toronto's assistant manager Hap Day recalled the afternoon that Sloan first visited Maple Leaf Gardens on a trip from northern Ontario. He skated on the ice wearing a pair of earmuffs. "He said it was the first time he had ever been inside a heated arena," Day remembered.

Sloan heated up the Maple Leafs that night, but the Canadiens kept coming on, in wave after wave. At 4:47 of the third period Montreal rookie Paul Meger captured a rebound from Doug Harvey's shot and beat Rollins.

Fortified with a 2–1 lead, the Canadiens had to tighten their defenses, hoping that McNeil could repulse the Leafs' drives. As expected, the Toronto players stepped up their attack with enormous gusto and several times appeared to have the tying goal on their sticks.

"It began to look as if, almost single handed, McNeil was going to beat them," said Dink Carroll. "How he stopped some of the shots they fired at him nobody knew, but stop them he did. There were times when he went to the ice and players of both teams, battling desperately, piled up in the crease. At the bottom of the pile would be little Gerry with the puck."

He baffled the Leafs until there was only one minute and thirty seconds remaining in the third period. The face-off was deep in Montreal's zone. Strategists on both sides immediately went to work.

Toronto coach Joe Primeau took the big gamble. He ordered goalie Al Rollins from the Toronto net and replaced him with crack center Max Bentley, whom he stationed at the blue line alongside defenseman Gus Mortson. The four remaining skaters—Teeder Kennedy, Sid Smith, Tod Sloan, and Harry Watson—were placed in a line facing the goal mouth.

Montreal coach Dick Irvin countered with his most diligent defensive players: Ken Mosdell, Floyd Curry, Ed Mazur, Tom Johnson, and Butch Bouchard. Referee Bill Chadwick ordered the players to line up for the face-off. The puck was dropped, and a wild scramble followed. Referee Chadwick whistled for another face-off.

Undecided about his strategy, Irvin sent Elmer Lach onto the ice to replace Mosdell; then he changed his mind and recalled Lach. Mosdell snared the puck from the face-off and nearly put the puck into the open Toronto net, but back-skating Harry Watson intercepted it in time. With sixty-one seconds remaining, the face-off was just outside the Montreal blue line. Day dispatched goalie Rollins back to the Toronto goal with instructions to speed off the ice if the Maple Leafs pushed the puck into Canadiens territory. Teeder Kennedy won the face-off and looped the puck to the boards, where players from both teams jammed heavily. Chadwick whistled a stoppage of play.

At this point Irvin committed the pivotal mistake. He removed his defensive aces and replaced them with Elmer Lach, Rocket Richard, and Bert Olmstead, his crack offensive unit. Lach skated opposite Kennedy for the critical face-off.

Sitting in the stands, Canadiens managing director Frank Selke fidgeted as the players lined up on the ice. He remembered how he had fought to obtain Teeder Kennedy for the Leafs and how it ultimately had cost him his job in Toronto. He knew that Teeder was the best face-off man in the business.

Kennedy dug his blades into the ice, riveting his eyes on the linesman's hand. The instant the black rubber hit the ice Teeder's stick flashed. The puck moved swiftly to the blue line, where Max Bentley trapped it and immediately skated in the direction of goalie McNeil. Lurching like a scared jackrabbit, Bentley finally decided there were too many bodies in front of the net to attempt a flanking movement. He shot the puck at the mass of legs and it bounced loose. Sid Smith, the Leafs' prime opportunist, snared the rebound and whacked a shot at McNeil. He beat the Canadiens' goalie, but the puck hit the goalpost and bounced free. It appeared that McNeil's luck would save him, but Sloan forced his way to a point just outside the goal crease, and when Smith's shot caromed free, Sloan swiped the rebound past the beleaguered McNeil and tied the score with only thirty-two seconds remaining in regulation time.

"The balance of power paid off for Toronto," said *Toronto Globe and Mail* sports editor Jim Vipond. "Leafs had strength in depth while Canadiens had heart and desire but couldn't match the manpower."

Still, with a break here or there and the great Rocket Richard firing, Montreal still could win the game in sudden-death overtime, the fifth consecutive heart-throbber.

"What the fans said out in the corridor during the ten-minute intermission sounded like gibberish," Dink Carroll remembered. "They mouthed words that made no sense, whacked each other on the back, and their hands shook when they lighted cigarettes."

When the intermission was over, the teams trooped onto the ice. The prime question was whether the Canadiens could withstand the psychological blow of losing the lead so late in the game. Primeau decided to use a line consisting of Howie Meeker, hero of past Cup triumphs, Cal Gardner, and Harry Watson, another play-off star. The coach had some qualms about sending defenseman Bill Barilko out on blue line.

"Bill had been committing himself too much, going on offense," Primeau later explained. "He would get caught out of position, which was dangerous with Rocket Richard on the ice. I finally told him I'd fine him if he didn't lay back and concentrate on defense."

Primeau decided to put Barilko on the ice, and Selke once again fidgeted in his seat. Earlier in the series the Canadiens' managing director said he hated Barilko so much that he wanted him on the Montreal team!

Referee Chadwick dropped the puck that launched the sudden-death overtime. Without hesitation the Maple Leafs took command and forced their way past the Canadiens' defense. Meeker took the first shot, but McNeil punted it out of danger. Montreal's attack was feeble, and in no time at all the Leafs captured momentum. "The Canadiens were inconsequential and indecisive," said Baz O'Meara of the *Montreal Star*. "The tired defense was wobbling in front of McNeil."

All the Canadiens needed, however, was someone to shovel the puck to Richard. With a quick burst he could round the Toronto defense and test the tall young Rollins. But the Montreal attack was deflated soon after it got going, and with more than two minutes elapsed Harry Watson's legs pumped mightily as he skated across the center ice to no-man's-land. Richard made a futile attempt at intercepting him, but Watson skimmed the puck into the Canadiens' zone with linemate Howie Meeker in speedy pursuit.

Meeker took control of the puck behind Montreal's net. His plan was simple—to swerve sharply in front of the goal and to take McNeil by surprise. The play almost worked, but McNeil covered up in time. He stopped the shot and the rebound drive by Watson. But McNeil couldn't control the second rebound, and he fell to the ice as the puck slid tantalizingly out to the blue line, where Bill Barilko should have been positioned.

But Barilko had remembered coach Primeau's warning about not drifting too deep into the enemy zone and had deliberately placed himself "safely" on the wrong side of the blue line. Suddenly he saw the puck coming at him. In that split second he had to decide whether to chance getting caught out of position and rush in for the puck or to play it safe and allow it to drift over the blue line, where he could organize another rush. Barilko gambled.

Literally running on the tips of his skates, Barilko lurched over the blue line, and in one motion he hurled his 5-foot, 11-inch, 185-pound body at the puck. "He looked like Dagwood catching a bus," said Smythe.

As he stroked the puck from his left, Barilko momentarily floated in the air, his legs spread out behind him, his hands clutching the stick, which was held horizontal across his body, and his head tilted slightly upward so that he could follow the trail of the flying puck.

Rocket Richard of the Canadiens was to Barilko's left, and Butch Bouchard was to his right, but neither was close enough to block the hard drive. Cal Gardner was directly behind Barilko. In that brief second of flight Barilko's eyes changed from an expression of anxiety to expectant glee. He was still aloft when the puck cleared McNeil's raised right glove and barely eluded the neck of his stick. Two minutes and fifty-three seconds after the start of the sudden-death period it hit the twine, at a height of three feet!

By the time Barilko landed he was practically atop McNeil's right skate. For one breathless second the 14,577 witnesses to one of the greatest hockey games ever played held their breath. Then they realized that it was over. "The walls of the rink vibrated with noise," said Carroll. "Toronto players left the bench and swarmed on the ice to join their teammates as they mobbed Barilko. The defeated Canadiens stood still, looking disconsolate, until they remembered their manners, and skated over to congratulate the winners."

Primeau, who had coached two Memorial Cup champion teams and one Allan Cup champion, was one of the first on the ice. He dashed to Barilko, hugged him several times, and shouted, "I won't fine you for charging on that one!"

20

The Best Coaches

THE BEST COACHES in hockey are easy to determine—they are the bench leaders who have consistently won big over a considerable period of time. They are the hockey bosses who grandly stand the test of time.

There is one exception, and that is Frank Boucher. Although he directed his Ranger club to only one (1940) Stanley Cup and one Prince of Wales Trophy (1942), Boucher was the most innovative coach to come down the pike and therefore deserves to be on the esteemed list.

The others were dynasty makers. Lester Patrick not only produced Stanley Cup winners, he personally came off the bench in one series and *played goal* for his club en route to the championship.

Dick Irvin was a galvanic coach in Toronto before moving on to Montreal where he was architect of the splendid Flying Frenchmen paced by Maurice "Rocket" Richard, Elmer Lach, and Hector "Toe" Blake. It was Irvin who helped *make* the Rocket, and quite by accident, almost broke him.

When Irvin left Toronto, he was succeeded by a rather innocuous-looking chap named Clarence "Hap" Day. In this case looks were deceiving. Day was a remarkable leader. He directed his Leafs to the extraordinary Stanley Cup comeback in 1942 when they were down three games to none against Detroit and rallied for a four-game sweep in the seven-game series. When manager Conn Smythe rebuilt the Leafs in 1946 it was Day who coached them to a then unprecedented three-straight Stanley Cup victories from 1946–47 through 1948–49.

Day's most successful rival was Detroit Red Wings coach Tommy Ivan, who had never played a big-league game in his life. But he knew how to coach and finished second in his rookie season, after which the Ivan-led Red Wings won six straight NHL championships.

If Ivan's work tended to overshadow Day's, it was Blake who made everyone forget Ivan. Successor to the ailing Dick Irvin in Montreal, Blake molded a newer version of the Flying Frenchmen, who, at one point, seemed to have a mortgage on the Stanley Cup.

After Blake they threw away the mold. As player power developed, the coach became more and more irrelevant. In Montreal, for example, two coaches—Al MacNeil and Claude Ruel—were fired immediately after they had won the Stanley Cup. Only a few of the old-school coaches remained. One of them, Billy Reay of the Black Hawks, was and is efficient, but in more than a decade behind the bench he has never won the Cup. Hence, he doesn't make the following list.

Lester Patrick (Rangers, 1926–27 through 1938–39)

Hockey's revered "Silver Fox," Patrick had long been an accomplished player before being summoned as an emergency replacement for Conn Smythe when the Rangers were organized in 1926–27.

Most respected critics believe that the Rangers would have been significantly less successful under the acid-tongued Smythe and might very well have failed. Frank Boucher, who played on the original Rangers, was one who believed that Patrick had the ideal touch, a perfect way with players.

"Through our first decade in New York," said Boucher, "there was a great comradeship and a maturity that could not have been possible under Smythe, the martinet.

"Smythe ruled by the sword. Lester had discipline, but he was one of us, too. Smythe could never have been. On top of that, Lester was the most knowledgeable hockey man I ever met."

Patrick's mannerisms, down to the minutest detail, suggested leadership. He had a habit of tossing his head back archly and according to Boucher betrayed the same imperial air as the actor John Barrymore. He had a vast vocabulary and never hesitated to use it on his awed, less-educated players.

"I sometimes thought Lester must search the dictionary or perhaps a thesaurus to come up with a ten-letter word," said Boucher, "that he could use in place of a shorter one. He could have been a lawyer, a teacher, or an actor."

But he coached the Rangers, and they immediately moved toward the top of the NHL. In seven of his first eight years behind the bench, Patrick was voted the NHL's outstanding coach. How did he do it?

"There's more to coaching a hockey club than standing behind the bench," Patrick would say. "That's almost the least important phase of the job—watching your men when a game is in progress. It is incumbent upon you initially to build up their morale and then maintain it, and before you can do that you must have acquired their confidence in your judgment, and you must know the men."

A hallmark of Patrick-coached clubs was an all-for-one-and-one-for-all spirit that seemed to be lifted from the pages of *The Three Musketeers*. To some it may have seemed corny, but Patrick believed in *esprit de corps* and did more than any other coach to create that happy feeling.

"Whenever a new player came to the club," said Patrick, "I took him into my office and talked to him. I questioned him about himself. I wanted to know if he had a family, and if so, if his family was in New York. If not, where was he living? Whom did he associate with? Did he have any troubles, professional, domestic, or financial? I invited his confidence. I wanted him to know that whenever he was confronted with a difficulty the door of my office was open to him. Before he put on a Ranger uniform I wanted him to feel at home."

Patrick contributed to the Rangers' *élan* in many ways. The most famous by far occurred in the spring of 1928 when the Rangers skated against Montreal's Maroons in the Stanley Cup finals. Lorne Chabot, the Rangers' regular goaltender, was injured, and no replacement was available. Patrick, who was forty-four at the time, put on the pads and guarded the Rangers' goal.

"Lester," said Boucher, "was an inspiration to us. And he seemed to be enjoying himself. Every time the puck came toward him he'd drop to his knees and smother it."

Patrick allowed one goal—a shot by Nels Stewart in the third period—which balanced the lone Rangers' score, and the teams went into sudden-death overtime with Patrick hanging in like a veteran goalie. But Lester held fast for seven more minutes, and then Boucher shot the puck past Maroons goalie Clint Benedict to win the match for New York. Thanks to Patrick's monumental effort the Rangers went on to defeat Montreal three games to two and win their first Stanley Cup.

Within seven years Patrick had won two Stanley Cups—1928 and 1933—and finished first twice. His club was always near the top of the standings, and his name became a legend in his time, not merely because of his goaltending exploit against the Maroons but because of that Patrick style. He had brains and class and he could teach hockey better than anyone, before or since.

"When it comes to teaching hockey to my young men," Patrick would explain, "I say as little as possible and avoid blackboards and diagrams. I've seen a lot of players who've been blackboarded half to death, so that when they go on the ice they're completely befuddled and the simplest plays hold terrors for them.

"I tell a boy how I want a play made and and then put him on the ice in practice when there's no pressure on him and have him go through that play. I go right out on the ice with him and take him by the arm and say: 'Look, here is how I want this play made, because this is the right way. Now let me show you what you are doing. I don't want you to do that because that's the wrong way. Simple, isn't it? Now do it my way.'

"Sometimes he does it right the next time. More often, he does it wrong again. I keep pegging away at him, but I don't lose my temper and bawl him out because if he does it wrong often enough I realize that he is a slow thinker or has a bad memory and simply can't get it right, no matter how hard he tries. I'm patient with him and then, someday in practice or some night in a game, he makes it right. Once, I had a fellow who made a simple play wrong for three years. One night in a tight game he made it right, and it won a game for us."

Patrick was blessed with several outstanding players, including the Cook brothers, Bill and Bun, and Frank Boucher. Lester would be very attentive to newcomers and veterans who he believed needed special instruction, but he never made a pest of himself with those in whom he had complete faith.

"Lester left our line completely alone," said Boucher. "Often during practices he would stay at one end of the rink with eight or nine players and let the three of us at the other end flip the puck around and work on our plays. He never interfered with our experiments. This, to me, pointed up his greatness as a coach. He gave us full credit for our success, never attempting to claim we were the products of his planning. His handling had much to do with the development of our confidence."

Dick Irvin (Chicago Black Hawks, 1930–31 and 1955–56)

Toronto Maple Leafs, 1931–32 through 1939–40; Montreal Canadiens, 1940–41 through 1954–55. A perfect counterpoint in style to Patrick,

Irvin was a dynamic player with the Black Hawks until his career was ended by a skull fracture from a check by Red Dutton of the Maroons.

Vitriolic and seemingly insensitive at times, Irvin began his coaching career with unusual success in Chicago where, like most coaches, he clashed with the Black Hawks' owner Major Frederic McLaughlin, even though he led Chicago to the 1931 Stanley Cup finals. A year later, Irvin was in Toronto working with the Leafs, and it was there that his coaching genius began to flower.

Fortunately for Irvin he found a friend in Toronto. Assistant Leaf manager Frank Selke, Sr., was a pigeon-fancier, and so was Irvin. In fact Irvin was convinced that there was a hockey lesson to be learned by studying the birds.

"Pigeons," Irvin explained, "are just like skaters. You send one out, and he's back in a minute, huffing and puffing. You send another one out, and he has no idea where he's going or what he's doing. You send a third out, and he knows exactly where he's going and what he's doing."

Irvin's mind was fertile and quick. Once, during a game against the Rangers, he ordered his injured players Charlie Conacher and Red Horner to dress for the match and sit on the bench. Both skaters had accumulated two major penalties in the season, and according to the NHL rules of the day, a third major would result in automatic one-game suspensions. The 1931–32 rule book also called for a major penalty to any player who took the ice while his team already was at full strength.

Midway in the game Irvin sent Conacher and then Horner on the ice, although the Maple Leafs already were at full strength. Both were given major penalties and suspended for one game, which was perfectly all right with Irvin, since injuries would have prevented them from playing in their next game anyway. So Irvin did away with the suspension while his Leafs edged New York, 5–3. Later in the season Irvin outwitted Lester Patrick, defeating the Rangers in three consecutive games of the Stanley Cup finals, and the Maple Leafs had won their first world championship. Irvin followed that with four first-place finishes in his next six seasons.

But that was just for starters. Irvin's best coaching years were still ahead, and prior to the 1940–41 season he received permission to negotiate with the Montreal Canadiens to become both manager and coach of the then faltering Frenchmen. "No man but Irvin could have restored order out of the Canadiens' chaos in so short a time," said Frank Selke, Sr.

One by one he acquired young players and infused them with confidence. One of them was Emile "Butch" Bouchard, a gangly youngster who came to the Canadiens' training camp on a bicycle. "When most critics laughed at Bouchard because he was a clumsy-looking rookie," said

Selke, "Irvin kept boosting him. After a while Bouchard became the number-one defenseman in hockey."

Irvin worshiped speed. Where once the Canadiens were plodders, the Irvin-coached club developed what later became known as "fire-wagon" hockey. "As long as they play this game on skates," said Irvin, "you have to be able to skate to win. Personally, I'll take a young pair of legs over an old head anytime."

To generate speed, a player had to be lithe, according to Irvin. There was no room for fat on a Montreal skater. "Irvin knew his stars so well," said *Toronto Star* columnist Milt Dunnell, "that he could almost tell by watching them skate whether they had a second helping of pumpkin pie with whipped cream for dinner a week earlier."

One night after a Canadiens star had scored two goals in a winning effort, the player expected congratulations from Irvin. Dick's reply was typical: "Son, you're four pounds overweight. You'll have to take it off to make this team."

By the 1943–44 season Irvin had melded English-speaking and French-speaking players together into a magnificent hockey machine. His best line was composed of Rocket Richard, Toe Blake and Elmer Lach—the "Punch Line." Bill Durnan, his crack goaltender, was a Toronto reject who, under Irvin's guidance, became the best by far in the business. Soon, Dick was being compared with Knute Rockne, the legendary Notre Dame football coach.

"Rockne had the ability to catch up a general truth in a brief phrase," said *Montreal Gazette* columnist Dink Carroll, "and Irvin could do the same thing."

Irvin's Canadiens finished first for four consecutive seasons beginning in 1943–44 and won the Stanley Cup twice in that period. He never finished first again but did win another Cup—his last—in 1952–53.

If Dick had a problem as he grew older, it was the fact that he became *less* mellow and more irascible. During the 1946–47 Stanley Cup series with Toronto, Irvin was accused of nearly inciting his team to riot after Lach had been injured. "Irvin apparently is anxious to incite mayhem," wrote Jim Coleman in the *Toronto Globe and Mail.* "If a riot results, it is probable that the names of a few of his own players will appear in the casualty lists and they should sue Irvin for the hospital bills."

The episode that finished Irvin in Montreal was the notorious "Richard Riot," which followed the suspension of Dick's superstar for assaulting an official in a game at Boston. Selke, who had become the Canadiens' manager, believed that Irvin had goaded Richard, and this goading had led to his squabbles and ultimate suspension.

Unknown to Selke at the time, Irvin was suffering through the initial stages of a bone cancer that cost him his life two years later. Selke informed Irvin that he could remain with the Canadiens in "another job" but not as coach. Irvin said he would rather coach and accepted a job back at his alma mater, the Black Hawks. He coached one more year before illness eventually took his life.

Frank Boucher (New York Rangers, 1939–40 through 1948–49)

Since he had studied under the old master, Lester Patrick, it was hardly surprising that Boucher emerged as one of the most innovative coaches in hockey. Were it not for World War II, he surely would have been one of the most successful. His Rangers won the Stanley Cup in his rookie year (1940) behind the bench and finished first two years later.

But the war decimated the Rangers' lineup more than that of any other NHL team—Boucher's ace defenseman Muzz Patrick (son of Lester) was the first NHL player to enlist—and the sure-to-flower dynasty was nipped in the bud. Still, Boucher did enough in a short time to establish his preeminence behind the bench.

He came up with the idea of removing a goaltender while play was in motion and also taught his men that the best way to defend against a power play was to take the offensive. "We chose [defenseman] Art Coulter as the anchor man," said Boucher, "instructing him to play the whole length of the opposing team's blueline while the three forwards—Neil and Mac Colville and Alex Shibicky—prowled like night fighters inside it. Over the season we outscored our opponents almost two to one when we were shorthanded."

Another successful Boucher invention that has become standard operating procedure today was the "box defense" against an enemy power play. "Our players," said Boucher, "formed a loose square in front of our goaltender and diverted incoming attackers to the sides so that any shots on goal were from bad angles and the goaltender needed only to play those angles."

Boucher later pioneered the two-goalie system, employing Chuck Rayner and Jim Henry in alternate games. As things developed, Boucher was several decades ahead of his time. Today, every club keeps two goaltenders available for a game.

"At first," Boucher explained, "I alternated Henry and Rayner because I couldn't decide which was better. And partly because a new philosophy toward goaltending was creeping into my mind. The game had speeded up by 1945, and goaltenders were confronted with new tensions and injuries almost unknown five years earlier."

Boucher not only alternated Henry and Rayner on different nights but occasionally switched them every few minutes in the same manner as he switched defensemen in the same game. The system finally was abandoned when the Rangers' farm club in New Haven sent an urgent SOS for goaltending assistance, and Henry was dispatched to Connecticut.

When Boucher's veterans returned from the war, most were over the hill, and the Rangers were unable to generate the power they had in 1940 and 1942 when they were among hockey's greatest teams.

Hap Day (Toronto Maple Leafs, 1940–41 through 1949–50)

Like Boucher, Day was an innovator. He used training techniques later adopted by the highly successful Russian National Teams. Day frequently would work out with his goaltender, Turk Broda. On the ice during practices, Day insisted that Broda face the shots *without* his big goalie stick. The coach prescribed handball as a tonic for sharpening the goalie's reflexes.

Day resolutely directed the Maple Leafs to a comeback Stanley Cup win in 1942. He did it again in 1944–45 despite a relatively weak club, which finished out of the play-offs the following season.

But when the 1946–47 campaign began, manager Conn Smythe presented him with a dozen youngsters and told him that he had three years to produce a winner. Day didn't wait. He won the Cup in 1947, 1948, and 1949.

If the acid in the Leafs' front office was supplied by manager Smythe, the glue belonged to Day. As a defenseman with Toronto he had never been reluctant to drape himself over an opponent. Likewise, his defensemen weren't either.

"When Day was playing defense," ex-Leaf Babe Pratt explained, "it cost the opposition triple money for sweaters. He used to rip them right off the players' backs with his clutch."

Under Day, Toronto's practice sessions were severe but never to the point of causing dissension. One afternoon Boston defenseman Pat Egan watched the Leafs complete the last minutes of a tortuous practice. "That's why they win everything," said Egan. "Day could tell those kids to go into the wall headfirst and they'd do it."

Although Day was more on the quiet side, he was a fighter and his players knew it, too. Once, in a victorious Toronto invasion of Boston

Garden during the 1947 play-offs, Day took on a few of the more rowdy Bruins fans.

"One fan threatened to hit me," said Day, "and I told him I'd be waiting at the end of the game. I turned around as soon as the game ended, and the two of us tangled. The worst part of it was that during the fight I slipped to the floor and lost my fedora."

When Day lost his captain and top scorer Syl Apps and veteran penalty-killer Nick Metz to retirement after the 1947–48 season, he still produced a Cup-winner. The three straight Stanley Cup triumphs constituted an NHL record and guaranteed Day's selection as one of hockey's supreme coaches.

Tommy Ivan (Detroit Red Wings, 1947–48 through 1953–54)

Of all the superior coaches who have graced the NHL, Tommy Ivan was the unlikeliest of all. He was the only coach who had never played professional hockey.

"I wasn't good enough to play it," Ivan admitted. "I played amateur hockey until a facial injury forced me to quit when I was twenty-six."

After that, Ivan turned to refereeing and scouting. "I helped Carson Cooper, who was Detroit's chief scout," said Ivan. "He patiently schooled me in hockey technique."

Eventually, the Red Wings asked him to coach in their minor-league system. He worked in Guelph and Brantford, Ontario, and later Omaha of the old United States League. Then, Detroit's manager Jack Adams promoted him to Indianapolis of the American League for the 1946–47 season. Adams retired as Red Wings coach the next year, and Ivan was selected his successor.

Tommy inherited such bright prospects as Gordie Howe and Ted Lindsay and molded them into winners. He annexed three Stanley Cups and finished first six straight years.

"Ivan," said Adams, "is the best thing that ever happened to me. He was a dandy coach, and we got along terrifically. I always had an open-door policy with him and never made a move without telling him about it. Tommy was a practical man when he was with us and a winner."

The Red Wings reluctantly released Ivan in 1954–55 when he became general manager of the Black Hawks. "Jim Norris came to me," said Adams, "and asked whether Ivan could help his team. I told him bluntly Ivan could help him if he was made general manager and given all the authority the job carries with it."

Ivan was quick to grab the opportunity, and the Red Wings were never the same after that. Tommy eventually developed the Black Hawks into a powerhouse. The Red Wings, with the players Ivan had developed, won one more Stanley Cup, in 1954–55, and then slipped into a permanent obscurity from which they've never recovered.

Toe Blake (Montreal Canadiens, 1955–56 through 1967–68)

When Dick Irvin left Montreal to coach Chicago in 1955, the Canadiens looked hard for a capable successor. The final choice was Blake, a former Canadiens star who had spent several years coaching in the minors.

Blake was Selke's choice because Selke believed that the "Old Lamplighter," as Toe was called, knew how to control the temperamental Rocket Richard. "Blake and Selke were trying to give the Rocket all they had by way of a tranquilizing program," said one observer. "They started giving him de-pep talks long before the season began."

The talks worked. Everything Blake did worked. He ruled the Canadiens like a benevolent despot, and they loved it. But the pivotal character would be the Rocket. If he got along with the new coach, everyone would. And he did.

"It didn't take very long to realize that we would work very well under Blake," said Richard. "Toe had one quality that marked him from Irvin. It was Irvin's policy to roast a player publicly for his mistakes. Blake would never give anyone hell in front of the other players. When he had something to say he would take them out to a private room, or his compartment on the train, or into his office and discuss it.

"Make no mistake, Blake was a tough man. You never heard a good word from him on the bench. If you made a good play he wouldn't walk over and pat you on the back. But that didn't really matter. In the dressing room you knew he was behind you, and as long as I played for him Toe was well liked by the players."

Of all the successful hockey coaches, Blake most closely resembled football's Vince Lombardi in temperament and technique. When it came to other coaches, Blake's strategy closely resembled his predecessor's.

"Blake and Irvin were practically alike," said Richard. "Toe emphasized skating and more skating—head-manning the puck and shooting whenever possible."

The simple formula paid rich dividends. Montreal took complete command of the NHL, winning the Stanley Cup five consecutive years, starting in 1955–56. They finished first in six out of Blake's first seven seasons.

"Sometimes," said Blake, "it's tough to coach players you once had as teammates. But these fellows went out of their way to make it easy for me. Even from the beginning we were like one big happy family."

That in itself was a miracle, since the Canadiens were a blend of Anglo-Saxons and French-Canadians who didn't always see eye to eye. Then, there was always the potentially explosive Richard. "Sometimes," said Blake, "I had to cool the Rocket on the bench. He'd glare at me, but he took it from me, too."

What about coaching style? "Your style of coaching," Blake explained, "has to depend on the players you have, because if you try to change the styles of your players you're in trouble.

"If you're connected with superstars as I was, you've got to let them go all out and let the defense look after itself. But I told my team that four or five stars don't make a team. Everyone in uniform is important. For example, sometimes your aces get heavily checked in the play-offs. When that happens you have to hope that your lesser lights can come up with a couple of goals and bail you out."

As the years progressed, Blake's problems became similar to Irvin's— Toe gradually turned more and more temperamental. Players who once tolerated his yelling and kicking became disenchanted with him. Still, Toe kept winning. On May 11, 1968, the Canadiens won another Cup for him. This was the last time. That night he announced his retirement. "I'd like to coach the Canadiens for a hundred years," said Blake, "but the tension is too terrific. On the days of some games this year, I was almost not human."

Odd. That's what his foes would say about Toe Blake—as a winner.

21

The Most Perfect Hockey Club— from Goaltender to Public Relations Man

As RONALD COLMAN once said, in *The Prisoner of Zenda*: "If I were king. . . ." With no monarchy in sight, I will lower my horizons and paraphrase Colman. "If I were a big-league hockey general manager and had twenty million dollars at my disposal. . . ."

I would spend five days in my study and emerge with the most formidable hockey club ever put together. Given the opportunity to launch a hockey club from scratch (and of course having enough scratch with which to do it), I would do things no other general manager would dare attempt. (They're a bunch of narrow-thinking *nudniks* as a group, anyhow.) And I would explore ice lanes previously untouched by human skates.

It would be a marvelous adventure and would begin with the selection of eighteen players, including two goaltenders. Since this is all fantasy and I would have available to me everyone from Bobby Orr to Rod Zaine, my most perfect hockey club would ignore current contractual entanglements in both major leagues. It would be named the Whippets and the roster would be as follows:

Goaltenders. Phil Myre and Bernie Parent

Myre, only twenty-six years old in November, 1974, is just approaching his prime. He is one of the last of the goaltending stylists from the Jacques

Plante School of Intelligent Netminders. This school, by the way, includes Les Binkley and Gilles Villemure, to name a few, none of whom is young enough or consistent enough, emotionally, to be my anchorman.

Myre not only is nimble, alert, and fearless but possesses a relaxed disposition (he's an accomplished guitarist) necessary in the National Hockey League jungle today. He will be expected to play in a minimum of thirty games.

His alter ego must be more experienced and confident enough not to be insecure about his partner. Parent has been a Stanley Cup winner and is acknowledged as one of the keener competitors among goalies, as he proved in the 1974 Stanley Cup play-offs.

Defense

Bobby Orr, Ed Van Impe, Brad Park, Guy Lapointe, Steve Durbano, and Pat Stapleton.

A melding of talent, experience, youth, and hostility are necessary to round out a defense that will also blend the best offensive and defensive qualities. Thus, Bobby Orr, whose offensive talents are obvious but who is defensively weak (that, chums, is relative to his attacking assets), will be matched with the best positional defensive defenseman in pro hockey, Van Impe. No matter how often Orr flits out of position, Van Impe *always* will be at his post, the spear-carrier *superior.*

The second unit will feature Lapointe alternating with Park or Durbano. Park will be employed against the strong teams; Durbano against the weaker ones, and whenever a policeman is needed. Both Park and Lapointe are equally adept at puck-carrying and hitting. When they are paired together Lapointe will be fined every time he skates more than ten feet inside the enemy's blue line. He must play defense in the Van Impe manner when he's working with Park.

For use on the power play, and as a general protection against overconfidence on the part of my regulars, I would hire Pat Stapleton, a master tactician and leader who, because of advanced age, would be ideal for occasional defensive chores.

First Line

Walter Tkaczuk, center; Bill Fairbairn, right wing; Steve Vickers, left wing. At least one unit on the club must be able to mesh like well-oiled gears and be vigorous skaters and checkers. They must be inspirational by their works, not by their verbs. They must, in short, provide full value offensively and defensively.

Tkaczuk, who will be twenty-eight in September, 1975, is the best *all-purpose* center in hockey today. He has been complemented on right wing by Fairbairn, the most tenacious forward to reach the NHL since Ted "Teeder" Kennedy (the original Mr. Tenacity and Grim Determiner) captained the 1949 and 1951 Toronto Maple Leafs Stanley Cup winners.

A first line must have a "bumper" (just as an automobile has one) to ward off trouble. Vickers, who has plastered such plasterers as Don Marcotte and Ken Hodge, should not be disturbed any more than hornets' nests. He is Cool Hand Luke: tough, multiplied by three. He can also score.

This unit, therefore, can be the match of anything on the opposition, as long as they aren't ground down to a walk by overwork during the regular season, as has happened in the past when Rangers coach–general manager Emile Francis insisted upon using Fairbairn and Tkaczuk as penalty-killers in nonsensical situations. They can score, defend, fight, and skate. What other line can make that statement with equal accuracy at each of the three positions?

Second Line

Phil Esposito, center; Mickey Redmond, right wing; Frank Mahovlich, left wing.

A line that can create a blizzard of pucks in the enemy end of the rink remains the dream of any general manager. This threesome can achieve that despite the obvious drawback in the over-thirty-year-old character of Esposito and Mahovlich.

Redmond, twenty-five, generates a superabundance of speed that can be employed as a defensive weapon if his partners fail on a scoring attempt and lack the energy to backcheck.

However, the essence of the line is total blitz that automatically psychs the opposition into a defensive posture and thereby eliminates the fear of a strong counterattack.

Both Mahovlich and Esposito have amply demonstrated over the years that there are few more devastating shooters or stronger hunks of hockey player. Thus, although they lack an innate belligerence, their bulk alone makes it almost impossible to use weight as armor against them.

It may be necessary to caution Esposito that passing will be a more valuable aspect of his repertoire than shooting when either Mahovlich or Redmond are in the clear. Too much shooting could spoil the froth.

Third Line

Gilbert Perreault, center; Yvan Cournoyer, right wing; Rick Martin, left wing. Perreault is a cliché center only because he is a reasonable (often superior) facsimile of Hall of Famer Jean Beliveau. There is absolutely nothing that Perreault cannot do with the puck, stick, and skates. His ice wizardry betrays only one weakness, an inability to handle his dukes, although some players will quarrel with that. However, there is a bromide to erase that argument, to wit: If you can't catch 'em, you can't hit 'em. Perreault is as easy to catch as a bullet.

One of the few objects faster than Perreault is Cournoyer. They call him the "Roadrunner" for good reason, but his scoring is more to the point. Perreault, an exceptionally unselfish playmaker, will skim passes (radarlike, as they say in the pulp magazines) to Cournoyer until the cows (or Cournoyers, if you will) come home.

Martin, who learned how to live with Perreault in Buffalo, is available to scoop up rebounds and assorted other garbage that will emanate from the panicking enemy defensemen whenever the French-Canadian Connection threatens.

Fourth Line

Bobby Clarke, center; Gordie Howe, right wing; Bobby Hull, left wing.

This unit fulfills two important tasks—it will satisfy nostalgia buffs who might have missed the "Big Fella" (Howe) and the "Golden Jet" in their prime, and it will be superadequate for penalty-killing functions.

Both Howe and Hull will have enough energy for occasional flashes of brilliance, since they will be used only occasionally. Clarke, the most acclaimed—and possibly the only—diabetic in pro hockey will be used for general plumbing; i.e., he will plug leaks on any of the other three lines, will alternate with Howe and Hull while generating enough enthusiasm (which he does better than a squadron of cheerleaders) for the entire team, and then some.

By now any hockey fan worth his weight in decibels should have asked the questions: How come Tony Espositio, Ken Dryden, Bill White, Vic Hadfield, and Ken Hodge were left off the team? What's the matter with J. C. Tremblay and Ted Harris? How come you didn't pick Derek Sanderson for no other reason than sex appeal? Et cetera, et cetera, et cetera. Viz. and to wit:

Obviously there are several players I would *not*—repeat, *would not*—want on my hockey club, especially the following:

Ken Dryden

Longevity is vital to the foundation of a team. With his law degree and his past record of walking out on and then returning to the Montreal Canadiens, Dryden is too big a gamble. However, he *will* be hired as the team attorney.

Tony Esposito

The younger member of the famed brother act nearly made the club but his consistent record of *not* coming through in the clutch play-off matches compelled me to drop him in favor of Parent, who did. And since Tony is over thirty, he lost out on the age factor to Myre.

Vic Hadfield

When he signs a no-cut contract with Team Canada, then and only then will he get a tryout with the team; besides he's over the hill.

Garry Unger

I may be wrong, but he appears to me to have received too much acclaim for too little production. The result can only be a young man with an inflated opinion of himself. Who needs that?

Stan Mikita

Absolutely no helmeted players will be permitted on the team; they photograph poorly.

It is impossible to cram everyone on the roster. J. C. Tremblay lost out on the helmet issue, while Bill White had to give way to Pat Stapleton who is just that much better. Ken Hodge is tough and can score but is too slow for a team that will be called the *Whippets*. Age bumped Harris. I can't afford Derek Sanderson.

Now for the easy choice, the coach.

A successful coach must have the trust of his owners and managers as well as rapport with the players. He must be contemporary enough to understand the hedonistic young players while balancing his necessary role as disciplinarian delicately enough to extract as much quality as possible out of his men. He need not be a *name* coach, since names do not necessarily make competent bench leaders. I'd immediately take Fred Shero of the 1974 Stanley Cup winners, but I think he wants to be a lawyer. Otherwise, he's my second choice.

Thus, one man uniquely qualifies for this role. His name is Aldo Guidolin, and he qualifies because (a) he's a good friend of mine; (b) he successfully coached the Baltimore Clippers of the American Hockey League when nobody but nobody could have been successful with that then nondescript outfit; (c) he has been a scout and manager *and* player—thereby touching all necessary bases; and (d) he is liked *and* respected by all players, a rare combination. Most important, he owns what few other coaches or managers, or anyone for that matter, owns—a sense of humor under pressure. Better still, he really doesn't want to be coach.

That means neither Scotty Bowman, Bep Guidolin (Aldo's cousin), Emile Francis, Red Kelly, nor Billy Reay will get the job. Bowman always has been too uptight with the press and his players. We will need excellent relations with the media. I'll never forgive Kelly for walking out on the New York Rangers in 1960, claiming retirement, and then signing with the Toronto Maple Leafs after Detroit had traded him.

As for Reay, if you think Bowman is difficult with the press, Reay makes him look like Little Red Riding Hood! The other chaps I won't even discuss. (They never discuss me either, if they can help it.) If I couldn't get Aldo, I'd gladly settle for Shero. He's a genius.

There will be a few departures from the normal rules for the Whippets. Our arena will ban organ-playing at all times between the start of a period to its finish. Air horns will be banished from the rink as well as liquor, carbonated soda water, and all smokes. Water and fruit juice will be dispensed.

In addition to the banning of helmets, there will be a *suggestion* that my players abandon the slap shot in favor of the wrist shot, that no curved sticks be used (no curve at all), and that goaltenders discard face masks. However, coach Guidolin will be the ultimate arbiter in these cases.

The Russian system of conditioning will be recommended, and once this is in use, all bed checks and curfews will be eliminated. The players will be too tired to fool around.

Wherever possible the team will travel by railroad instead of plane so that more good hockey yarns, which have nearly been eliminated by jet travel, can be created. These can only be told on the long train rides.

If Guidolin approves, two assistant coaches will be hired—Maurice "Rocket" Richard to teach scoring and Glenn Hall, alias Mr. Goalie, to instruct the netminders.

There also will be a resident psychologist.

By midseason, headlines will be blaring from Montreal to Los Angeles: BREAK UP THE WHIPPETS!

22

Fischler's Guide to the Best Hockey-Writing in the World

THE FOLLOWING ARE my favorite hockey writers, *not* in order of preference or performance, and my reasons why:

Furman Bisher, Atlanta Journal

He knows little about hockey but a hell of a lot about words. When Furman writes about the Flames you get your money's worth in entertainment.

Jerry Nason, Boston Globe

A columnist unafraid of the Boston Bruins front-office clout—which makes Nason a rarity—who has wit and a deep knowledge of the sport going back decades.

Leigh Montville, Boston Globe

Montville is one of the best of the new breed who will quickly expose those he regards as phonies and will even prick the balloons of superstars such as Bobby Orr.

John Porter, Oakland Tribune

Charlie Finley didn't like Porter, which was John's first big plus. He has a nose for hot news, and despite the fact that he has covered the lowly Seals he is highly regarded across the continent.

Bob Verdi, Chicago Tribune

Fair, hard-hitting when necessary, and a rapidly improving writer, Verdi is ready for a big bust-out as soon as he can free himself from *The Hockey News* and some of the flack magazines for which he still writes.

Bill Brennan, Detroit News

As knowledgeable about hockey as anyone and more worldly than most hockey writers, Brennan has been head and shoulders above his competition, Jack Berry, and a beacon zeroing in on the many defects in the erstwhile Ned Harkness–Red Wings machine. Nobody has more guts among scribes than this man.

Joe Falls, Detroit Free Press

Nostalgia is his forte but he also handles the contemporary scene with acumen and was withering in his criticism of the "spoiled-brat" Detroit hockey players of 1973–74. His style is free and easy; very readable.

Charley Hallman, St. Paul Pioneer Press

Insightful, steeped in hockey basics, Hallman trained his Argus eye well on both North Stars and Fighting Saints.

Claude Larochelle, Le Soleil, Quebec City

One of the foremost French-language journalists, Larochelle has the contacts and the courage to print just about anything. The pity is that his prose is not available to the English-speaking hockey fan. If it were, he might be regarded as the best in the world.

John Robertson, Montreal Star

A superb stylist, Robertson was one of the very few to stand up and call Team Canada's win a phony. He properly scathed Al Eagleson, Harry Sinden, and the boorish NHL players, while displaying the perspicacity to predict Team Canada's problems with the Soviets long before most others did. Unfortunately, he has left writing for radio work.

Jacques Beauchamp, Le Journal de Montreal

Many colleagues knock him, but Jacques is the same guy who was the Canadiens' spare goaltender during the Rocket Richard era. His gossip is good and his background unsurpassed.

Ben Olan, Associated Press, New York

A creative magazine editor, Olan has a more comprehensive knowledge of hockey than his New York confrères. When he writes, he's objective, clever, and fair to the underdogs, which is more than can be said for his associates.

Hugh Delano, New York Post

At one point this very nice man was *too nice* to the New York Rangers. He has since turned into a perceptive analyst who writes more hockey, day to day, than anyone in Gotham.

Al Coletti, Canadian Press

A veteran all-purpose journalist, Coletti is on top of secret NHL meetings when nobody else knows about them. He makes the nitty-gritty and the obscure just as easy to read. Al is a pro's pro.

Red Foley, New York Daily News

Although Foley doesn't cover hockey as much as others, he has a finely sharpened stiletto that knows where to probe. He knows the game, and unlike many, he can make you laugh better than most.

Gerald Eskenazi, The New York Times

The Rangers are happy that he's off hockey, but when he covered on a regular basis Eskenazi was an exceptionally conscientious reporter who could stickhandle phrases from the left and right sides.

Dink Carroll, Montreal Gazette

One of the last of the Old Guard that included Baz O'Meara and Elmer Ferguson, Carroll proves the value and beauty of the simple style. Before you know it, you have read to the bottom of his piece and loved every second of it.

Jack Chevalier, Philadelphia Bulletin

A chronicler of the Flyers since their inception, Chevalier can wield a stiletto as well as a harpsichord. He is both knowledgeable and entertaining.

Frank Orr, Toronto Star

Nobody knows the junior hockey scene better than Frank. He's doing more NHL work now, with a light touch combined with a sensitivity for his subjects. His contacts are among the most reliable around.

Dan Proudfoot, Toronto Globe and Mail

Dan's stories on Team Canada and its mutinies were examples of first-rate journalism. Now he's a free-lance ace.

Milt Dunnell, Toronto Star

The best-liked columnist in Canada, Milt has splendid contacts and a delightful style, but he can be abrasive, as the NHL Establishment has often discovered.

Rex MacLeod, Toronto Globe and Mail

Although Rex no longer covers hockey on a regular basis, he is my personal favorite. Nobody is wittier, more insightful, nor more readable. He can handle a column as well as a game story with equal ease and readability. The pity is that he's been grossly underplayed by his paper. At the very least he should be a regular columnist.

Jim Proudfoot, Toronto Star

Jim is a serious columnist with an eye toward improving the game as well as a keen ear for dialogue. There are few more intelligent commentators around.

Jim Taylor, Vancouver Sun

Hard, hard, hard, and very, very funny; maybe the best of his kind on the beat.

Dick Beddoes, Toronto Globe and Mail

Although Dick tends to be too cutsey at times and occasionally appears to be in the NHL's pocket, there's no denying that he *can* write powerfully and humorously when he's on.

Jim Kearney, Vancouver Sun

Day in and day out, Kearney produces one of the most readable columns in North America. Neither the Canucks nor the Blazers have escaped his clever pen.

Alan Malamud, Los Angeles Herald-Examiner

Even though the Kings aren't worth watching half the time, Malamud is worth reading all the time. Ask Jack Kent Cooke.

John MacFarlane

Author of *The Death of Hockey*, this Toronto-based editor has a great love for the game and a greater love for words. Trouble is, he doesn't write enough.

Ira Gitler

A New York free lance, Ira has the advantage of being an active amateur player, which gives him a dual perspective. He writes well and has a dandy sense of humor to go with it.

Trent Frayne, Toronto Star

Unfortunately, Frayne is a general feature writer and handles hockey rarely. But he has been at it for years, and his interviews can cut to the quick. Ask Al Eagleson, whom Frayne once withered in a *Maclean's* magazine article.

Scott Young, Toronto Globe and Mail

Like Frayne, he's been off hockey on a regular basis, but he stays close to the game and has led some classic battles against Clarence Campbell and the NHL.

Wayne Overland, Edmonton Journal

He has some of the best inside information about the WHA and knows how to make it readable.

Tim Burke, Montreal Gazette

Having had a solid background covering general assignment stories, Burke brings an important additional quality to his work. He is fearlessly impartial and one of the finest interviewers to grace the sports pages. He frequently has been the best hockey writer on the entire beat.

Reyn Davis, Winnipeg Free Press

Another highly knowledgeable WHA scribe who occasionally has become too enamored of the home team. He writes well and is a good reporter.

Vic Grant, Winnipeg Tribune

Sardonic when the episode merits such treatment, this chap has written some classic columns that too few people have seen.

Jim Kernahan, Toronto Star

The WHA has created a lot of opportunities for a lot of people. In Jim's case it was a chance to write hockey. He has made the most of that and currently is one of the better young men on the beat.

Bob Mellor, Ottawa Journal

A first-rate columnist who produced the best little inside book about hockey players' greed and the birth of the WHA. It's called *Left Wing and a Prayer*.

Jack Matheson, Winnipeg Tribune

Very funny, very sharp machete. Not to be trified with.

Gary Ross, Toronto Life

A very clever free lance who edited the Toronto Toros program magazine and made it the best in hockey.

Frank Bertucci, Philadelphia Free Lance

This pleasant young man emerged from out of nowhere to become star of the short-lived weekly, *The Hockey Spectator*, and has since written some excellent magazine articles.

Chuck Newman, Philadelphia Inquirer

A no-nonsense type who has managed appropriately to twit the Establishment. He recently left the hockey beat.

Earl McRae, The Canadian Magazine

His player profiles have, over the years, been the most entertaining on either side of the border.

Mark Mulvoy, Sports Illustrated

Having overcome his earlier Boston bias, Mulvoy has become one of the more respected analysts of the game and a damn good writer.

Shirley Fischler, Co-Editor, Action Sports Hockey Magazine

Many women have tried to write about hockey, but none has the feel for it that Shirley has. In this case it's not even close.

23

The Best Episode

ONE AFTERNOON DURING THE 1973–74 SEASON, rookie Denis Potvin of the New York Islanders missed his team's bus, which was leaving from Long Island for a short trip to Philadelphia where the Islanders were to play the Flyers that night.

Instead of trying to find alternate means of transportation to Philadelphia, Potvin, who was earning approximately $130,000 a year, chose to remain at home. That night his club was badly beaten by Philadelphia.

Potvin, an articulate, intelligent young man, offered several alibis for his deportment. He explained that a snowfall had deterred him from hitchhiking and that he didn't know his way around the area well enough to seek an alternate means of transportation from New York to Philadelphia. His rhetoric was considerably better than his reliability.

Whatever his reasons, this much was clear: Potvin really didn't try all that hard to reach Philadelphia and help his club although he had more than six hours in which to try. It also is evident that Potvin symbolizes the wealthy, highly pampered young player who is a startling contrast to the hard-bitten aces of yesteryear.

When Potvin stayed home on Long Island that day, several hockey commentators remarked, "Eddie Shore would never have done a thing like that." They were right because Eddie Shore once nearly killed himself in order to reach his hockey club after missing a train. And that's why it's true when they say, "They don't make hockey players like that anymore."

On January 2, 1929, the Boston Bruins took the night train to Montreal for a National Hockey League game with the Montreal Maroons the following evening. As the Pullman slowly rolled away from the platform, Boston manager Art Ross walked through the sleeping car, counting his players. When Ross reached the last berth he realized that one of them—All-Star defenseman Eddie Shore—was missing.

"Mr. Ross didn't know it," said Shore, "but I was running down the station platform trying to jump on the last car of the train. I didn't make it and had just missed the train because my taxi had been tied up in a traffic accident coming across town."

Shore was determined to reach Montreal in time for the game, however. The Bruins already were shorthanded because of injuries, and Shore was well aware of the $500 fine Ross levied against any player who missed a road-trip train. He first checked the train schedules and found that the next express wouldn't reach Montreal until after game time. He tried the airlines and was told all plane service had been canceled because of a sleet storm. He then decided to rent an automobile but changed his mind when a wealthy friend offered him his limousine and a chauffeur.

At 11:30 P.M. Shore and the chauffeur headed north on a 350-mile trip over icy, snow-blocked New England mountains. It was sleeting, and there were no paved superhighways, no road patrols, no sanders.

The chauffeur drove through the storm at three miles an hour. "I was not happy at the rate he was traveling," says Shore, "and I told him so. He apologized and said he didn't have chains and didn't like driving in the winter. The poor fellow urged me to turn back to Boston."

At that point the car skidded to the lip of a ditch. Shore took over at the wheel and drove to an all-night service station where he had tire chains put on. By then the sleet storm had thickened into a blizzard. Snow caked either side of the lone windshield wiper, and within minutes the wiper blade had frozen solidly to the glass. "I couldn't see out the window," said Shore, "so I removed the top half of the windshield."

His face was exposed to the blasts of the icy wind and snow but he still managed to see the road. At about 5:00 A.M., in the mountains of New Hampshire, "we began losing traction. The tire chains had worn out."

Slowly, Shore eased the car around a bend in the road where he could see the lights of a construction camp flickering. He awakened a gas station attendant there, installed a new set of chains, and weaved on. "We skidded off the road four times," he says, "but each time we managed to get the car back on the highway again."

The second pair of chains fell off at 3:00 the next afternoon. This time Shore stopped the car and ordered the chauffeur to take over the wheel. "I felt that a short nap would put me in good shape," he said. "All I asked of the driver was that he go at least twelve miles an hour and stay in the middle of the road."

But the moment Shore dozed off, the chauffeur lost control of the big car, and it crashed into a deep ditch. Neither Shore nor the chauffeur nor the car suffered any damage, so Shore hiked a mile to a farmhouse for help. "I paid eight dollars for a team of horses," says Shore, "harnessed the horses, and pulled the car out of the ditch. We weren't too far from Montreal, and I thought we'd make it in time if I could keep the car on the road."

He did, and at 5:30 P.M. Shore drove up to the Windsor Hotel, the Bruins headquarters. He staggered into the lobby and nearly collapsed. "He was in no condition for hockey," said Ross. "His eyes were bloodshot, his face frostbitten and windburned, his fingers bent and set like claws after gripping the steering wheel so long. And he couldn't walk straight. I figure his legs were almost paralyzed from hitting the brake and clutch."

Nevertheless Shore ate a steak dinner, his first real meal in twenty-four hours, and refused the coach's orders to go to sleep. "I was tired all right," Shore said, "but I thought a twenty- or thirty-minute nap would be enough, then I'd be set to play."

An hour later Dit Clapper and Cooney Weiland of the Bruins entered Shore's room and shook him gently. Nothing happened. They rolled him over the bed and onto the floor. Still nothing happened. Weiland filled several glasses with water and poured them over Shore's face. This time he woke up and immediately insisted on playing.

Ross didn't want him to. "I knew how durable he was," the coach said, "but there's a limit to human endurance. I finally decided to let him get on the ice, but at the first sign of sleepwalking I'd send him to the dressing room. I had to worry about him being groggy. What if he got hit hard and wound up badly hurt?"

The game was rough and fast. The powerful Maroons penetrated Boston's defense often, but Shore always helped repulse them. Once he smashed Hooley Smith to the ice with a vicious body check and drew the game's first penalty. Ross considered benching him at this point but changed his mind. When the penalty had elapsed, Shore jumped on the ice and appeared stronger than ever. Shortly before the halfway point in the second period, he skated behind his net to retrieve the puck. He faked one Montreal player, picked up speed at center ice, and swerved to the left when he reached the Maroons' blue line. He sped around the last defenseman and shot. "I would say I was fifteen feet out to the left," Shore recalled. "I can remember exactly how my shot went. It was low, about six inches off the ice, and went hard into the right corner of the net." The time of the goal was 8:20 of the second period. The Bruins led, 1–0.

Shore still showed no signs of his ordeal during the third period (he had another two-minute penalty), and almost twenty-four hours after he had chased the train down the North Station platform the final buzzer sounded. Apart from the two penalties Shore had played the entire game without relief, and what's more, had scored the only goal of the game. Coach Ross never fined him for missing the train.

Part Five

Fischler's Worst

24

The All-Dirtiest-Toughest Team

THE DIFFERENCE BETWEEN a dirty hockey player and a tough hockey player is about the same as the difference between sleet and snow. There is practically no difference. What is dirty play to one viewer is nothing more than tough play to another.

When Bobby Clarke of the Philadelphia Flyers skates against the Montreal Canadiens the Montreal coach invariably labels Clarke a dirty player. "But," said a member of the Canadiens, "if Clarke was on our team, we wouldn't call him dirty, we'd call him a good, tough player."

As a result, I make little distinction between the two unless a player such as a Jean Beliveau is so impeccably clean—in spirit if not always in fact—that he can *only* be called tough, and rarely dirty.

My All-Dirtiest-Toughest Team covers every hockey era, but special emphasis is placed on the post-1930 era, since my information about pre-1930 ruffians was gathered by research and not firsthand viewing. I'm not *that* old.

In evaluating the list, the reader must bear in mind that toughness and dirty play are relative to the era in which the players performed. There is absolutely no question in my mind that the contemporary players were pussycats compared with those who played in the preexpansion post–World War II era.

Likewise, I am convinced that those who skated in major leagues during the "prehistoric" era—1910–20—were the toughest and dirtiest players of all. A man who played during that and subsequent eras, Frank Boucher, bears out this point.

"Games were tougher," said Boucher, "and blood flowed even more freely then."

Boucher recalled the night when Hall of Famer Jack Adams, playing for Toronto, was carved up by the Montreal Wanderers so freely that "he came out looking like the loser of a saber duel at Stuttgart."

Adams was taken to Montreal General Hospital, where his sister happened to be working as a nurse in the admitting room. "Jack," said Boucher, "was so battered and bloodied that she didn't recognize her own brother until she recorded his name at the admitting desk."

Later, the wounded player dismissed suggestions that he was the victim of a wanton gang attack. "It wasn't an unusually tough game," said Adams. "When you got cut, you skated to the boards where the trainer sloshed off the blood with a sponge he kept in a bucket and patched you up with a slice of adhesive tape. That night most of my tape must have sweated off."

With that in mind, I present Fischler's All-Dirtiest-Toughest Team:

Eddie Shore (NHL, 1926–40)

No big-league hockey player came closer to killing an opponent in a game than Shore, a Boston Bruins defenseman who had 978 stitches laced over 80 wounds on his torso.

Shore almost killed Toronto Maple Leafs forward Ace Bailey during a game at Boston Garden in 1933. During a particularly bloody battle, Shore checked Bailey, a generally peaceful man, from behind. Bailey's head struck the ice, and he was carried off with a cerebral concussion. For several days Bailey teetered between life and death in a Boston hospital. He eventually recovered but never played hockey again.

The fact that Shore wantonly charged a peaceful man like Bailey—apparently Shore mistook Bailey for another Leaf—while Bailey had his back turned and was totally unprepared for the blow, and damn near killed him, puts Shore at the top of the list.

Shore eventually got his comeuppance years later when he started a fight with Phil Watson of the Rangers. Watson's teammate Murray Patrick intervened and flattened Shore for the count. Patrick had once been amateur heavyweight champion of Canada.

Ted Lindsay (NHL, 1944–65)

Lindsay was equally potent with his stick or his dukes, depending on the occasion. During a game between Boston and Lindsay's Detroit Red Wings in 1951 Lindsay and Bill Ezinicki of the Bruins dueled with their sticks and then exchanged punches. Ezinicki lost one tooth and needed nineteen stitches to close assorted wounds.

"It was a case of self-survival," said Lindsay. "He had hit me over the head after the whistle and cut me at the hairline, so I tapped him back. Then he dropped his stick and his gloves, so we ended up in a fight."

Lindsay's flailing stick was used as often as an intimidating device as it was for scoring. He is personally credited with running at least one player out of the NHL with his menacing tactics. Some critics charged that Lindsay was tough only when his powerful linemate Gordie Howe was around.

"I interpret toughness with ability to back up any situation which may arise," said former Montreal Canadiens manager Frank Selke, Sr. "I cannot place Lindsay in this category because he is mean and quick with his stick but cannot back it up with his dukes."

The majority opinion had it the other way. Before he died, former Toronto Maple Leafs president Stafford Smythe said of Lindsay: "He is tough because he is dirty!"

Leo Labine (NHL, 1951–62)

As a member of the Boston Bruins Labine made a policy of head-hunting the superstars, especially Maurice "Rocket" Richard. He nearly killed Richard one night, blindsiding him with a combination knee to the groin and crosscheck to the head. Richard was carried unconscious from the ice but later returned to score the winning goal.

Labine could fight with his fists but like Lindsay was notorious for his quick stick, usually waved around an opponent's mouth. "I don't know anybody who likes to eat wood," said Labine, "unless he's a beaver."

Unlike many marauders Labine was as terrifying with his tongue as he was with his stick. One night a piqued Rocket Richard jammed a butt end of his stick into Labine's ribs. Leo barked: "Look, Rocket, you've got thirty-two teeth. Do you want to try for sixteen?"

Labine had several bloody run-ins—parting the scalp of Chicago's Gus Mortson with his stick, trading punches with tough Tod Sloan, and fencing with Richard.

In his old age Labine mellowed. One night in Toronto Eric Nesterenko then of the Maple Leafs broke a hockey stick over Labine's head. "You shouldn't do such things," said Labine. "You'll get a penalty!"

Gordie Howe (NHL, 1946–71; WHA, 1973–present)

Dozens of players, coaches, and managers have branded Howe as the greatest *and* dirtiest player of all time. With surgical precision Howe has used his stick blade against the most formidable opponents. Once, he nearly removed Ranger defenseman Lou Fontinato's ear. Another time he bashed in Fontinato's nose.

"Howe," said Phil Watson, ex-Rangers coach and more recently Vancouver Blazers manager, "gets away with murder. Cross-checks, high-sticks, the works. He's been doing it for years."

Former teammate Ted Lindsay was one of the few—besides Gordie himself—to defend the Howe style. According to Lindsay it is less than fair to call Howe a dirty hockey player.

"What is dirty?" said Lindsay. "If dirty means protecting yourself, Gordie is dirty. When you're the best, you can't let the other team take chunks of flesh out of you. In other words Gordie has been protecting himself."

When Gordie played in the NHL a poll among managers placed him at the top of the list among "toughest players in the league." More than a decade later, in 1973–74, WHA bosses were saying the same thing.

Fernie Flaman (NHL, 1944–61)

A mean and highly competent defenseman, Flaman once nearly took Ranger Andy Bathgate's eye out with a stick, and another time, almost skewered Camille Henry of the Rangers. "Flaman," said Henry, "was absolute murder to play against."

Although Flaman had a Milquetoast look about him, more than one NHL tough guy confided, "I wouldn't want to come face-fo-face with him in a fight."

Flaman rarely lost his cool, but once former Red Wings coach Jimmy Skinner antagonized him from the bench. Flaman skated over to the Detroit bench and smacked Skinner in the face.

One night in a play-off game against the Canadiens, Flaman lifted Henri Richard of Montreal off the ice with his two hands as Richard was in flight and then hurled the Canadien *back* on the ice in one motion.

"Flaman," wrote Jack Zanger in *Sport* magazine, "was the most dangerous Bruin to tangle with."

Washington Capitals manager Milt Schmidt, who once coached Flaman in Boston, called him "a solid bodychecker who was at his best when things were rough."

Edouard "Newsy" Lalonde (NHL, 1917–22)

According to one veteran hockey writer, Lalonde "spilled enough corpuscles to gratify any blood bank on the continent."

Prior to formation of the NHL, Lalonde played in various Canadian pro leagues. His clashes with "Bad" Joe Hall, who later became a teammate on the Canadiens, were studies in jungle brutality, but Newsy never reserved his venom for Hall.

Once, Newsy bashed Hall across the head with his stick, opening an eight-stitch wound. The next time they met, Hall crashed Lalonde so hard Newsy required ten stitches for his wounds.

In another match Lalonde hit Odie Cleghorn viciously enough to inspire Odie's brother Sprague to charge across the rink and smash Newsy across the forehead with his stick. The blow just barely missed Lalonde's eye, and he required twelve stitches to close that gaping wound.

"Without question," said Dick Beddoes of the *Toronto Globe and Mail*, "Lalonde could buckle a swash with any ruffian alive."

Tony Leswick (NHL, 1945–58)

If you were to take the trouble to ask each NHL player during the late forties or early fifties for his opinion of little Tony Leswick, the reply would be "pest" or any number of synonyms thereof.

Ted Lindsay, who was Leswick's teammate after Tony was traded from the Rangers to the Red Wings in 1941, liked to greet Leswick with the observation, "You little toad!"

Leswick was little (five feet, six inches; 160 pounds) and he was tough. He usually took on bigger men and frequently lost but always came back for more. Once, rugged Howie Meeker of the Maple Leafs grappled with Leswick, lifted Tony about the waist, and dispatched him to the ice with a thud. The unconscious Ranger was taken to the infirmary, revived, and eventually returned to the game with a turbanlike bandage swathing his head.

"Tough Tony," as New York fans liked to call him, also was dirty, nasty, sneaky; you name it, that's what they called him. "He was the chippiest bloke in the league," said former teammate Don Raleigh.

Toronto defenseman Garth Boesch put it another way: "Leswick would get under your arms and between your legs. He'd annoy the life out of you."

His style was similar to Leo Labine's. He'd use his tongue as effectively as his stick. "Tony would get up close and laugh at his opponents," said former teammate Nick Mickoski. "He'd do anything to get under their skin. Once, when I played against him, we went into the corner and he winked at me, like we were good friends. I let up for a second and then, *wham!* He knocked me right out of the play."

Some of Leswick's more notable targets were Jean Beliveau, Bill Ezinicki, and Maurice "Rocket" Richard. The Rocket once bluntly summed up his feeling about Leswick's decorum this way: "I have nothing good to say about Tony Leswick."

Carol "Cully" Wilson (NHL, 1919–27)

The post–World War I era produced a large number of brutalized skaters who would think nothing of shoving a stick down an enemy's throat and often tried it. Cully Wilson was one of them.

In 1925, when Wilson was playing for the Calgary Tigers, he cross-checked Dick Irvin's teeth into his tongue. When Irvin recovered he knocked Wilson cold, using his stick as a bludgeon.

Wilson's most memorable battle has long been regarded as hockey's most private fight and symbolized the ferocity of the old-time game.

It was 1917 and Wilson had been feuding with Cy Denneny, a star with the Ottawa Senators. Their running battle had extended through a whole season without noticeable result, and both players were thirsting for blood.

They realized that a full-scale brawl during a regular-season game might be damaging to their respective teams as well as bring suspensions upon themselves, so they waited until an exhibition All-Star game was to be played on non-NHL turf in Cleveland.

"The two of them knew," said hockey historian Bill Roche, "that they would be free from fines and suspensions, since the NHL had no supervision over the game."

The match was played in Cleveland's old Elysium rink, and according to witnesses, it was one of the most vicious ever to take place on or off the ice. Hall of Famer Frank Nighbor, who was there at the time and who had played in hundreds of games, called it "the hardest and longest fight" he had seen.

"Neither the rink nor the city police were inclined to interfere," said Roche. "The result was a draw in what was hockey's most thoroughly private bout."

Lou Fontinato (NHL, 1954–63)

Nicknamed "Leapin' Louie" because of his antics whenever a referee whistled him off the ice, Fontinato is more remembered for the bouts he lost—especially the decision to Gordie Howe—than those he won.

Muscular and fearless, Fontinato made the previously passive Rangers a respectable team in 1955 by beating up on the opposition large (Jean Beliveau) and small (Henri Richard). Louie knew every dirty trick in the book and once went public when a New York newspaper had him give photographic demonstrations of hockey's illegal play. Fontinato gladly complied. Louie's last NHL years were spent in Montreal.

His enemies were numerous. One of them, Bert Olmstead, once reportedly stabbed Fontinato with the point of his stick and sidelined the New York defenseman. When Louie returned to action he pursued Olmstead all over the ice and finally nailed him with a death-defying crosscheck that nearly severed Olmstead's head from his neck.

Another constant foe was Vic Stasiuk of the Bruins. In March, 1958, they were sharing the penalty box at Boston Garden when several fans—friends of Stasiuk's—taunted Fontinato until finally in a rage he took out after them. Boston police finally stopped the riot and pressed charges against Fontinato and some spectators. Stasiuk was a witness against Fontinato in the court proceedings.

Louie never forgave Stasiuk for that. Long after the episode the Bruins and Rangers embarked on a twenty-four-game European exhibition tour. The games meant nothing but still Fontinato and Stasiuk kept at each other. "I remember one game," said a Ranger, "when Vic was playing with three sore ribs. Fontinato could have given him a break, under the circumstances, and eased up. He didn't, though."

Fontinato's career as a Canadien was prematurely ended in 1963 when Vic Hadfield checked him into the end boards. Louie broke his neck and never regained proper use of it.

George "Red" Sullivan (NHL, 1949–61)

Never renowned as a fighter, the lightweight Sullivan was a forechecking specialist for the Bruins, Black Hawks, and later the Rangers, who used his stick in every possible manner.

He completely disregarded the unwritten rule that goaltenders are off limits when it comes to mugging; and as a result, Sullivan frequently pursued and pummeled Montreal's wandering netminder, Jacques Plante.

Many of Sullivan's less-than-clean techniques were neatly subtle, except to the victim. Red was most notorious for his habit of "kicking skates," a method of dumping an opponent by allowing him to move in front of you in the corners, then kicking the back of his heel. The usual reaction is to fall on one's head.

If the victim survives, as did defenseman Doug Harvey of the Canadiens, the assailant is in trouble, big trouble. Harvey vividly remembered how Sullivan had nailed him. "It got so," said Harvey, "that there was no defense against it except spearing. I don't like it but I don't like to be taken either."

Harvey finally caught up to Sullivan on Madison Square Garden ice and nearly killed him with a plunge of his stick in Red's stomach. "Sully was cutting for the goal," said teammate Andy Bathgate, "when Harvey shoved his stick in Red's gut. It looked like Harvey was using a fixed bayonet."

Sullivan collapsed on the ice and was removed to the hospital, where an emergency operation was performed on a ruptured spleen. A Catholic priest administered last rites. The operation was successful and left Sullivan with a souvenir forty-five-inch scar across the stomach.

"I thought I was going to die," said Sullivan.

25

The Two Classic Chokes

C-H-O-K-E IS THE DIRTIEST WORD in hockey.

Up until the seventies it was heretical even to allude to a hockey team or player as a choker. But the New York Rangers made "choke" a respectable term simply by choking so many times during the coaching reign of Emile Francis from 1965 through the present that by 1974 not only was it possible to discuss the art of getting the apple with a Ranger but New York newspaper headline writers freely referred to the Rangers as the "Broadway Chokers."

The modern Rangers, however, were amateurs when it came to choking compared with past NHL clubs, including an earlier New York club. Compared with the Detroit Red Wings of 1941–42 and the 1958–59 Rangers, the contemporary chokers just couldn't hold an apple to them.

By far the classics of them all were the Red Wings of 1941–42 because they had the Stanley Cup in their grasp, having won the first three games of the final series against the Toronto Maple Leafs. *But they then did something no other NHL team has done in more than seventy-five years of Stanley Cup competition*—they lost the next four Cup final games in a row and thereby blew a world championship. There has never been a choke like it before or since.

The 1958–59 Rangers club had a comfortable lead in the race for a play-off berth in the last month of the season. Then they fell apart like a house of cards and finally lost their play-off berth on the final night of the season under extraordinary circumstances. It was by far the worst choke during a regular season.

What made these two teams so unique, so collapsible? Consider the circumstances that follow:

Detroit Red Wings, 1941–42

World War II was in full fire when manager Conn Smythe of the Maple Leafs and Jack Adams of the Red Wings were putting the finishing touches on what they hoped would be major hockey powers.

Smythe had made much more progress than Adams. The Leafs revolved around two players, center Syl Apps, Sr., and goalie Walter "Turk" Broda. Apps was big, fast, clean, and durable, literally the All-Canadian Boy. The pudgy Broda often appeared too clumsy to be efficient, but he was at his best in the clutch. Their leading goal scorer was an exciting shooter named Gordie Drillon, and their defense was anchored by a pair of behemoths, Wilfred "Bucko" McDonald and Rudolph "Bingo" Kampman.

How the Red Wings managed to clamber up to the finals remained a mystery to those who had not followed Jack Adams' club closely in the last months of the season. True, the Wings did finish a distant fifth, *fifteen points behind* the Maple Leafs, and were nearly ousted in the first play-off round by the Canadiens. But Detroit-watchers knew that the Red Wings had jelled in the last month from an inept, loosely coordinated team into a crisp winner. They proved it by upsetting the Bruins two games to none in the Stanley Cup semifinals. Utilizing bruising defensemen such as Jimmy Orlando and Jack Stewart, they intimidated the enemy; and practicing a completely new offensive technique—the Detroit forwards would skim the puck into the opposition zone and then race after it rather than pass their way in—they befuddled the traditional-minded foe.

"We may not be the greatest hockey club in the world," said Adams, "but we're loaded with fighting heart. And if there's anything that wins championships, it's just that!"

Despite the obvious superiority of the Leafs—on paper—a subtle air of anxiety trickled forth from parts of the Toronto camp. It was due partly to the Leafs' continuous inability to win the Stanley Cup as well as a suspicion that the Red Wings had the equipment to go all the way. Coach Day himself betrayed a certain anxiety when he labeled the Red Wings "a bunch of hoodlums." Major Conn Smythe, who had completed training and was preparing to leave Canada with his army group for Europe, surveyed the scene and delivered an uncharacteristically gloomy view of the series even before it had begun.

"Don't underestimate this Detroit club," warned Smythe. "They can skate, and they're going to run at us. Unless we match them check for check and stride for stride, we're going to be in trouble."

Right from the opening face-off, Adams sent his speedy skaters on their mission: Toss the puck in and dash after it, forecheck the Leafs into errors. "It was not pretty hockey," said Stanley Cup historian Henry Roxborough, "but it was effective."

It was so effective that the normally poised Toronto skaters fumbled their way around the rink like battle-weary warriors. The Red Wings' harassment tactics worked on two levels, physical and mental. Tough Jimmy Orlando handed out several thudding body checks and sent young Bob Goldham bleeding to the bench after clobbering him in the head with his stick. Don "the Count" Grosso scored twice for Detroit, and the jubilant Red Wings skated off with a 3–2 upset triumph.

Anticipating his imminent departure for Europe, Major Smythe walked into the silent Leafs' dressing room and sensed despair wherever he turned. "I'm worried about this club," he told his aide Frank Selke. "It's going to be quite a job for Hap to straighten them out."

But the Maple Leafs were only one game down in a best-of-seven series, and they had lost by only one goal. Surely the next match, at Maple Leaf Gardens on April 7, would revitalize them. But it didn't.

Before the second game had even started, manager Adams disregarded the cautionary policy adapted by his colleagues and openly predicted that his Red Wings would win the Stanley Cup in six games. Nothing that happened in the second game indicated that he was wrong, except the chance that Detroit might require fewer games than six.

Toronto fans were transfixed as they watched the Red Wings skate away with a 4–2 win. Grosso again scored twice, and teammates Mud Bruneteau and Jim Brown each tallied once. The beleaguered Leafs were able to get scores from Sweeney Schriner and Wally Stanowski, but the big guns of Apps and Drillon were strangely silent. Even worse, the usually reliable Bucko McDonald was proving to be especially vulnerable on defense when the Detroiters tried their new skate-and-run style.

On April 9 Motor City fans flocked to Olympia Stadium with glee to see whether what they had heard and read about their club was on the level. At first they thought it all was a joke. Toronto's Lorne Carr put two shots past goalie Johnny Mowers in no time at all, and the Leafs appeared to be in control for the first time in the series. Then the Wings skimmed the puck into the Toronto zone, and the Leafs backliners began falling over themselves trying to keep up with the Detroit sprinters. Before the period had ended, Gerry Brown and Joe Carveth had been set up for scores by Detroit defenseman Eddie Bush. The fact that center Sid Abel had retired with a badly bruised cheek seemed to inspire them to even greater efforts.

Bush proceeded to organize goals by Pat McReavy and Syd Howe; then he added one himself, and the underdog Detroiters suddenly found themselves favored to capture the play-offs in an incredible four straight games. It was easy to understand the logic behind such talk. The usually reliable Drillon had been completely defused and had gone for seven play-off games without scoring. Needled by Bush and Orlando, Broda played his worst game of the series, and McDonald, the former Red Wing, was skating in mud on the Toronto defense. "You got the idea," wrote Vern DeGeer in the *Toronto Globe and Mail*, "that it was all over but the shouting."

Certainly everyone in Toronto thought so, and they heaped their abuse on coach Hap Day. "Smythe never should have allowed [coach] Dick Irvin to go to Montreal," said one fan. "Day can't handle this club."

And so it went. "They hooted Day's name," wrote Canadian writer Ron McAllister, "and told him to go home. He'd never been a player or a coach or a referee; he was just a stumblebum who didn't know anything."

Quitting in the face of defeat had never been Day's style, and he was not about to start. He coolly pondered the situation, seeking answers to the question of why his machine wasn't functioning the way it should. At last he thought he had the solution, but to be sure he phoned Smythe, who was stationed in Petawawa, Ontario. Conn endorsed the plan, as did Selke, although it was very possibly the most daring plan ever tried in a championship sports series anywhere.

Day benched his ace scorer Gordie Drillon and his veteran defenseman Bucko McDonald. That in itself was startling enough, but Hap then revealed that they would be replaced by the most unlikely players imaginable. Drillon's substitute was Don Metz, kid brother of Nick Metz, who had scored only two goals all season and who had not played for about two weeks. McDonald was replaced by raw rookie, Ernie Dickens, who had played only ten NHL games in his life.

In Detroit the move was interpreted as panic of the highest order. Every correspondent covering the series predicted a quick demise for the Toronto club, and a record 13,694 fans turned out to see the Red Wings do the honors. Apart from the dramatic benching of Drillon and McDonald, Day attempted to explore all avenues of hope, including a letter he had received from a fourteen-year-old girl.

Just before the game, Day walked into the Toronto dressing room and read the letter to his players. The young girl expressed her conviction that the Leafs really were capable of rallying to win the Stanley Cup. Somehow her belief actually inspired as hard-bitten a warrior as Day, and when he read the letter he oozed with such conviction that the Toronto players were similarly affected. A few seconds after Day had finished his reading, old pro Sweeney Schriner clambered off his bench and said, "Don't worry about this one, Skipper, we'll win this one for the little girl." Then Billy Taylor shouted, "We're not licked yet!"

First Mud Bruneteau and then Sid Abel scored for the Red Wings, and with the game more than half over, Detroit held a commanding 2–0 lead. Mowers seemed to have the Red Wings' net boarded up for the night, and the fans in Olympia could almost taste the Stanley Cup champagne. There was only one problem—the Maple Leafs forgot to quit.

Toronto needed one goal to ignite their frozen attack, and they finally got it at 13:54 of the middle period when Bob Davidson took relays from Pete Langelle and Johnny McCreedy to beat Mowers. They were beginning to warm up and within two minutes they were hot. Taylor moved the puck to Schriner, who lateraled to Lorne Carr. Carr brought the score to 2–2, and it stayed that way through the end of the second period.

The Leafs' rally seemed to arouse the Red Wings to new strength in the third period, and despite Broda's courageous display, Carl Liscombe lifted Detroit into the lead again at 4:18 of the third. The screams of delight that reverberated off the walls of Olympia were frightening, because the fans believed that Liscombe's goal had applied the *coup de grâce* to Hap Day's stunned skaters. But the Leafs seemed to possess a persistence about them that would not tolerate defeat. Before the fans had calmed themselves over Liscombe's goal, Apps roared into Red Wing territory and delivered a smoking shot that beat Mowers. Then with seven minutes and fifteen seconds remaining in the period, Apps and Don Metz collaborated on passes to Nick Metz, who fooled the Detroit goalie. Broda held fast, and Toronto pulled off an astonishing 4–3 triumph. The first of the choke had taken place.

The realization that they had come so close to the Stanley Cup and then allowed it to elude them had a disturbing effect on several Detroit players even before the final buzzer sounded. This inability to accept defeat was to have a far-reaching effect on the Red Wings and their Stanley Cup future.

Not long after Nick Metz had scored what was to be the game's winning goal, Wings defenseman Eddie Wares was handed a misconduct penalty by referee Mel Harwood. Instead of accepting the decision, Wares ignored Harwood's command and then insulted the official by handing him a hot-water bottle he obtained from the Detroit bench. Wares eventually skated to the penalty box, but not before Harwood had added a $50 fine to his sentence.

By then Jack Adams was livid, and he virtually exploded when Harwood gave Detroit another penalty for having too many men on the ice. Grosso was designated to antagonize Harwood, dropping his gloves and stick in front of the embattled referee. Harwood replied with a $25 fine.

The game finally continued to its conclusion, and all would have been well had Adams not decided to resume hostilities with the referee. The Detroit boss leaped over the sideboards and charged at Harwood, hurling blows at him until linemen Don McFadyen and Sammy Babcock intervened—accompanied by the local police. One spectator taking all this in with consummate interest was NHL president Frank Calder. Calder fined Wares and Grosso $100 each, and Adams was suspended indefinitely.

As the teams returned to Toronto for the fifth game, at Maple Leaf Gardens on April 14, speculation mounted over Day's decision about Drillon and McDonald. Benching the veterans for one game was all right, but surely he wasn't going to try it again.

Day daringly answered the question a day before the game when he announced that he had still another ploy up his sleeve. He was promoting nineteen-year-old left wing Gaye Stewart to the Maple Leafs, although the rookie was less than a year out of junior hockey. Stewart was to replace Hank Goldup, a three-year NHL veteran.

Few could interpret precisely what effect Adams' suspension would have on the Red Wings. The Detroit high command decided that veteran Ebbie Goodfellow, who was no longer useful as a player, would coach the team in Adams' absence. The question was whether Detroit could recapture the momentum lost at Olympia or whether Day's unique experiment would work again.

The answer was supplied by the chief subject in the experiment, Don Metz. Metz scored a three-goal hat trick, driving the Leafs to a 9–3 shellacking of the Wings. Thus Toronto was down only three games to two, but the sixth game was slated for Olympia Stadium, and the Red Wings were ready to do anything to settle the issue on their home rink.

Led by Count Grosso and Sid Abel, the Detroiters mounted assault after assault in the first period. Their repeated shots seemed to zero in on Broda like tracer bullets, but he was more than equal to the occasion. When Grosso and Abel failed, coach Goodfellow tried to steal a page from Day's battle plan by sending out rookies Gus Giesebrecht and Doug McCaig. But they were not in the class of Don Metz and Ernie Dickens.

Broda's defiant stand in the first period deflated the Red Wings, and before the second period was fifteen seconds old, Don Metz had done it again; a quick shot put Toronto in the lead, and it was followed by goals from Bob Goldham and Billy Taylor. The Leafs, who only a week earlier were teetering on the brink of elimination, had pulled themselves into a 3–3 tie in the series.

One Detroit spectator hurled a dead fish on the ice late in the game.

"That dead fish," wrote Toronto writer Ed Fitkin, "seemed to be symbolic of Detroit fans' reaction to the collapse of their Red Wings."

The collapse had begun with Wares's and Grosso's tantrums late in the fourth game, and it was furthered by Adams' attack on referee Harwood. "The wild outbursts," said historian Roxborough, "did not help the morale of the Detroit players, and neither did the loss of their coach, who had to be replaced by a less experienced leader."

Still, the Red Wings, like the Maple Leafs, had one more chance. The final game was played on the night of April 18, 1942, at Maple Leaf Gardens, where 16,240 spectators, the largest crowd in Canadian hockey history up to that point, came to see what fabric made up the Maple Leafs. They remembered the collapses of the past, and they wondered if it would happen again.

It certainly looked as though the Leafs would blow the duke again as they had in the past. Syd Howe put Detroit ahead, 1–0, and Toronto's attack suddenly fizzled, as it had in the first three games of the set. At one point goalie Mowers blunted the Toronto shots with his team two men short, and Detroit skated out for the third period guarding the 1–0 lead.

The Leafs needed a break, and they got it early in the third period when referee Bill Chadwick whistled Jimmy Orlando into the penalty box for two minutes. Coach Day sent the Schriner line out for the power play instead of Apps and the Metz brothers. "Sweeney was a big man," wrote Charles Coleman, "a fast skater and very nimble in his play."

Never was Schriner more nimble than he was in front of the Detroit net with his Maple Leafs on the brink of defeat. Sweeney awaited the pass, but the puck rolled to him on its side. In order to handle the rubber, Sweeney had to turn his back to the cage. He did just that and rapped the puck past the startled Mowers to tie the score. The Maple Leafs were alive again!

Spectators crumpled programs in excitement; others leaned so far forward in their seats that they jammed their knees into the backs of those in the rows ahead of them. Everyone waited and hoped for the moment when Toronto could pull the string that would drop Detroit out of contention. But they worried about the Red Wings' propensity for coming from behind.

In the next two minutes the Red Wings' forwards attempted to puncture the Maple Leafs' blue-line corps, but Day's "substitutes" came through nobly. Rookies Ernie Dickens and Bob Goldham would not be breached, and Don Metz checked zealously on the forward line.

A whistle was blown, and Day changed squads. He sent young center Pete Langelle on left wing with veteran Bob Davidson and Johnny McCreedy on the right side. Immediately they stormed into Red Wing ice with McCreedy leading the way with a shot on Mowers. The Detroit goalie moved far out of his cage to deflect the drive, but the puck rebounded back into play, and Mowers was stranded away from the gaping net. In a desperate lunge the Detroit defense tried to cover Mowers' abandoned net, but Langelle pounced on the puck like a leopard seizing his prey and smacked it into the cage.

When the thunderous roar of the audience had diminished, Turk Broda knew that it was his game to win. The Maple Leafs were closer to the Stanley Cup than they had been in ten years. Joe Carveth, Carl Liscombe, and Gerry Brown of Detroit's first line tested the Turk with shrapnel, but Broda displayed the brand of goaltending that was to earn him a reputation as the most dependable money goalie in NHL history. After one sortie Turk punted the puck ahead to his defense as Schriner picked up speed at center ice. Sweeney took the pass and scored for the second time in the game. With less than five minutes to play, Toronto was ahead, 3–1.

One man more than any of the thousands in the arena fixed his eyes on the clock as the Maple Leafs battled to retain the lead. It was Conn Smythe, who had been granted permission by his army superiors to leave the Petawawa military base in order to watch his team in their most critical battle since he organized the Toronto hockey club. To Smythe the seconds seemed like hours as the hands on the clock moved toward the finish.

Try as they might, the Red Wings could not secure a bridgehead in Toronto territory. The clock began to tick off the final minute of play, and the 16,240 spectators helped it along with a second-by-second chant until they recited the final "*five . . . four . . . three . . . two . . . one!!*" And the bell sounded ending the series.

In his book *Turk Broda of the Leafs*, Ed Fitkin described the last seconds: "Pandemonium broke loose on the ice and in the stands at the final bell. Every player on the Leaf bench leaped over the boards and rushed out on the ice to grab and hug a teammate, while the crowd roared with the ecstasy of the moment . . . the moment they had waited ten long years to witness.

"Broda, grinning and whooping, was mobbed by every Leaf at the final bell. Young Bob Goldham, who had been a great play-off performer, hugged him enthusiastically and said: 'Guess we showed 'em, Slip! You old sonofagun, you were terrific!' Probably the most excited man on the ice was Captain Syl Apps. Blood streaming from a cut down the side of his nose, Syl dashed to the Leaf bench and said: 'C'mon, Conny, and get the Cup.' "

Never before and never again has a team lost the first three games of a Stanley Cup series and then pulled itself together to win the next four and the championship. "That was a night I shall long remember," said broadcaster Foster Hewitt, who had seen more hockey games than anyone in the world. "It was a thrilling tribute to hockey's outstanding comebacks, a team with the fight to turn a rout into a triumph."

Conn Smythe, who had so often leaped over the sideboards to assail an enemy player or referee, this time vaulted the timbers and marched proudly to center ice, where NHL president Frank Calder awaited him with the gleaming silver trophy. Captain Syl Apps pumped Smythe's hand, and the players congratulated one another; suddenly Goldham realized that his coach was not among them.

Hap Day, the man so bitterly reviled by spectators and the press during the early days of the finals, was watching the proceedings from the sidelines. Goldham spotted his mentor and escorted him to the jubilant throng at center ice. The moment Day stepped on the rink his appearance touched off a tumultuous ovation, as if the Maple Leafs had just won the Stanley Cup again.

For a time it seemed as though the cheering would never stop. The Leafs' dressing room was surrounded by thousands of well-wishers long into the night. It was as though ten years of frustration were finally being released by the Toronto hockey enthusiasts. The celebration didn't really end until late the next day, after a reception at the Royal York Hotel in downtown Toronto.

For months after the Stanley Cup finals hockey experts analyzed the arresting Toronto triumph, trying to ascertain precisely what had brought about victory when defeat seemed so imminent.

One theory had it that Red Wings manager Jack Adams had "blown" the series after the fourth game when he erupted at referee Mel Harwood and invited suspension for the remainder of the play-offs. Adams, of course, was able to transmit his strategy to acting coach Ebbie Goodfellow, but his eruption seemed to have a debilitating effect on morale in the Detroit camp. "If the Red Wings had maintained their composure," wrote one critic, "there is no question that they would have kept the edge on Toronto and won the Stanley Cup. In big-league hockey a 'cool' club often can defeat a superior team that panics, as the Red Wings did in April, 1942."

By contrast, Hap Day had remained cool. His awesome benching of Gordie Drillon and Bucko McDonald bore that rare touch of genius, as was proved by Ernie Dickens and Don Metz, the replacements who performed so well under fire. "We couldn't have won the Cup," said captain Apps, "if the Skipper didn't have faith in us. He won the Cup more than anybody."

New York Rangers, 1958–59

In the 1955–56 season, after several depressing years, the Rangers appeared to be skating on a golden river that ultimately would lead to the Stanley Cup. Their high-strung, vitriolic coach, Phil Watson, was blessed with an abundance of young forwards such as Andy Bathgate, Dean Prentice, and Camille Henry who led the Rangers to play-off berths for three straight seasons. In 1957–58 the Rangers finished second, and many experts believed that they were capable of reaching first the following year. While the New Yorkers were finishing second, their Canadian rivals, the Maple Leafs, had wound up in the cellar. Toronto's front office had ordered a full-scale housecleaning, and George "Punch" Imlach was given the job of reorganizing the Leafs as manager and orchestrating them as coach.

Imlach figured that he was at least a season away from producing a big winner, although he remained the supreme optimist from the very start. Watson scoffed at Toronto's chances. Punch, in turn, predicted early in December that the last-place Leafs *would*, in fact, rise up and smite the Rangers, coached by volatile Phil Watson, and finish in a play-off berth.

"Imlach can crow all he wants," laughed Watson. "But it will be the same this year as last. The Rangers will make it, the Leafs won't."

Thus a feud between New York and Toronto that would grow more bitter with each passing month had begun. With a play-off team, Watson was riding high, while Imlach was still struggling, trying to make a winner out of the Maple Leafs. In an attempt to confuse the opposition, one night thoroughly bald Punch started a lineup of five defensemen—Carl Brewer at center, Noel Price at left wing, Bob Baun on the right, and Tim Horton and Al Stanley playing back. But the Leafs were still last in January, and Watson's needles became sharper.

"All the time," Watson snapped, "Imlach is saying, 'I did this and I did that. I've won so many games since I took over.' Before that it was always 'we' or 'those guys.' Always he's predicting what Leafs are going to do. The only crystal ball he's got is on his shoulders. What a beautiful head of skin!"

Although it was not evident to most casual observers, the Maple Leafs *were* shaping up under Imlach. Carl Brewer had developed into a mature rookie defenseman, Johnny Bower had played a solid goal, and youngsters such as Frank Mahovlich and Dick Duff were complementing such diligent and dependable veterans as Bert Olmstead and Allan Stanley.

Punch tried deals wherever possible, using his minor-league experience as a guide. He remembered how Gerry Ehman had scored forty goals for him at Springfield, and he dealt Willie Marshall for Ehman. Placing Ehman on right wing with center Billy Harris and Frank Mahovlich gave Imlach two solid lines; the other was a unit centered by Bob Pulford with Ron Stewart on right wing and Bert Olmstead on the left. As February, 1959, came to a close, the Leafs appeared far from a play-off berth, and speculation about a new Leafs coach was rampant.

One thing was certain: If the Leafs were to make the play-offs, they would have to do so at the expense of one team, Phil Watson's Rangers. Torn by dissension and unnerved by Watson's temper tantrums, the Rangers started to wobble early in March but recovered to defeat Detroit, 4–2, on March 8 at Madison Square Garden. On March 11 the Leafs lost, 6–2, to the Canadiens in Toronto. *Imlach's team was nine points out of fourth.*

The Maple Leafs were dead. Phil Watson thought so; Madison Square Garden Corporation thought so; and the NHL schedule-makers thought so.

The Garden Corporation began printing play-off tickets. The NHL schedule-makers prepared play-off dates for Montreal, Boston, Chicago, and New York, omitting Toronto.

While Watson awaited the play-off clincher, Imlach kept telling himself and his players that there was still time for a miracle. Only two weeks remained, and the staggering Maple Leafs were still a big nine points away from fourth place.

Imperceptible as it was at the time, the turnabout began in Manhattan on Wednesday night, March 11, while the Leafs were losing, 6–2, to the Canadiens in Toronto. On that same night the Black Hawks invaded Madison Square Garden and delivered a 5–3 defeat to Watson's Rangers.

The stage was set for the New Yorkers to deliver their *coup de grâce* to Imlach and his Leafs. On Saturday, March 14, Watson brought his Rangers to Maple Leaf Gardens for the first of a home-and-home series with Toronto. All New York required was a single victory on either night in order to finish the Queen City sextet. The New York victory on Saturday night would give the Rangers a nine-point bulge over Toronto, and with four games remaining on their schedule after that, the Leafs couldn't make up the difference.

Only the most insightful critic would have given Toronto a chance—and then only by the slimmest margin. The Rangers were just short of open rebellion against Watson at the time. He had worked them to exhaustion in practices, and in the process he had tired his lighter forwards such as Camille Henry and Red Sullivan. Once, Watson actually put his team through a full-scale workout immediately after a loss!

Imlach hoped against hope that he could capitalize on the negative

Ranger factors. On the other hand, the New Yorkers had several top professionals, including high-scoring Andy Bathgate, Dean Prentice, Bill Gadsby, and goalie Lorne Worsley. In spite of Watson they wanted the play-off money as much as the Maple Leafs did.

Try as they might, the Rangers could never get themselves untracked on that Saturday night. George Armstrong scored for Toronto at 7:23 of the first period, and Frank Mahovlich got another one for the Leafs at 16:26. Dick Duff scored twice for Toronto in the second period, and Mahovlich collected his second goal in the last period. Final score: Toronto 5, New York 0.

The victory, balm that it was for Imlach, did not torpedo Watson or his Rangers. They never expected a win at Maple Leaf Gardens; even a tie would have been gravy. But on Sunday night, March 15, in New York, Watson *did* expect a victory, the final chop of the guillotine against Imlach and the Leafs.

New York defenseman Bill Gadsby delivered the first blow less than four minutes after the game began, putting the Rangers ahead, 1–0. But Duff and Armstrong rallied Toronto with a pair of goals, and the game soon took on wild proportions. Bathgate tied the match, 2–2, early in the middle period, only to have Mahovlich and Armstrong put Toronto into a 4–2 lead. Then Jimmy Bartlett of the Rangers narrowed it to 4–3 a few minutes before the second period closed.

Imlach nearly crushed his fedora in his palm when big Hank Ciesla tied the contest for New York at 5:37 of the last period, and he almost leaped off the bench when Armstrong put him ahead again at 12:40. But Bower was having an unusually inept night in the Toronto goal, and at 15:21 Red Sullivan scored for the Rangers, and the game was tied once more.

With only four minutes remaining, Watson beseeched his players to concentrate on defense, and they did just as he ordered. At last the Toronto attack seemed to be defused, and Worsley was expected to repulse what long shots were hurled at him from center ice. Watson fixed his eyes on the round time clock hanging from the mezzanine directly across from the Rangers' bench. His calm was restored when he saw that defenseman Gadsby and Harry Howell were throwing a fortress across the New York blue line.

Punch Imlach hoped for a miracle. Then it appeared. Allan Stanley, in his inimitable plodding style, moved the puck away from Bower and toward the Rangers' zone. He passed it to Bert Olmstead on the left. Two more strides, and Olmstead detected Bob Pulford in motion at center ice. The pass was true, but Pulford chose not to bisect the Rangers' defense. Instead, he cracked his wrists and sent a rather ordinary long shot at Worsley. Imlach's hope was that the Rangers' goaltender would deflect it to the corner, where a Toronto player could retrieve it for a close-in play on goal.

With the stunned silence that inevitably follows disaster, the packed crowd at Madison Square Garden sat thunderstruck as Pulford's shot breezed past Worsley's arm, glove, and leg pad. Toronto won the game, 6–5, and pulled to within three points of the Rangers with three games remaining.

Panic descended on New York. Rangers manager Muzz Patrick blasted Worsley, and Watson singled out hard-rock defenseman Lou Fontinato for criticism. Earlier in the season Fontinato had been beaten up in a fight with Gordie Howe of Detroit and had played poorly ever since. "Fontinato was my policeman," Watson lamented. "But he became a changed man since the fight. He went into a shell. I don't know why."

Still, the odds favored the Rangers, who next would play the Bruins on Wednesday night, March 18, at Madison Square Garden. Boston put three goals past Worsley by the five-minute mark of the second period, and when the Rangers appeared to rally, low-scoring Larry Leach of the Bruins beat Worsley on a stoppable drive, and the Rangers went on to lose, 5–3. "If any one player can be singled out for the collapse," said Muzz Patrick, "it's Worsley. I can't understand why he's lost his touch."

Imlach moved on to Montreal with his team for a Thursday-night game against the Canadiens at the Forum. The Boston team had also arrived there for a Saturday-night match, and when Imlach saw Fleming Mackell of the Bruins, he asked about the win over New York. "Watson," said Mackell, "took it as if he was being hit in the head with a mallet. He sank slowly behind the boards, over on their bench. I could see less of him every time I looked."

Imlach's confidence had reached the bursting point. "I told the Boston guys," Imlach wrote in his autobiography, "then, in public, with some of the Leafs listening and grinning, that we were going to play them in the playoffs, because we were going to finish fourth, and they were going to finish second."

But the Leafs were still trailing, and they needed a win over league-leading Montreal. Punch needed another stroke of luck, and he got it. Montreal's Vezina Trophy–winning goalie Jacques Plante was sidelined, and the Canadiens imported raw rookie Claude Pronovost as a replacement. The Rangers brass screamed "Foul," but Pronovost took his spot in Montreal's nets on March 19.

Phil Goyette lifted Montreal into the lead, beating Bower at 12:04 of the first period, but the aroused Leafs rebounded with four straight goals and swept the game, 6–3. For the first time in the season Toronto had won three consecutive games and had pulled to within one point of the

Rangers. Fourth place would not be settled until the final weekend of the season.

Just to make things more difficult for Imlach, Watson finally rallied his club on Saturday afternoon when the Rangers defeated the Red Wings, 5–2, in Detroit. Toronto, three points away from fourth, was to play Chicago on Saturday night and the Red Wings at Olympia in Detroit on Sunday. All the Leafs needed to expire was a loss to the third-place Black Hawks.

The Leafs reacted with the same vigor that they had displayed against the Canadiens and virtually swept Chicago out of the rink. Pulford and Mahovlich scored to give the Leafs a 2–1 lead after two periods; then Stewart, Ehman, and Mahovlich sealed the victory with third-period goals.

On Sunday night, the final night of the season, the Rangers played host to the Montreal Canadiens, a team that had clinched first place and was trying to avoid injuries before the play-offs. Instead of using goalie Claude Pronovost, the Canadiens elected to play substitute goalie Charlie Hodge.

The Rangers opened the game as if they intended to demolish the Canadiens. Within six minutes defenseman Harry Howell had put a long shot past Hodge, and the Madison Square Garden crowd went wild with joy. If the Rangers were to win or if Toronto should lose, New York had the play-off berth. But the Canadiens didn't turn over and die. Dickie Moore and Jean Beliveau got goals in the first period, and Henri Richard added another for Montreal at 6:17 of the third. Trailing 3–1, the Rangers desperately pushed their way into the Canadiens' ice, and Camille Henry scored at 14:38 to make it 3–2, Montreal. Beliveau counterattacked and scored again, and the Rangers lost, 4–2.

The Toronto-Detroit game had started one hour later in Detroit, and the Leafs still needed a victory to beat New York. By the time the final score of the Rangers game was flashed, Toronto was behind, 2–0. The score stayed that way until 2:41 of the second period, when Larry Regan beat Detroit's excellent goalie Terry Sawchuk. Then Bobby Baun tied the game for the Leafs.

Norm Ullman gave Detroit a 3–2 lead, but Brewer and Regan scored for Toronto. Then Marcel Pronovost scored for the Red Wings, and the second period ended with the teams tied, 4–4. In New York's Madison Square Garden the Rangers' dressing room had emptied except for a few lingering players. A friend walked over to trainer Frank Paice and made an offer. "If Detroit holds Toronto," the man said, "you give me a hockey stick."

Downcast Camille Henry overheard the conversation and interrupted. "Hell," snapped Henry, "I'll give you five and buy you a beer to boot!"

In another corner goalie Worsley was telling a newsman how little he

,ought of his coach. "That Watson makes plenty of mistakes himself," said Worsley, "but he's always looking for someone to blame."

General John Reed Kilpatrick, president of the Rangers, sat in the press cage overhanging the mezzanine. He was accompanied by his publicity assistant, Marvin Resnick, and a reporter. They watched the Western Union ticker report the third period of the Maple Leafs–Red Wings game from Detroit. "Let's hope the wire doesn't move until the end of the game," said Resnick. Kilpatrick remained silent. He was thinking of the $90,000 worth of play-off tickets the once-confident Rangers had sold in advance.

The minutes passed but not fast enough to outrace the Maple Leafs. Suddenly the wire machine next to Kilpatrick jerked, and all heads peered at the metal fingers pounding out the news.

It was a score—but for whom, Toronto or Detroit?

One minute earlier there had been a face-off in Maple Leafs zone. Regan cocked his head next to Dick Duff and whispered loud enough for Duff to hear: "Dick, you're going to get the winner. I'm going to give it to you. Just be there."

Regan won the face-off and dipsy-doodled so adroitly through the Red Wings' defense that he reminded onlookers of Max Bentley at his best. But the curly-haired center had skated too far to the side to make a play. Instead, he kept control of the puck and wheeled behind the Detroit net; he saw Duff skating headlong to the goal. Regan's pass was true, and Duff walloped the puck past Sawchuk almost in the same motion. On the Madison Square Garden ticker it read: DUFF, 2:51—TORONTO 5, DETROIT 4.

Kilpatrick turned to Resnick. "It looks bad," he said, and his face was crimson with anger. Morbid silence reigned until twelve minutes had elapsed. Then there was more clicking, perhaps a Detroit goal.

Seconds before the ticker began, Billy Harris had skated into the Detroit zone and skimmed a pass to Bob Baun at the blue line. Baun shot the puck two feet off the ice toward the net. Harris saw it coming and arched his stick as a baseball batter might in attempting a bunt. The puck deflected off the wood and caromed past Sawchuk. The ticker clicked: HARRIS, 14:40. The general said nothing. More minutes passed, and then more clicking: ONE MINUTE TO GO. 30 SECONDS. GAME OVER.

One area of Detroit's Olympia Stadium was bedlam as the Maple Leafs and their small but vocal retinue of well-wishers celebrated the miracle. In its way the occurrence matched the immortal Toronto comeback of 1942. Screaming at the tops of their lungs, the jubilant Leafs trooped into the dressing room and continued to whoop and holler.

Imlach, the man who would never give up, strutted from skater to skater, pumping each hand. "He had the dazed, glazed look of a man who has come through shell-shock," wrote Scott Young in *The Leafs I Knew*. "Bob Pulford broke down in one corner and could not compose himself for a minute or two."

Later, Imlach added: "I feel sorry for Phil Watson. I won't gloat about the man who didn't make it."

Imlach's discretion was not shared by New Yorkers who vilified Watson and his Rangers for their choke. Nobody but nobody would have dreamed that the New Yorkers would fold the way they did.

In his autobiography Imlach offered this retrospective look at the Rangers' fold-up:

"Even a week before the season ended, you could have got a hundred to one against us even making the playoffs. I remember hearing later that Conn Smythe had said to somebody on Toronto's hockey committee, 'What did you get when you got Imlach, a coach or did you get a madman?' This because I kept saying, 'We're gonna make it, we're gonna make it.' They got a madman all right, but they didn't know it at the time."

But the Rangers did, and maybe that, in part, explains why the boys from the Big Apple got the second biggest apple in NHL history.

26

The All-Time Worst Teams

THE WORST TEAMS in major-league hockey are playing today—right now in the NHL and WHA. They are infinitely worse than any teams on my All-time Worst list because contemporary hockey is a shade of its former qualitative self.

Expansion has done it. Expansion and a steadily decreasing talent flow that will only change in the next few years when more American-born players and more Europeans are lured to the North American continent.

In selecting the All-Worst it would be simple to name the California Golden Seals during Charlie Finley's regime; or the New York Islanders in their first year; or the Washington Capitals; or the Kansas City Chiefs. That, however, would not be fair. I am categorically eliminating any post-1967 expansion team from the list and will divide the choices into three eras—pre–World War II, wartime, and postwar.

The worst of all was the Philadelphia Quakers (1930–31); second worst, the New York Rangers (1942–44, two seasons); and third worst, Chicago Black Hawks (1947–51, five seasons). Here are my reasons why:

Philadelphia Quakers

Prior to expansion, a line in the *NHL Record Book* succinctly said it all about the worst team in major-league hockey: *Fewest wins, one season—4, Philadelphia Quakers, 1930–31, 44-game schedule.*

It was the height of irony that Philadelphia's Quakers were owned by a man who almost never lost, former lightweight champion Benny Leonard. Unfortunately for Benny, the Quakers made up for all of his nonice triumphs and then some.

In fact the Quakers had a legacy of losses even before their opening face-off. Leonard originally had bought the club in 1928–29 when it was the Pittsburgh Pirates. Not only did the Pirates lose games with ease, they also lost fans, and in October, 1930, the NHL approved Leonard's request to move the team to Philadelphia.

"The Quakers," said an overenthused Leonard, "are to ice hockey what the Athletics are to baseball."

Well, not quite. The A's were then the world champions. The Quakers had yet to step on the ice. And when they did they slipped and went right on slipping for the rest of the season.

Their goaltender, Joe Miller, was mediocre; the defense was virtually nonexistent, and the only scoring threats were Hib Milks and Gerry Lowrey. All of these minuses jelled on opening night, November 11, 1930, against the Rangers. Philadelphia lost, 3–0.

After losing their first three games the Quakers began to show promise of improving although it later was to prove to be a false promise. They tied Ottawa, 2–2, and finally won their first game on November 25, 1930, defeating Toronto, 2–1. Almost immediately, though, disaster piled on disaster. The Quakers failed to win a single game from November 29, 1930, to January 10, 1931, setting a league record—fifteen straight losses—that still stands.

The Quakers literally could do nothing right, not even get hurt. One night Philadelphia defenseman Stan Crossett was brutally sandwiched between a pair of Detroit defensemen and knocked flying into the air. Crossett was hit so hard he was unconscious *before* he even hit the ice. Ordinarily, a penalty might have been called against the perpetrators but with typical Quakers luck the unconscious Crossett got the penalty. He had accidentally hit one of the Detroit players with his stick as he flew through the air. The referee gave Crossett a five-minute penalty for drawing blood while he was stretched out unconscious on the ice!

Inept as they were, the Quakers never shied away from a good fight. They lost, 8–0, to Boston on Christmas Day, 1930, but came out even in a series of intense brawls that caused officials to send for a battalion of Boston police.

The Quakers scored a moral victory when they returned to Boston for a rematch with the Bruins. This time they held the vastly superior home club to a 3–3 tie. Meanwhile, Leonard was losing money faster than his Quakers were losing hockey games. When the Montreal Canadiens offered him a first-rate defenseman for only $5,000, Benny said thanks-but-no-thanks; NHL hockey in Philadelphia was, for the time being, doomed.

In their final match, the Quakers tied the Canadiens, 4–4, and then disbanded. And rightly so. They had won four games, lost thirty-six, and tied four. Major-league hockey has never suffered so terrible a team since.

New York Rangers

Prior to America's entry into World War II the New York Rangers had fused one of the most powerful clubs the NHL had known. Featuring such high-scorers as Bryan Hextall, Sr., Lynn Patrick, and Phil Watson, the Rangers won the Stanley Cup in 1940 and the Prince of Wales Trophy (first place) during the 1941–42 season.

But armed forces enlistments drained the New York sextet of its best players, and when the 1942–43 campaign began, the Rangers were but a shade of their former powerful selves. In fact not only were they bad, they were ludicrous.

Even before the season began, events were moving from the ridiculous to the absurd. With Jim Henry and Chuck Rayner already in the Canadian Army, the Rangers *did not even have a single regular goaltender with whom to open camp.*

Both club president Lester Patrick and manager Frank Boucher sent an SOS to Ranger scouts advising them to find a goaltender, *any goaltender!* The bird dogs took the advice literally, and when training camp finally opened in Winnipeg a young man named Steve Buzinski skated between the pipes for the Rangers. Never has there been a more unlikely-looking goaltender.

"He was a skinny, scrawny guy," said Boucher, "a little fellow who was the most bowlegged goaltender I ever saw. You could easily shoot a puck between the space created by his legs and his goalie pads."

It took a few days for Boucher to realize just how bad Buzinski was. "Not only was he not a big-league goaltender," the manager lamented, "but he was not a big-league *wartime* goaltender."

One man disagreed. Steve Buzinski. He thought he was gangbusters.

"One night," said former teammate Lynn Patrick, "Steve nabbed a puck that was sailing wide of the net. With all the cockiness in the world he smiled and said, 'Y'know, this is as easy as pickin' cherries from a tree.' A few nights later Buzinski caught another long one and this time threw it into our own net."

Perhaps the most bizarre aspect of Buzinski's brief NHL career was Lester Patrick's affection for him. Lester, hockey's "Silver Fox," was regarded as a superb critic of playing talent. And Patrick thought Buzinski was good, too.

"I think you'll be pleasantly surprised with him," Patrick assured a dubious Boucher.

But the only surprises involved Buzinski's repertoire of strange tricks. There was the night at Maple Leaf Gardens when Steve was knocked to the ice by a Toronto player. "From the bench," said Boucher, "I could see Steve flat on his back. Then he was in a sitting position. Then he was flat on his back again. Lynn Patrick came skating from the goal-mouth pileup to our bench, and he was laughing so hard he was shaking.

" 'You'll never believe this,' said Lynn. 'We thought Steve had been knocked out. We were yelling for a penalty to Davidson for high-sticking. Davidson said he didn't hit him. It was the puck. He got hit in the head with the puck. That's when Steve, lying there cold as a mackerel, sat straight up and said to the referee, 'That's a damn lie. He high-sticked me,' and fell flat on his back again with his eyes closed.' "

After six games and fifty-five goals scored against him Buzinski could see the handwriting on the dressing-room wall. He was finished as a Ranger regular.

As a team the Rangers were so bad that none of Buzinski's replacements made much of a difference. They won only eleven of fifty games and finished sixth among the six teams. It appeared that the New Yorkers could not possibly get worse, but they did! A year later they won only six out of fifty games.

Patrick began to think Boucher's coaching might be the problem, but Lester got the answer on January 23, 1944, when Boucher took the night off to attend his brother's funeral. Patrick took Boucher's place behind the bench that night in Detroit's Olympia Stadium and played a part in one of the most humiliating defeats ever in the NHL. With Ken "Tubby" McAuley in the nets for New York, the Red Wings scored fifteen consecutive goals and won the game, 15–0.

The game set records for (a) most consecutive goals, one team, one game; (b) most points, one team, one game; (C) most goals, one team, one period; and (d) most points, one team, one period.

"I think," said Boucher, "this particular game persuaded him that there was something even more fundamentally wrong with the team than my coaching."

The only thing wrong with the Rangers was World War II. After hostilities ended, the soldiers came home, and by 1945–46 the Rangers were competitive again. By that time poor goalie McAuley had nearly been vulcanized by all the rubber that had hit him and never stayed around for the Rangers' renaissance.

"McAuley, bless his heart," said Boucher, "he should have been awarded the Croix de Guerre, if not the Victoria Cross, for bravery above and beyond the call of duty."

Chicago Black Hawks

In Chicago's very first year of NHL hockey, a curse purportedly was put on the Black Hawks that was to have long-lasting repercussions. It happened when club owner Major Frederic McLaughlin criticized his coach, Pete Muldoon, for not winning the Stanley Cup in their maiden season.

"You're crazy," shouted the incensed Muldoon at his boss. At which the Major handed his coach a pink slip and told him to find work elsewhere.

Muldoon stared down McLaughlin. "I'm not through with you," the just-fired coach reportedly warned the Major. "I'll hoodoo you. This club will *never* finish in first place."

Whether the events happened exactly as told is hardly relevant. What matters is that Muldoon's hex, or whatever it was, must have worked. Year after year, no matter how good the Black Hawks might have been, they never finished first as long as the Major was alive.

When McLaughlin died in 1944, the Black Hawks were a mediocre club on a treadmill to oblivion. Then things began getting worse. The Major was succeeded by his aide, Bill Tobin, who managed to do just about everything wrong that was possible with a good franchise.

He failed to build and maintain an adequate farm system. He lacked a comprehensive scouting program. His trading philosophy was medieval, and he had little rapport with his coaches. Otherwise, Tobin was a veritable hockey genius.

Naturally, it all came out in the standings. From the 1946–47 season through 1951–52, the Black Hawks finished last five times and fifth once. "I couldn't put the Black Hawks on the rink as my home team," said an NHL coach. "After seeing them once, everybody would stay as far away as they could get. Chicago must be the greatest hockey city in the country to keep on supporting them."

Chicago *was* a great hockey city—as great as the Black Hawks were terrible. Capacity crowds at mammoth Chicago Stadium were the rule, and that, in part, explains the front-office flops. "The management had it too easy for too long," said a Black Hawks' critic. "They knew that no matter how bad the team, the fans would show up. They became lax and didn't work at the job."

At the end of World War II, Chicago had the nucleus of a contender. Max and Doug Bentley were two of the best scorers in the NHL, and linemate Bill Mosienko was coming on strong. But they needed help, and that's where Tobin failed them. He failed to cultivate farm clubs in Western Canada, where the Black Hawks were extremely popular because the Bentleys came from Saskatchewan.

"We trained at Regina for the 1945–46 and 1946–47 seasons," said then Chicago coach Johnny Gottselig. "That gave us a foothold in the territory. Our club was tremendously popular in the area then. The Bentleys were the idols of Canadian youngsters in that section. 'We want to play where the Bents play,' was a popular refrain.

"If the proper steps had been taken then, we could have cornered the whole West for amateur talent. But the next year the club moved the training site, and we missed our great chance. When we failed to press our advantage in the West, Detroit moved into the territory and wrapped it up."

One of Tobin's biggest blunders was the breakup of the famed Bentleys. Early in the 1947–48 season, he traded Max Bentley, hockey's greatest scorer of the day, to Toronto along with Cy Thomas for three forwards and two defensemen. Tobin not only relinquished high quality for quantity but also demoralized Doug Bentley in the process. That the trade was an abject failure was underlined in the spring of 1947. The Black Hawks finished dead last while the Maple Leafs, led by Max Bentley, finished first and won the Stanley Cup.

Frequently, Tobin would sell players for cash, a move that inspired a rival to term it "the height of stupidity."

"He'd sell players for ten or fifteen thousand dollars, instead of trading them for the rights to promising youngsters," one NHL official said. "I told Tobin, 'You can't play thousand-dollar bills at those wing positions.'"

Tobin made one good move—he hired veteran center Sid Abel as player-coach in 1952. With Abel behind the bench and excellent goalkeeper Al Rollins between the pipes, the Black Hawks actually finished fourth in 1952–53. But it was just a mirage. A year later they were sixth again, winning only twelve, tying seven, and losing fifty-one games. "That club," said Detroit hockey writer Tommy Devine, "was one of the weakest teams in NHL history."

The Black Hawks of that season were so bad that their leading scorer, Larry Wilson, scored only nine goals. Rollins was the only ray of hope, and he was buried under a barrage of rubber. Worse still, fans for the first time began staying away from Chicago Stadium by the thousands. Hard as it was to believe, the Black Hawks were close to folding their operation.

In September, 1952, Jim Norris and Arthur Wirtz purchased the club. They studied the mounting losses and had to make a decision—either quit hockey or pour millions into the franchise in the hopes of reviving it.

They decided to save the Black Hawks.

Tobin was shunted to an inconsequential front-office position. He was replaced by clever Tommy Ivan, who had coached the Red Wings to a couple of Stanley Cup triumphs.

Using Rollins and defenseman Bill Gadsby as a nucleus, Ivan began building. It took a while for Ivan to construct a farm system, but he did, and by 1958–59 the Black Hawks had climbed to third place. In 1961, led by Ivan discoveries Stan Mikita and Bobby Hull, they won the Stanley Cup. And in 1967 they actually broke the forty-year-old Muldoon jinx and finished in first place.

27

My Case Against Hockey Writers

HOCKEY WRITERS as a group are, professionally speaking, one step away from Hamburg whores. Whether they're a step above or below depends largely on the quality of free grub being distributed in the press room of the home team that week. Usually, it's one step below.

Hamburg whores make no pretense about their business; hockey writers do. They pretend that they're honest, objective, that they know what they're writing about and that they're not on the take. It is a measure of the caliber of shinny reportage that for twenty-five years only one weekly hockey paper appeared on the market and that one—*The Hockey News*—is so bad I use it in my journalism classes as the best example of the worst kind of sportswriting.

There are several key exceptions to my condemnation of the hockey-writing fraternity, and these are mentioned separately. But remember, these precious few good ones comprise about 1 percent of the shabby, tweedy crowd. And that ain't good!

Hockey writers are lousy reporters for several reasons, which I'll enumerate here and then explain in detail a bit later:

1. They are easily intimidated by players, coaches, and managers.
2. They frequently can be "bought"—directly or indirectly—either by a home team or a league.
3. They become too closely involved with the home team or certain

players, and develop into cheerleaders, rooting in print for their club.

4. They are dull, noncreative, and fail to tell it like it really is for a number of reasons.

5. Sadly, with few exceptions, hockey-writing is regarded by most newspaper editors as the lowest rung on the sports department's competence ladder. *Ergo:* The worst writers cover hockey.

6. Hockey writers consider their beat one of the easiest in the business and will do anything to keep from losing it.

Now to explain these points:

Intimidation

For any number of reasons—some obvious, some subtle—hockey players, coaches, and managers are held in awe by writers. Hockey people cultivate this situation to the degree where they literally hold the newspapermen in their palms. If any journalist dares cross the hockey man, he can expect the fires of hell to wither him.

Of course every now and then some of the good ones stand up to the hockey men. Bob McDevitt of the Canadian Broadcasting Corporation is one such good journalist. McDevitt approached Team Canada coach Harry Sinden after the 1972 series with the Russians. The dialogue went something like this:

> McDEVITT: Harry . . . Harry Sinden? Would you mind stepping over here for a few words on the CBC?
>
> SINDEN: I hear you cut us up pretty good on one of your sportscasts, McDevitt?
>
> McDEVITT: I just told it like I saw it, Harry.
>
> SINDEN: Well, go *bleep* yourself, then!

Unlike other hockey reporters McDevitt was lucky. He does not cover the National Hockey League as a regular beat and therefore is not beholden to Sinden or anyone else for stories. But imagine if he did write Boston hockey on a regular basis. He might have to put up with the abuse Dan Proudfoot suffered in September, 1972, from Sinden.

Writing in the *Toronto Globe and Mail*, Proudfoot courageously disclosed Team Canada's morale problem and that several players were on the verge of quitting. It was accurate, and as things developed, prophetic. Proudfoot's reward?

"Sinden chewed out Proudfoot publicly and obscenely at a Team Canada practice," said John Robertson of the *Montreal Star*, "for that one."

Although writers are not likely to admit it, such high-decibel vituperation by hockey men frequently does wear down the journalist who figures he can do without the yelling from management.

This often happens when the home club is playing badly, and the home club's executive would like to believe—and more important, would like the writers to believe—otherwise. If that doesn't work, there are other methods of reprisal—dressing-room bans, noncooperation from the team publicity (propaganda ministry) department, actual violent acts against writers by players, etc. The writers know this and usually get the message. It takes a lot of balls for a reporter to resist a blanket barrage, or even a small threat. As a result most hockey writers cave in to the Establishment.

Buying the Press

Most newspapermen consider themselves underpaid and therefore seek ways of embellishing their incomes. Hockey teams know this and try to "help" them by supplementing their income—for a price, of course. The price is being nice to the home club.

Out-and-out bribery is taboo. Buying the press occurs in more subtle forms. The most common technique is to have hockey reporters write "stories" for the home-team program. Usually the stories take about a half hour to complete. Payment is anywhere from $75 to $100. At $100 an hour, a writer just might be willing to overlook some otherwise printable stories that the home club would dislike. So, everybody is happy. The writer is making a few easy bucks. The home team is keeping a nasty story out of the paper. Only the fan is getting screwed, if the writer caves in.

Another form of "payment" is the free trip, or junket. For example, at Stanley Cup finals time the NHL has paid the round-trip transportation and room and board for any "approved"—approved by the NHL, of course—writer. Quite often, individual teams will do the same for hometown journalists. The Rangers for years footed the traveling bill for *New York Post* hockey writers and even paid the writers' daily meal money.

A simpler bribe is the "freebie." That's a ticket—usually a pair of ducats—to each game, mailed to the writer's home with his own free press ticket to every home contest. Reporters like to get freebies because they give them to friends and feel like big shots. The free ticket has been the standard "payoff" for decades. Only recently, with the advent of sellouts in many rinks, has it been abolished.

Other payoffs come in the form of lucrative Christmas gifts (Madison Square Garden used to send an annual $25 gift certificate) ranging from cash to color television sets. Paul Rimstead of the *Toronto Sun* once told me about the time he was given a color TV by Maple Leaf Gardens. "I returned mine," said Rimstead, "but I can't say the same for some of the other guys."

Cheerleading

Most writers who regularly travel with a team automatically become friendly with the players. Inevitably, they develop close ties with certain individuals, and these alliances make it virtually impossible for them to write critically and honestly about these people. More than anything, cronyism is the curse of hockey journalism, and you don't have to go farther than Boston or Madison Square Garden to see what I mean.

It is a fact of life that Boston fans are considerably more sophisticated than their writers, who worship at the very mouths of Phil Esposito, Bobby Orr, and Harry Sinden. When the Bruins lose, they mourn as if they were members of the team, and when Boston wins, they exult. The following episode tells it well:

A press conference was held at Boston Garden prior to a match during the 1972–73 season. The subject was Derek Sanderson's return to the Bruins from the World Hockey Association. The conference seemed to drag on endlessly until finally a veteran Boston scribe snapped: "Screw Sanderson! Let's go out and win a hockey game!"

Maybe he didn't realize it at the time but the writer sounded more like a coach than a writer. He was cheerleading more than some of the Bruins themselves do in the dressing room before a game.

"Owning an NHL hockey team," said Canadian author John MacFarlane, "means never having to spend a buck on promotion. The press flogs the game for nothing." In their book *The Death of Hockey* MacFarlane and Bruce Kidd wrote:

"No one has ever written a story about *how* Bobby Orr plays hockey. 'Bobby Orr is fast' . . . 'Bobby Orr can do anything' . . . 'Bobby Orr is the greatest' . . . that is what passes for technical analysis of the most talented practitioner of hockey among the people whose business it is to write and talk about it."

Only a few hockey reporters actually expose the crap that comes out of press conferences, the league offices, and the mouths of players. These few good writers define players and issues as *they*, the reporters, perceive them, not as the coaches, managers, governors, attorneys, and press agents want them perceived.

One who wasn't afraid to buck the system was Dave Marash, a sports commentator for WCBS-Radio, who in September, 1972, was offered a job as play-by-play announcer for the New York Rangers. Marash was interviewed by Rangers general manager Emile Francis and was asked, among other things, whether I was a friend of his. Since we weren't what you'd call friends, Marash said no. Then Francis asked whether Marash planned to remove his beard if he got the job. Marash said no, he wasn't going to remove his beard. Francis said he couldn't hire him. "We don't allow facial hair for our players," said Francis, "so we can't make an exception for our broadcasters."

Marash then was offered a similar job by the New York Islanders. This time Islanders president Roy Boe said Marash would have to shave off the beard. "We're appealing to a suburban audience," Boe explained. "I don't think they would like to see one of our broadcasters wearing a beard." With a thanks-but-no-thanks, Marash refused to eliminate his beard at the price of losing the potential job. Shortly thereafter he was hired by WCBS-TV as the anchorman on its prime news program—beard and all.

"The experience with the Rangers and Islanders was very interesting," Marash said in retrospect. "For one thing the issue of my wearing a beard didn't come up in the conversations until all else had been settled. It seemed that I had the jobs, in both cases."

At the time Marash was not riding high, and while not desperate, regarded both the Rangers and Islanders jobs as broadcasting plums. Yet he refused to compromise. "I told Francis," said Marash, "that I'd lost better jobs than the one with the Rangers, and that was that."

Occasionally an independent nonhockey journalist happens on the beat and is stunned by the provincialism that oozes out of every dressing room. *New York Post* columnist Larry Merchant made such a discovery in April, 1970, before long hair became the vogue among professional athletes.

Covering a play-off game between the Rangers and Black Hawks, Merchant encountered Chicago coach Billy Reay in the aisle near the Hawks' dressing room after the match and asked Reay if he could speak to the Chicago players. Reay eyed Merchant's shoulder-length hair dubiously and then denied the request. Fearless, unlike most of the others who have confronted Reay, Merchant ironically snapped: "You sure show a lot of class."

To which Reay replied, "You show a lot of class, too, you long-haired jerk."

Dull Writing

There are several reasons why hockey reportage is dull. Those who cover the beat frequently are not the most creative types around. Then, their subjects are so insipid as to make any interview a chore. Consider the following interview conducted by Murray Chass of *The New York Times* following a 5–3 Pittsburgh win over the Rangers in November, 1972.

Chass wondered why a splendid team like the Rangers could be beaten twice in a row by a terrible club like the Penguins. He asked both coaches, Red Kelly of Pittsburgh and Emile Francis of New York, what the Penguins had on the Rangers. Since Kelly was a former member of the Canadian Parliament and Francis is regarded as one of the most voluble hockey professionals around, he expected eloquent replies to the interesting question, What *do* the Penguins have on the Rangers?

"So far, goals," said Kelly. End of answer.

"What do they have on us?" said Francis. "They have two wins, that's what they have on us." End of answer.

Don't Lose the Beat

It's fun being a hockey writer—fun, that is, if you don't take the job seriously. You travel well, see the continent, stay at good hotels, eat decent food for next-to-nothing, and get your name in the paper several times a week. In the eyes of some fools, you are what they call an expert. You get to know players and therefore are in a position to bring autographs home to kids on the block and in a very small way you are a big deal. Lots of people like it that way, and that's why most hockey writers won't rock the boat. If they rock the boat, they lose the beat.

The same fans who, ten years ago, had to scour the newspapers for hockey coverage are now bombarded by what they can recognize as mediocre writing. It doesn't take much to recognize the hometown rooters, the writers who distill publicity handouts instead of digging for their own stories, and the deference to management to smooth out the working relationships.

Writers, of course, see it, too. The trouble is that too many of the reporters who know what's wrong still succumb to the temptations for which they berate their peers. And there's the problem.

28

The NHL's Hall of Fame Farce

DOUG HARVEY'S REFUSAL to attend the Hockey Hall of Fame induction ceremonies in Toronto on August 23, 1973, was more than a farsighted individual act of rebellion against the nearsighted hockey Establishment.

This is the same ridiculous Establishment that once barred Bobby Hull from skating for Team Canada; and the same bunch who, by their absurd, indifferent behavior, forced Gordie Howe to the World Hockey Association.

Harvey's nose-thumbing at the Hall of Fame was a symbolic act, not for Doug alone, but for all those ice worthies who have been locked out of the shrine because of ignorance, petty hockey politics, or unnecessary dilly-dallying.

Absolutely no excuses can be summoned for this behavior; at least not after the National Hockey League opened the gates of the Hall of Fame to Montreal defenseman Tom Johnson in 1970 and kept Harvey out until 1973. Johnson made the NHL first All-Star team only once in his life. Harvey made it ten times.

If Harvey could be omitted from the Hall of Fame for three years while Johnson was a member, it follows that other notables have been neglected. Offhand, I can think of twelve former players who belong there right now and should receive immediate consideration when the NHL thinkers consider good men for entry in future years.

These are my choices:

Marcel Pronovost

If Detroit Red Wings general manager Jack Adams allowed this marvelous defenseman to rush the way the Bruins let Bobby Orr roam, he'd have been a scorer like Orr. Marcel always was a better defensive defenseman than Orr. Pronovost played in 1,206 regular-season games, scored 88 goals, and had 257 assists for 345 points. In play-offs he was good for 8 goals and 23 assists for 31 points in 134 games. Pronovost was first All-Star twice and second All-Star twice; he played on five Stanley Cup winners and seven first-place clubs.

Harry Lumley

There have been few better goaltenders, certainly none better today. "Apple Cheeks" Harry played 804 regular-season games for a 2.75 goals-against average. His play-off average was 2.62 for 76 games. He played for some bummers in Boston and Chicago, but also won the Vezina Trophy, played on one Stanley Cup winner and two first-place clubs.

Pierre Pilote

If he doesn't make it soon, something is screwy. This slick Chicago defenseman was a first All-Star five times and second All-Star thrice. He played on one Stanley Cup winner and one first-place club while winning the Norris Trophy three times. He also was tough as an armadillo.

Cecil Dillon

Strictly for old-timers. He was a super New York Rangers forward in the thirties when goals were dearer by half than they are now. Cecil was once a first All-Star right wing and three times a second All-Star. He played on one Stanley Cup winner for New York and one Prince of Wales champ. Which is more than any contemporary Ranger can say.

Bill Quackenbush

Quackenbush starred for the Red Wings and Bruins as a genuine defensive defenseman. Three times he made first All-Star, and twice second All-Star. He was the first defenseman to win the Lady Byng Trophy (1949) and played for two first-place clubs.

Lorne Carr

One of several golden Maple Leafs—also a prize New York American—he scored 204 goals at a time when that was considered only the work of titans. Lorne was twice first All-Star right wing and played on two Stanley Cup winners for Toronto. Style is what he was all about.

Gordie Drillon

Another Toronto right-wing ace, Gordie suffered by comparison with Syl Apps, Sr., then the all-Canadian idol and his linemate. But nobody could light the red bulb better than Drillon. He was a two-time first All-Star, once second All-Star, and won the Art Ross and Lady Byng trophies in 1938.

Bob Davidson

It is possible that Davidson invented the art of backchecking. He was Apps's defensive specialist and a very important reason why Toronto won a pair of Stanley Cups, once coming from behind to take four straight games after losing the first three to Detroit in 1942.

Edgar Laprade

He could not shoot worth a darn, but Edgar did everything else right—especially think, stickhandle, and pass. He was one of the most beautiful centers since Frank Boucher. Laprade was Rookie of the Year in 1946 and Lady Byng Trophy winner in 1950.

Al Rollins

As a Maple Leaf rookie in 1950–51, his goals-against average was 1.75 in the regular season and 1.50 in the play-offs. This tall, angular, perfectly artistic goaltender won the Vezina Trophy for Toronto and later the Hart

Trophy with one of the worst Chicago sextets ever. When you're the NHL's Most Valuable Player with a subterranean club, you must rate pretty high with the experts. Rollins did, and fully deserved it.

Jim Thomson–Gus Mortson

Although they should be voted in separately, they were the "Gold Dust Twins" of Toronto's golden era when the Hap Day–coached Leafs won the Stanley Cup in 1947, 1948, 1949, and 1951. They each played on a first-place club, played together, and worked splendidly as a team, Thomson laying back while Mortson did the rushing. Neither lost many fights.

29

The Unofficial NHL
All-Nasty Team

Presenting the first-ever All-Nasty Team, a selection of hockey men who have demonstrated outstanding rotten qualities. The picks have been made by four hockey writers polled for this purpose. Several stars won mention.

Whether they fit in just one of the categories—disingenuousness, phoniness, or orneriness—or in all of them, the fact remains that, like All-Stars, they deserve recognition.

There are All-Star teams, awards for gentlemanly behavior, most popular, and fans' favorite polls. Now, at last, a comprehensive list of our favorite game's most *un*favorite people.

Naturally, not every player, coach, or executive deserving of nomination could possibly be named. There is only so much space, even though the sport has an astounding number of unlikable characters.

Of course there are many, many more nice guys than creeps. Right? But the nice guys get most of the space in the piles of literature produced about the game, so there's a need for this compilation of people who make hockey noticeably less palatable.

To arrive at the All-Nasty Team, we employed four highly knowledgeable spies in National Hockey League cities. They were veteran hockey-watchers, carefully ordered to keep a sharp eye. The full-time reporters were promised anonymity in exchange for the inside stories on the people they most disliked in hockey.

Mention of any individual here does not mean total condemnation—the

254

individual mentioned may very well keep his wife and kids fed, his boss's back well-patted, or his opponents' nets well-filled. No, even a single nasty incident can win nomination to the team.

So, congratulations to those frowning faces who made the first annual team. And to those who just missed, such as Eddie Shore, Toe Blake, Don Murphy, and assorted difficult types,—better luck next time, fellows! Keep growling!

Now, without further ado, the list compiled by the four scribes.

First, the special categories:

The Superstars

Ask waiters in late-night spots wherever the Boston Bruins congregate. PHIL ESPOSITO can be the most inelegant man in the NHL, shouting, ordering, and insulting at a level right up there with teammate Wayne Cashman. But to Espo's credit, he makes a lot of noise without much meanness, so he doesn't rank among our top twenty on the nasty list, despite his constant crying and complaining about the tough checks he takes on his way to his fantastic scoring levels. Will aging superstar Espo ever grow up completely? As long as he doesn't, he has a shot at the All-Nasty. Not this time, though. Sorry, Phil!

BOBBY ORR hides from reporters, and when caught, often answers questions evasively, with little frankness. His mind seems programmed by his Toronto lawyer, Alan Eagleson, to be completely inoffensive. Nevertheless, the game's number-one player often *is* offensive, taking stupid penalties (or deserving them but not getting them) when an opponent checks him as though he's just another player.

Orr once had a telephone that answered automatically with a recording of his voice saying, "Roses are red, violets are blue, leave your number and I'll call you." He often didn't. And that's supposed to be superstar style?

The Virtue-Overcomes-Negativity Category

GILBERT PERREAULT has a public personality quotient just above zero. But other players say it's because he's still unsure of English, and he's really a swell guy. Maybe so. Regardless, he's such a swell hockey player to watch he cannot rank on the All-Nasty Team—until he's learned enough English to prove he has a zero personality.

SAM POLLOCK, the Montreal Canadiens general manager, has fast-talked so many incompetent hockey executives into bad deals that the Better Business Bureau should talk to him. Here's the thing, though, with Sam: Whenever Pollock tells a fib, observers report that his nose and eyes run and he has to pull out his handkerchief. Therein lies the clue.

So, Sam's nasty quality is too easy to detect, and too funny for words. Sorry, Pollock can't make the team.

SID SALOMON, III, SIDNEY SALOMON, JR., owners of the St. Louis Blues, have been cruel in their constant firing of coaches and perhaps unwise in their interference with their hockey executives' jobs. Yet, the Salomons did revolutionize NHL treatment of players by giving the Blues such rewards as post-season Florida vacations, presents for extra effort, and dinners at the Salomon home. All this, before formation of the WHA forced most NHL teams to treat their players with dignity. So, despite their bungling, the Salomons don't make All-Nasty. Can't help it!

At last:

The All-Nasties

JIM PAPPIN, the Chicago Black Hawk, can score goals but he can't score with fans by refusing to sign autographs. He shows no class, brushing by youngsters. Anyhow, they know enough to get autographs from Pit Martin, the center who makes right-wing Pappin go.

MARCEL DIONNE hurt his Detroit Red Wing teammates in 1973–74 every time he mouthed off about getting out of the Motor City as soon as his contract expired after the 1974–75 season. Yapping is nothing new for Dionne, a superior team player on the ice who has been spoiled from his junior days in St. Catharines, Ontario.

WREN BLAIR, former general manager of the Minnesota North Stars, called Dean Prentice a quitter in 1973–74 when Prentice, forty-one, tried to retire in midseason. Prentice was averaging twenty goals a year way back when Blair was still a milkman, so where does the Bird get the right to call his player a quitter? Another example of Blair's ability to irritate people unnecessarily.

RICK FOLEY, back in the minor leagues after displaying his blubber in three NHL uniforms, has conned record numbers of coaches into believing he's going to try to get in shape and take hockey seriously. Considering his gifts for the game, he should be ashamed not to have developed himself.

BOB PULFORD, Los Angeles Kings coach, once told a group of reporters his players weren't ready for the postgame interviews. Some reporters waited outside the dressing room, and finally Pulford told them they could come inside. But all of the players had escaped out another door. In that episode Pully displayed a blissful ignorance of the necessity for selling the Kings and hockey in the Los Angeles area.

PAUL HENDERSON emerged as a superstar in the 1972 Canada-Russia series, but since then he has starred consistently only in bad manners. A Toronto newspaper revealed with a single picture how he threw a temper tantrum in a 1973 rehearsal with the Toronto Symphony. Several players appeared as guests in Haydn's *Toy Symphony.* Paul smashed a toy trumpet to the floor when it wouldn't work. This is a variation of Henderson's frequent tantrums when he cannot score.

JOHN BELL gets the award as most difficult public-relations man in the NHL, because of his obvious and oily phoniness in promoting the Detroit Red Wings. Runner-up is DON MURPHY of the Chicago Black Hawks, who at least isn't usually phony about being annoying.

DENIS BALL, New York Rangers farm system director, took exception when several players kidded him about trying to usurp Emile Francis' position as general manager because he once sat in the same spot in the airplane the absent Francis would have chosen. Ball is typical of many minor executives with NHL teams—a great talent for acting more important than he really is and no sense of humor beyond slapstick. Maybe Francis likes keeping a clown in the office.

PHIL WATSON is blessed with a vicious blend of double-talk. In 1972–73 when his WHA team was in Philadelphia and Bernie Parent was his goalie, game after game, he testified that Parent was great in the dressing room, a real leader. Now, with Parent back in the NHL, Watson says he had to beg the goaltender to keep playing. Somewhere, at some point, Phil was fibbing. Meantime, Parent led NHL goaltenders and Watson's Vancouver Blazers floundered in 1973–74 without Bernie in the nets.

VIC HADFIELD cried and complained as long as Larry Popein coached the Rangers in 1973–74. For these public outbursts, and his own less-than-perfect play, Hadfield gets a nomination and a ticket to Pittsburgh.

DON RUCK, NHL vice-presidnet, has told reporters what the newsmen insist are outright fudges, without missing a puff on his dreadful pipe. He tries selling NHL hockey to networks.

HARRY SINDEN, once friendly and outgoing, is careful and guarded now that the pressure is on him as Boston Bruins general manager. Afraid of bad scenes, he avoided such players as Ed Johnston and Don Awrey during the time between their falling into his disfavor and their being traded, making things far worse than necessary. Honesty pays, Harry, even when it's uncomfortable.

JACK KENT COOKE gets a nasty nomination as owner of the Los Angeles Kings, for unprecedented interference in team operation, while flaunting the biggest ego in the league.

To PETER MAHOVLICH and DEREK SANDERSON, special nominations for deeds in the past. To Mahovlich, congrats for being stupid enough to rip up a paper Ken Dryden was carefully writing by hand for the law course he was taking. Mahovlich thought it was a funny prank, which tells you a lot about big Peter. To Sanderson, congrats for accepting a huge WHA contract for the 1972–73 season and then doing nothing to justify it.

To RICHARD MARTIN, a nomination for leading both leagues in surliness, except, of course, when there's money to be gained by being pleasant.

And finally, a farewell nomination to CHARLIE O. FINLEY, who when he owned the California Golden Seals indeed did prove his middle name should be Zero. Under his ownership hockey suffered in the Bay Area, but not nearly as much as the players and others who worked under him.

◦   ◦   ◦   ◦   ◦   ◦

As my boyhood idol, columnist Dan Parker of the *New York Daily Mirror* might have said, I have gone over hockey once over lightly, if not politely. If anything, I hope the knocks are interpreted constructively, and that the digs at the assorted and sordid characters of The Game are simply a function of reportorial candor.

But don't get me wrong, I LOVE HOCKEY!

Index